The University of Alberta Library

THE FIRST HUNDRED YEARS, 1908–2008

Merrill Distad

UNIVERSITY OF ALBERTA
LIBRARIES

Published by
University of Alberta Libraries
5–02 Cameron Library
Edmonton, Alberta, Canada   T6G 2J8

LIBRARY AND ARCHIVES CANADA CATALOGUING IN PUBLICATION

Distad, N. Merrill (Norman Merrill), 1946–
    The University of Alberta Library : the first hundred years / Merrill Distad.

Includes bibliographical references and index.
ISBN 978–1–55195–245–1

    1. University of Alberta. Library—History.
I. University of Alberta. Library II. Title.

Z736.U395D48 2009   027.77123'34   C2009-901837-3

Dedicated to staff of the University of Alberta Libraries,
past, present, and future

for Melody Kaban,

Merritt Fleed

24 April 2009

Contents

Foreword

MILESTONE ANNIVERSARIES are marked in many ways that
acknowledge and celebrate achievement. A century ago Mr Alexander
Cameron Rutherford, Alberta's first Premier, stood in the middle of
a 258-acre patch of half-cleared scrub that overlooked the valley of
the North Saskatchewan River, a plot designated "River Lot 5" on a
surveyor's map, and conjured up a vision of a great university. Others
who lacked his imagination dismissed his idea as premature at best,
or foolhardy at worst. But Rutherford was not a man to be denied, and
he pursued his vision with tenacity and the power of government
behind him.

Over the past century, Rutherford's vision was realized in ways
that he would surely have found remarkable. River Lot 5 has gradually been transformed into a university with 40,000 students and
10,000 academic staff and other employees, to become one of the City
of Edmonton's largest employers. At the heart of the University is
one of the largest academic libraries in North America. The size and
complexity of the University and its Library would have delighted
Mr Rutherford, particularly the Library's vast collections, for he was
himself a passionate book collector. But the realization of Rutherford's dream of a great university was no more certain than it was
predictable, and few people today are aware of the enormous challenges that were met and overcome in the process.

Professor Rod Macleod's excellent *All True Things: A History of
the University of Alberta, 1908–2008*, published by the University of
Alberta Press to mark the University's centenary, is the most recent
of several histories of the University, or of its individual faculties, to have appeared over the years. But, other than a very short,
summary history of the Library that the late Mr Bruce Peel produced

as a pamphlet, more than thirty years ago, the absorbing story of our Library's growth and development remained to be told. Dr Merrill Distad's *The University of Alberta Library: The First Hundred Years* has now captured much of that history in the pages that follow.

ERNIE INGLES
Vice-Provost & Chief Librarian
March 2009

Acknowledgements

WHOLEHEARTED THANKS are owed first and foremost to Ernie
Ingles for inviting me to write the Library's centenary history, for
giving me a free hand in doing it, as well as for submitting to a
probing interview. Former colleagues Rod Banks, Peter Freeman, and
Sieglinde Rooney also consented to be interviewed.

Other Library and University colleagues, past and present,
who supplied reminiscences, information, encouragement, and/
or general support include: Karen Adams, Anna Altmann, Chantal
Beesley, Carl Betke, Josh Bilyk, B.J. Busch, Kathy Carter, Pat Clements,
Cathie Crooks, Kathleen DeLong, Nancy Goebel, Jeannine Green,
Jim Heilik, Tina James, David Jones, Martina King, Loretta Klaren-
bach, Margaret Law, Rod Macleod, Sharon Marshall, Juliet McMaster,
Rob Merrett, Shirley Norris, Skye Rodgers, Mary-Jo Romaniuk, Alan
Rutkowski, John Teskey, Kathy West, and Janet Williamson.

University Archivist Bryan Corbett and UofA Archives staff
members Jim Franks, Raymond Frogner, Kevan Warner, and Doug
Bracewell were endlessly helpful in locating documents and photographs, and Bryan performed extra yeoman's service verifying all my
archival citation references.

Thanks for supplying additional photographs are owed to Richard
Siemens of UofA Creative Services and to Melina Bowden and
Michele Greig of the Vancouver Public Library

Special thanks are due to Allan Marble of Dalhousie University for
information about Miss Eugenie Archibald, the UofA's first librarian;
to Barbara Brydges, Director of the Doucette Library of Teaching
Resources, University of Calgary, for sharing her work on the
history of the University of Calgary Library; and to President Indira
Samarasekera and Provost Carl Amrhein, for their remarks.

UofA Press designer Alan Brownoff has given the book its distinctive appearance, and Bonar McCallum and his colleagues at McCallum Printing have ensured its swift and timely passage through the press.

Last but not least, the book owes its existence to my resident editor, proofreader, indexer, principal critic, and wife, Linda. Any of its faults and shortcomings, however, rest squarely and exclusively upon my shoulders.

MERRILL DISTAD
Edmonton, April 2009

Preface

OVER THE COURSE OF ITS FIRST CENTURY, the University of
Alberta Library has grown from the humblest of beginnings to rank
as the second-largest library in Canada, and one of the twenty largest
academic research libraries in North America. Today, more than 70
librarians and 200 associate staff members provide information
and research services to the students and faculty of the University of Alberta, as well as to a host of other clients locally, nationally,
and internationally. With local collections that by 2008, its centen-
nial year, exceeded 7 million titles, equalling more than 10 million
physical items, as well as licensed, on-line access to hundreds of thousands of electronic books and journals, the University of Alberta
Library plays a vital role in preserving and providing access not
merely to the latest published results of scholarly research, but, as a
library of record, to the vast historic catalogue of human civilization
in all its recorded forms.

The story of the University of Alberta Library's growth and
development is a testament to the dedication and labours of several
generations of dedicated staff and supportive faculty and administrators who, despite the setbacks and disappointments engendered by
two World Wars and the Great Depression, never wavered in their
vision of the Library as the heart of the University. As well as a story
of a great institution, this is their story.

For surely there is nothing that renders a Library more recommendable
than when every man finds in it that which he is in search of, and
nowhere else encounters; this being a perfect maxim, that there is
no book whatsoever, be it never so bad or decried, but may in time be
sought for by some person or other.

GABRIEL NAUDÉ (1600–1653)
French scholar and librarian,
Instructions concerning erecting a library,
translated by John Evelyn (London, 1661)

The true university of these days is a collection of books.

THOMAS CARLYLE (1795–1881)
Scottish historian, essayist, and critic

No university in the world has ever risen to greatness without a
correspondingly great library....When this is no longer true, then our
civilization will have come to an end.

LAWRENCE CLARK POWELL (1906–2001)
University Librarian and first Dean of UCLA Library School

1

Origins and Humble Beginnings 1908–1921

THE HON. ALEXANDER CAMERON RUTHERFORD, first Premier of Alberta and also, as Minister of Education, the visionary founder of the University of Alberta, succeeded in securing passage of a University Act in May 1906, when critics believed it rated a low priority in a frontier province with a population of scarcely 300,000. The following year, Rutherford secured the purchase of a 258-acre parcel of land on the south bank of the North Saskatchewan River, opposite Edmonton, the recently established capital of the new province, and announced that it would be the site of Alberta's provincial university. Only three weeks earlier, Rutherford had secured the incorporation of the town of Strathcona (population 7000) as a city, whose borders were expanded to include the site for the new university campus. Coincidentally, it was Rutherford himself who represented Strathcona in the Provincial Legislature.[1]

Mr Rutherford revealed himself to be a crafty politician by these manoeuvres, to the chagrin of political opponents, and not a few of his own supporters, who represented other urban centres across Alberta. He also proved to be a shrewd judge of character when he recruited Dr Henry Marshall Tory of McGill University to translate his vision of a university into reality. Tory had recently worked to create extension programs in British Columbia on behalf of McGill, at that time the preeminent English-language university in Canada; this experience would prove invaluable as he fulfilled Rutherford's commission. He also came highly recommended as someone uniquely well suited to the somewhat informal culture of the West:

> *Dear Mr. Rutherford, I have been thinking over our conversation...*
> *concerning a Principal for your new University, and have come to*

A.C. Rutherford.
[UAA 69–153–4]

3

Henry Marshall Tory.
[UAA 69-153-4]

the conclusion that of all the men I know Dr. Tory is by far the best
suited for the position. Have you met Dr. Tory? If you have you know
that his personality will appeal to the western people. He is not the
ordinary 'frock coat type' of professor, but rather the type of a western
rustler. He is a man to meet and impress all classes of the community
with his tact and good common sense, and is strong enough to
do without the frills often necessary for weaker individuals.

In writing as above I do not for a moment wish you to understand that
Dr. Tory is at all of the class of objectionables who bluster and think they
know everything. He is an excellent scholar and teacher, and...his work in
the west in regard to the McGill extensions have [sic] given him a greater
practical knowledge of schools than is possessed by any other Canadian.[2]

In the years following his appointment, full measures of tact and diplomacy were certainly necessary, but Dr Tory, a man of vision and energy, proved to be an ideal choice, who was more than up to the challenge. As Professor Robert K. Gordon later recalled:

> The chief inspirer of hopes and dreams, the eager encourager of great expectations, the incorrigible believer in progress was the President, Henry Marshall Tory. A strange mixture of idealist and politician, he was a good man to build up a university in a community which had just said goodbye to its pioneer days. He could rouse the indifferent and win over the sceptics. He made the people aware that they had a university and convinced them that it was worth spending money on. He did not, I think, much like sitting at his desk. He was not an office man. He liked to go out and look at what was going on. The place was still small enough for him to have a finger in every pie. One would see him hurrying across the campus....and then he would dash across the river and seek to convince the Premier that a cut in the university estimates would mean black disaster....His drive and warmth and the rich humanity in him more than made up for all defects.[3]

At the first meeting of the University Senate, on 30 March 1908, it voted to create a Faculty of Arts and Sciences, to admit students for the following September, and "that Dr. Tory be authorized to expend a sum not exceeding $5,000 on books and equipment for the Library." After this meeting, President Tory departed for the East to recruit staff, buy equipment for a science lab, and acquire "the nucleus of a library." Premier Rutherford had his own suggestions to offer about the Library's collection needs, so on 14 April Tory wrote to Rutherford: "I came to Ottawa yesterday and have spent most of the time since looking into library matters. I find I can get a lot of things free and many that the list you had proposed does not contain. Dr. Doughty is going to make a collection from the Archives including some old prints of Western Canada." From Boston, Tory wrote to Rutherford: "I have been working hard on the book problem...and am making good headway. The publishers are meeting me generously with regard to discounts. I am making satisfactory permanent arrangements." Recruiting faculty members, however, was proving more challenging, as he explained to Rutherford:

> I have been almost in despair with regard to a Professor of English and a Professor of Modern Languages. Neither of these men are to be

*had in Canada unless I take third-rate men. I think I have been able
to solve the difficulty about English however as I have just met a man
at Harvard with the highest recommendations....The only drawback is
he is an American not a Canadian but he is a southerner, and a perfect
gentleman, cultured and earnest....he looks like the man I am after.*[4]

Years afterward, that young Harvard scholar, long-serving
Professor of English E.K. Broadus, recalled his meeting with Tory:

*It was across a luncheon table in a hotel in Boston in the early spring of
1908....He was telling me of a University that didn't exist; in a province that I
had never heard of; in a country that I had never been to. And then and there,
amid an atmosphere of Parker House rolls, and staid proprieties, I got an
impression which has remained with me ever since as the peculiar essence of
Dr. Tory. He had dreamed a dream and there was a passion of fulfillment in
him....He seemed somehow to belong in a place where things hadn't yet been
done, and where his restless spirit could loose itself to the doing of them. And
he had a way with him which made you want to go along and see him do it.*[5]

On this, as well as subsequent recruiting and purchasing exped-
itions, Tory demonstrated his negotiating skills and shrewd
judgment of character, as well as a high degree of charisma.

Classes began at the new University of Alberta on 23 September
1908, in temporary quarters at the Duggan Street (now Queen
Alexandra) School in Strathcona, where President Tory and four
professors lectured to 37 students; 8 more arrived for the winter
term. Over the Christmas holidays the entire University operation was moved seven blocks north to the top floor of the newly
completed Strathcona Collegiate Institute (now Old Scona High
School), where, "a very pleasant large south room became the
library where the presiding spirits were Miss Jennie Carmichael...
the president's secretary and Miss Eugenie Archibald, the university's first librarian. Already some valuable volumes were appearing
on the shelves; the senate's five thousand dollar vote was showing
results."[6] That the results were still somewhat modest, however, was
shown by the fact that a single wagon-load sufficed to transfer all of
the University's books and equipment to what served as its new quarters until Athabasca Hall was ready for occupancy in September 1911.

In addition to the University Senate's special allocation of
$5000 for library books — a very substantial sum when contrasted

with the University's first-year operating budget of $25,000 for salaries and all other expenses — it also authorized the creation of a University Bookstore, and directed "that any profits which may be made from the sale of books etc., be utilized in further equipping the library."[7] Also, Premier Rutherford not only donated 500 of the Library's first 2000 volumes, he also solicited donations of books from a number of sources, including the Library of Parliament, the Premiers of Manitoba and Quebec, and Lord Strathcona, who was then serving as Canada's High Commissioner in London. The Librarian of Parliament, Martin Griffin, responded to Rutherford's appeal by sending "books of which we have several useless copies here," and promising that "more will go at intervals." Quebec Premier Jean-Lomer Gouin was pleased to report the dispatch "by Express" of 787 volumes; Manitoba Premier Rodmond Roblin arranged for the shipment of "copies of our Statutes, Journals and Public Documents of the Legislature of Manitoba"; and Lord Strathcona arranged with His Majesty's Stationery Office in London "to present to the University of Alberta the series of the annual Parliamentary Debates (including both the House of Lords and House of Commons) from the session of 1909 onwards." In addition to the success of Premier Rutherford's importuning solicitations on behalf of the new University Library, he was himself an enthusiastic and discriminating book collector, whose personal collection, including many great rarities of Canadiana and Americana, is now preserved in the University's Bruce Peel Special Collections Library.[8]

Besides the hiring of faculty members, President Tory had busied himself during the spring and summer of 1908 purchasing, "not only a set of the ordinary texts required for undergraduate courses, but also a list of all the reference books then in use, in the other universities in Canada. Work was therefore beginning with a fairly substantial library on hand."[9] The Library's earliest acquisitions were carefully recorded in accession registers, along with the prices paid. Pride of seniority goes to Edgar Allan Poe, whose Collected Works, purchased for $7.50, constituted the first ten volumes, followed by collected editions of Washington Irving (numbers 11–24 at $14), George Eliot, Jean Froissart, Henry Fielding, Edward Gibbon, Charles Lamb, Thomas Babington Macaulay, Walter Scott, William Shakespeare, and Robert Louis Stevenson. The first 200 volumes also included literary works by Jane Austen, Victor Hugo, Rudyard Kipling, and Tobias George Smollett; hist-

President Tory and administrative staff meeting in the Library.
[UAA 70–69–008]

ories by J.R. Green and Henry Hallam; and works by John Stuart Mill. In addition to these, which reflected what might be found in the library of any moderately affluent and cultured home, there were also practical treatises in fields such as engineering, surveying, horticulture, and animal husbandry. President Tory also sought and obtained the permission of the Senate before he purchased a 136-volume set of *Annalen der Chemie und Pharmacie* for $950, a sum more than sufficient at that time to purchase a modest house.

Following a trip abroad in the summer of 1909, "President Tory briefly outlined to the Senate the result of his trip to England. A considerable amount of equipment had been purchased and an agreement had been entered into with some of the principal book dealers whereby the University would get discounts ranging from 20 to 40 percent on all books purchased for the University Library." Tory remained closely involved in the selection and purchase of library materials, for which purpose he corresponded with McGill University Librarian Charles Henry Gould and Alberta Provincial Librarian John Blue. As well, President Tory and Professor W.H. Alexander, like Premier Rutherford, made personal donations of books to the Library.[10]

At a ceremony on 29 September 1909, with Premier Rutherford behind a horse-drawn plough, ground was broken for the Arts Building, but its completion was delayed until 1915. So in September 1911, Athabasca Hall, the first of the three original residential halls to be completed, housed students (35 men and 7 women) as well as providing a temporary home for all University offices and instruction, including the Library, which then housed 6000 volumes on the third floor. A student writing in *The Gateway,* the students' newspaper, described it as, "well and even hondsomely [sic] appointed, the library being especially large and comfortable." With the completion of Assiniboia Hall in October 1912, both the University's administrative officers and the Library were moved yet again; in Assiniboia Hall the librarian occupied an office on the second floor, while the reading room and books were located at the north end of the ground floor.[11]

The University's early growth was rapid in the years leading up to World War I. Enrolment more than doubled in the second year, when more than 100 students were registered in the autumn of 1909. By 1912 the faculty had grown to 26, and the student body to 320. By 1914 their numbers were 34 and 440 respectively. Over the next four years programs were established in Applied Science (i.e., engineering), Medicine, Law, Pharmacy, and Accounting, to bring the total number of teaching departments to 15. An Extension Department was established as early as 1912, headed by Albert Edward Ottewell (1882–1946), one of the University's first graduates. Ottewell was fondly described by a colleague as "a man of great size and warm geniality, full of common sense, kindness, and humour, who knew every corner of the Province and won friends for the University wherever he want."[12] Later Ottewell served as University Registrar.

As head of the Extension Department, Ottewell recruited Miss Jessie Fleming Montgomery, who served as the Extension Librarian for the next 32 years. Together they presided over a library collection which held 4000 volumes by 1922 and for decades supplied books to rural residents throughout Alberta.

> The extension library renders an important service to the province. It consists at present of over twenty thousand volumes, about half of which may be borrowed by individuals with no charge except for postage. The remaining books compose the travelling libraries, and some three hundred of these are in constant circulation throughout the province. A library consists of about forty books and may be kept in a community for three months. Upon

Above: A.E. Ottewell
at his desk in the
Extension Library
with his assistants.
[UAA 71–202]

Right: Miss Jessie
Fleming Montgomery,
Extension Librarian,
1913–1945.
[UAA 81–117–97]

its return another selection is sent out. There is a waiting list of applicants
of from twenty-five to fifty. No charge is made except for transportation.

In addition to loaning and shipping books, Ottewell toured
rural Alberta each year to deliver hundreds of lectures illustrated
with lantern slides and films, which realized part of Dr Tory's
promise that the University would serve all of Alberta's people.
Professor Robert Gordon later wrote of his own experience:

> *To small communities all over Alberta his Department shipped boxes of*
> *books which gave pleasure and sustenance to thousands of people through*
> *the long, isolating winter. From time to time all of us served the Department,*
> *and at its bidding went forth to offer our wares. One might go and deliver*
> *a single discourse at, say, Red Deer or Calgary, and so home, but there was*
> *also the grand tour; that was the great adventure. You gave seven or eight*
> *lectures and were away about ten days. Medicine Hat, Lethbridge, Macleod*
> *were the three largest places on the itinerary; and at them you were expected*
> *to face your audience in the full splendour of dress shirt and dinner jacket.*[13]

Between 1911 and 1915 the University Library's collection had
doubled to 12,000 volumes, making repeated moves increasingly
impractical. The pressure for space was relieved when the new Arts
Building was officially opened in October 1915. Despite the pall cast
by war, the completion of one of the most expensive buildings yet
constructed in Alberta provided the occasion for a celebratory convocation. "Everyone was dressed splendidly, the lieutenant governor
attended, and Premier Sifton was one of many who spoke. Eleven
honorary degrees were awarded — a record." The program featured
the ceremonial presentation of a gilt key, and "so many speeches
that the last three were mercifully cancelled."[14] The Library moved
into Room 110 of the Arts Building, an oak-panelled room at the
south end of the main floor with seating for 80 readers. Current
periodicals were displayed in an alcove, while the book stacks,
located on the ground level, below the reading room, housed the
Library's collection. Alas, this facility, though initially ample, was
filled to overflowing within ten years. Annual acquisitions averaged 1000 volumes, so that by 1920–1921 the collection numbered
17,000 volumes; by the spring of 1925 it had increased to 26,438.
Building a university-level library collection from scratch
presented an enormous challenge, of which the selection and

purchase of books and journal subscriptions was only a part. Housing an ever-expanding collection was, at least in those early years of regular moves from building to building, primarily a matter of logistics, although accommodation for collections remains a challenge to this day. But the organizing and cataloguing of books by subject, once they began arriving in the summer of 1908, might have been expected to tax the ingenuity of the small staff. Dr Tory sought the advice of McGill's Librarian, C.H. Gould, on various library issues, including collection development. The initial implementation of the Cutter Expansive Classification System, one of the most innovative of its day, was made by the University's first librarian, who came to Edmonton from the McGill University Library, where the Cutter System was already in use.[15]

First Librarians

Miss Eugenie Archibald (1877–1943), the University's first librarian, was born in Truro, Nova Scotia, and educated at Dalhousie University in Halifax (BA, 1899). She was recruited from McGill, where she had worked as an assistant librarian since 1904, and where the Cutter System was already well established. Her appointment reflects the strong influence of C.H. Gould and of Tory's McGill connections. Possessed of a restless spirit, Miss Archibald left Alberta in 1911, and later worked at the Forbes Library in Northampton, Massachusetts, in Saskatchewan, and at the Vancouver Public Library, before pursuing post-graduate studies at the University of Michigan, and, finally, returning to Halifax to work at the Public Archives of Nova Scotia and, later, the Dalhousie University Library. Miss Archibald was remembered by contemporaries as "frail in body but great in spirit" and as "the woman who knows everything."[16] During her brief tenure, working in the cramped, borrowed quarters afforded her and her single assistant, Miss Green, she nonetheless established the new University's library on a progressive trajectory, which her successors did well to continue. When she left, she was replaced, on a temporary basis, by Mr Cecil Race (1876–1927), the University Registrar, who was named Acting Librarian.

In 1912, Mr Frank Gresty Bowers (1863–1921), a native of Chester and graduate of Oxford University, was appointed University Librarian after a career as a schoolmaster at Bath in England, Nassau in the Bahamas, and Toronto, and as a civil servant in the Alberta Attorney-General's office. Known as a man of considerable culture,

Eugenie Archibald, the University's first librarian. Courtesy of the Vancouver Public Library, Special Collections, ca. 1927.

erudition, and charm, and himself a committed book collector, Bowers served during a period of the University's very rapid growth, slowed only by the advent of World War I, but the last years of his tenure were blighted by chronic ill-health that preceded his early death.[17]

Although Bowers lacked formal library training, he applied himself earnestly to the study of current "best practices" in academic libraries. In 1913 he requested and received a $200 travel grant to visit university libraries in Toronto, Madison, and Chicago, "to improve my knowledge of the working of a University library in particular and library work in general." That same year, in his first report as University Librarian, Bowers noted that:

> On entering on my duties as Librarian to the University in September last I found that 7283 volumes had been entered up to that time in what is known as the Accession Book. Probably half had been classi-fied and properly labelled under the Cutter system of classification; the remainder had been placed on the shelves in the divisions of the library allotted to each Department. I found that the catalogue consisted of

*an Author index of which the entries varied from a full and proper
entry to a mere memorandum which will require to be replaced.*

During the previous year,

*1100 books have been added to the library at an approximate cost
of $2000. These have been classified and labelled and Author cards
giving full particulars have been made for all while rather more than
half have been fully catalogued as to titles and subject matter, from
three to ten cards, or even more, being required for each volume.*

*In addition...there has been a large amount of purely manual labour
in connection with fitting the books for use, page cutting, pasting
in borrowers' card pockets, and the like. The catalogue entries
have been made so far on slips of paper of the standard size but
these will ultimately be replaced by thin cards, type-written.*[18]

It was fortunate that Mr Bowers remained committed to that
relatively newfangled library tool, the card catalogue. This late-nine-
teenth-century American innovation had gained wide acceptance in
libraries, but had not yet entirely extinguished enthusiasm for more
traditional ledger catalogues, which consisted of entries on small slips
of paper pasted into large, often awkward, scrapbook-like volumes, or

the perceived prestige of printed book catalogues. When a proposal
was made that the University Library should publish a printed catalogue, Bowers dutifully obtained cost estimates, and, in a letter to
acting President Kerr, reported that the Library's current stock of
almost 16,000 volumes would require at least 1500 pages to list by
author and title, and that at something like $3 per page, an edition of
500 copies would cost roughly $4500 to produce, a sum nearly suffi-
cient to cover the Library's staff payroll for a year. It was not merely its
high cost, but also its immediate obsolescence that prompted Bowers
to declare: "I cannot speak about this subject without entering an
emphatic protest on other grounds than expense against the idea of a
printed catalogue."[19] And with those last words, the idea was quashed.

The sheer volume of work, and a growing backlog of uncatalogued or only partly catalogued volumes, prompted a search for
an experienced assistant librarian to serve as a cataloguer. Calgary
Public Library Director Alexander Calhoun replied in March 1913 to
an inquiry from Professor J.M. MacEachran by recommending none
other than his own sister, Miss Kathleen Calhoun. A graduate (BA)
of Queen's University, with "a good reading command of French
and German and a fair knowledge of Latin," as well as several years
of teaching experience, and some months' experience of library
work, Miss Calhoun was then completing her formal library training
at the University of Wisconsin. Before Miss Calhoun had even

*South end of the
Old Arts Building,
home to the Library,
1915–1951, and Law
Reading Room on the
top floor, 1923–1951.*
[UAA 72–58–1591]

submitted her formal letter of application, Albert Ottewell had interviewed her, and reported favourably to Bowers: "You asked me to see Miss Calhoun if possible. I have met her and she is O.K. in every particular so far as I can tell. She has a prepossessing appearance and a pleasing personality. The report from her practice work at public libraries, which I saw, is excellent. Her instructors tell me she is one of the best in the school." Miss Calhoun clearly passed this test, since Ottewell went on to report on her salary expectations: "Now it will require $65 or possibly as high as $75 per month to buy her. She has abundant opportunity at the lower figure. Miss Hazelti[n]e [the] principal of the Library School is very anxious to know if we want her as she has already recommended her to Moose Jaw but thinks the university position would be better for her." Miss Calhoun was, indeed, hired, and, except for a year's leave to work in Ottawa as an editor and librarian with the Military Hospitals Commission's Department of Soldiers' Civil Re-Establishment, she served in the University Library for a decade, until her departure at the end of 1924.[20] Before returning from her leave in September 1919, however, Miss Calhoun sought to obtain a salary increase from $1200 to $1500, but Tory would only concede $1350 with a promise to recommend $1500 for the following year, a clear indication that her services were valued. As Professor Gordon recalled, years later, "Nobody could make dollars go farther than Dr. Tory. Whatever mistakes he made — and what man in his position could avoid them? — he certainly never made the mistake of overpaying the staff."[21]

It was fortunate that Miss Calhoun did return, for the following year Mr Bowers' deteriorating health posed some hard choices. When an advertisement in Library Journal for a library cataloguer elicited only two applicants, both unsuitable, Tory turned to Dr Gerhard Lomer, C.H. Gould's successor at McGill, to recommend potential librarian candidates. Lomer replied, "I cannot at the moment suggest anyone. Possibly when the vacancy is assured and you can definitely state the salary I may be able to refer applicants to you. Our most promising student in the Summer Library School refuses to leave the city." Dr Lomer added that other institutions were experiencing difficulty recruiting, including "Queen's [which] was looking for a head cataloguer for months. I am told that in the United States the supply of library assistants is far short of the demand." Lomer recommended that "if you would consider an American, you might...apply to the Library School at the University of Wisconsin...which has an excellent course and a very good reputation." A month later, George Locke, Chief Librarian of the Toronto Public Library, wrote Tory to recommend "a chap by the name of Mr. Jamieson, graduate in honours at the University of Toronto and who has already made a name for himself in this New York City Library School. He is a coming man, and especially adapted to University Library work." Faced with a dearth of suitable candidates, Tory "instructed Miss Calhoun that, once incoming books were entered on the Accession Book, and so made available to Professors and students, she and her one assistant should give their attention entirely to caring for the ordinary library service and should allow the cataloguing to stand until a future date."[22]

University Development During the 1914-1918 War
For both its faculty and its students, "A backwoods university, far from great libraries and on the fringe of the world of learning, has its drawbacks," as Professor Gordon later reminisced, but,

> We were very lucky, and we knew it. The present was good, and we were sure the best was yet to be. The youth and stir and zest of the place are unforgettable but not easy to recapture in words. The west was young, and so were we; and we went on our way, never doubting that, if 1913 was rich in blessings, 1914 would be still more bountiful. War was something we never dreamed of; the skies were clear in Alberta, and we assumed they were almost as clear elsewhere.[23]

The skies elsewhere were not clear, though, so a total of 484 students and staff, including President Tory and half the faculty, volunteered for war service, of whom 82, or 17 percent, were killed in action. Although enrolment dropped by as much as 30 percent, to a low of 309 in 1916–1917, expansion of the curriculum continued during the war years, in fulfillment of Tory's original vision of a full-fledged university. In 1915 Agriculture was established as a full faculty; Pharmacy was elevated to the status of a school in 1917; Dentistry, Household Economics, and classes in soils, mining, and economics were added in 1918; the University stock farm was purchased in 1919; and work was begun on the new medical building in 1920. Well could Tory boast in a letter that year to a donor living in England:

> It seems only the other day that...the University was in its beginning. It has grown to have rather an important place in the life of the

Province, having had over eleven hundred students last year and our
staff, which...was only four some years ago, consists now of seventy full
time people and a considerable number of assistants...making a total
of nearly a hundred. In addition to our Faculty of Arts and Science, we
have developed our Faculties of Agriculture and Engineering and now
have a rapidly growing Medical Faculty which will doubtless be one
of the big medical schools of Canada in the course of a few years.[24]

Supporting this widening of the University's curriculum
placed an additional and growing burden upon the
University's Library. Thus, with an eye to the future, in 1915
a Committee on Graduate Study was established, and, two
years later, a Library Committee was established at the

recommendation submitted by the President...that the expenditure of
ordinary appropriations, provided for the purchase of books for the
library, should be entrusted to a committee composed of the following: The
President, Dean Kerr [Arts & Sciences], Dean Howes [Agriculture], Professor
Alexander [Classics], Professor Broadus [English], Professor Sheldon
[Mathematics], Professor Lewis [Botany], Dr. Jamieson [Bacteriology],
with the Librarian, Mr. Bowers, as Secretary of the Committee.[25]

The Library Committee met for the first time on or about
10 January 1918, but its earliest surviving minutes date from
27 May 1920, by which time the membership had expanded to
include Professors MacEachran (Philosophy), Revell (Anatomy),
and Wilson (Applied Science), as well as Dean Rankin (Medicine).
At the Library Committee's meeting on 22 December 1920, "The
President also reported that Mr. Bowers' health was very precarious and it was not quite clear yet how long it would be before
he would be back in the library; that he intended to continue the
library as it is." A month later, on 25 January 1921, Mr Bowers died.
Remembered by his friends "as a book lover and himself in possession of [an] extensive private library" and as "a man with a highly
cultivated taste in literature and art, of unusually wide reading
and marked individuality...He was very proud of the library over
which he presided and nurtured its growth with loving care."[26]
 In the summer of 1917, President Tory recommended to the
Government of Canada the creation of "a university in khaki" to allow
soldiers to continue their education while they awaited demobiliza-

tion. Instructors would be drawn from among the ranks, and classes organized in military camps across the United Kingdom. Charged with implementing his own proposal, Tory left for England, leaving Arts and Sciences Dean W.A.R. Kerr to act as President; Tory returned to Edmonton in August 1919. While directing this "Khaki University," Tory met Rev. Mr Donald Ewing Cameron (1879–1946), an army chaplain and a remarkable man of many talents. By securing his future services for the University of Alberta, Tory quite unwittingly shaped the future of the University Library for a quarter of a century. Cameron was born in Stanley, Perthshire, Scotland, and educated at St Andrews University and the University of Edinburgh (MA), where he won the gold medal as a divinity student at New College; he pursued further university studies at Göttingen in Germany. An ordained minister of the Presbyterian Church, he served in parishes in London's East End and in Manchester, before moving to Canada for his health in 1913, where he accepted a clerical charge in Cardston, Alberta, a tiny community first settled by Mormon immigrants from the United States, and, unlike his previous parishes, blessedly free of slums. Commissioned in 1916 as a major in Canada's 192nd Regiment, he served as a chaplain on the western front, and was later transferred to England, where he joined the Khaki University, and met Dr Tory.

Appointed as Assistant Director of the Extension Department in 1919, Cameron returned to Alberta, and spent the next two years working for Extension Director Albert Ottewell. The untimely death of Bowers, the University Librarian, and Tory's recent frustration in recruiting suitable librarians, led him to appoint Cameron to replace Bowers as University Librarian. This gesture of confidence proved a shrewd choice, and, inasmuch as the Extension Department ran its own province-wide lending library service, Cameron did not lack for experience in administering a library. Tory announced the appointment at the Library Committee's meeting in May 1921, and later informed a correspondent that, "Cameron has ceased to be connected with the Extension Department and has become Librarian of the University and is doing very well indeed." How well, may be judged from the testimony of his friend John Macdonald, published a decade after Cameron's death:

> Mr. Cameron was a man of insatiable intellectual curiosity, ranging over
> the whole field of knowledge, with a direct acquaintance with the world
> of books that was a source of perpetual astonishment to his academic

colleagues. For nearly three decades, no figure around the university was more familiar or more beloved than that of 'D.E.' The Library began in a modest way and in modest quarters, but it had a librarian who would have been an asset to any university library anywhere.[27]

2

Mr Cameron's Library, 1921–1945

ALTHOUGH THE POST-WAR YEARS witnessed a decline in agricultural commodity prices, and thus straitened provincial finances, the University's curriculum and library resources continued to grow, as did student enrolment, which rebounded to 1106 in 1919–1920, and the staff to 100. Although the University's operating budget leaped from under $500,000 in 1919 to more than $750,000 the following year, fluctuating revenues throughout the decade of the 1920s imposed an ongoing building moratorium that postponed construction of any major, new facilities. A chronic shortage of space presented Mr Cameron with his greatest challenge during his 25 years as University Librarian. Although space was to become an increasing and chronic problem, noisy and distracting behaviour was a more common complaint in the immediate post-war years. The Library at least provided sufficient space to house travelling art exhibitions provided by the Dominion Art Gallery in Ottawa, the Carnegie Corporation, and local artists.[28]

In 1921, the year of Mr Cameron's appointment, the United Farmers of Alberta (UFA) defeated the provincial Liberals in an election. Annoyed that President Tory ranked development of the medical faculty ahead of agriculture, the newly-elected UFA government threatened to withhold the University's appropriation. This threat was only avoided, President Tory later claimed, by the timely arrival of a cheque for $500,000 from the Rockefeller Foundation to support the Faculty of Medicine. In 1921, agricultural engineering and public health nursing were added to the curriculum, the former perhaps offered as a sop to the UFA government, while the latter was undoubtedly inspired by the recent influenza pandemic that had turned

Donald Ewing Cameron.
[UAA 81–117–1–57]

Pembina Hall into a temporary infirmary and morgue. In 1924, the School of Nursing was established within the Faculty of Medicine.[29]

Donald Cameron moved quickly to address the Library's dual shortages of money and space. In 1922 he succeeded in implementing an annual student library fee of $5 to generate a guaranteed annual budget for the acquisition of books, including duplicate copies of some of the titles in greatest demand. He also established the right to retain and carry forward any unspent balances from one fiscal year to the next. This unique perquisite acknowledged the fact that not all orders for books might be delivered and paid for within a single budgetary year. The student library fee continued to be collected as a levy separate from tuition until 1958–1959. To supplement the limited study space available in the Library, Cameron opened satellite reading rooms; medical and agricultural reading rooms were opened in the Medical and North Labs buildings in 1922, and a law reading room on the top floor of the Arts Building in 1923.

The students appear to have accepted the need to levy the library fee in addition to tuition: "Since the library fee has been imposed, there seems to be no special need to point out to students that we have a Library; it has become one of the things that thrust themselves

even on the most shrinking student," wrote the editor of *The Gateway*, who, "hoped, however, that the students will be stimulated to make enough use of the Library to turn the fee into a sound investment. As the demand grows, increased service will be given; there is pleasure in being crowded into doing more for students that want to read." Unwilling to leave this totally to chance, the editor wrote that he had been, "haunting the librarian's office...and at last, to sympathetic questioning, propounded his great idea. The Library should advertise. Every student should know that we have such a thing as a Library, and should use it regularly....Would the librarian help, perhaps by writing a bit in The Gateway about it? Certainly, with the greatest of pleasure. (Hand-shaking business.)" This article went on to encourage students to acquire an early acquaintance with the Library and its 25,000 volumes, counselled "good citizenship" in their use, and warned that infractions of the Library's rules would be reported to the Provost.[30]

The editor's "great idea" led Mr Cameron to publish an appeal in *The Gateway* the following fall semester: "The staff of the University invites all students to make full use of the Library during the term. According to the wisdom of the old hands, it pays to begin as early as possible; books are not always to be had, when too many put off asking for them until the last minute." He went on to list the Library's several branch reading rooms, briefly explain the Cutter System, and urge students not to "hesitate to consult the library staff, which will do all it can to help you. This invitation means anything the library can do for you, short of allowing you to fill your fountain pen out of our ink bottle." Finally, like a latter-day Presbyterian Jeremiah, he concluded:

> Use the library to the full, but do not abuse it or its books. Remember that others want the books as well as you. Don't shake your fountain pen in the library. Don't mark the books. We do not desire to put a plaster on your caution money, but we don't shrink from the idea.
>
> You have to pay a library fee. We shall try to give you value for it, but it is up to you to get it.[31]

In 1922–1923 the Library was open daily from 8:30 A.M. to 5:30 P.M., with extended evening hours from 8:00 P.M. to 10:00 P.M. five nights a week. Because study space remained at a premium, the Library was generally filled to capacity, and students took maximum advantage of evening hours, as Mr Cameron noted in his annual report for 1924: "During the last three weeks of the term the Arts Reading Room was open every day for 11.5 hours, and only lapsed to summer hours when the last student, after falling asleep at 9:30 P.M. on the last evening for study, wakened up at 9:35 and walked out. It is worth noting that on every day there are some who will remain to the last minute, no matter what the hour is."[32]

Crowded conditions prevailed in the Library throughout the decade of the 1920s. As the collections grew to service the expanding curriculum in the professional schools, growing enrolment necessitated the purchase of duplicate copies of many titles; the Library was lending about 25,000 books a year. Cameron summed up conditions in his 1928–1929 annual report: "During the year the Library has been greatly used, and our problem during many mornings has been that of accommodation for readers....we have noted that many look in and go away, as they see no available seat. The crowding is not to the advantage of steady work, but in the circumstances we must tolerate the pressure on space." He went on to recommend further dispersal of books and the extension of evening hours as stop-gaps: "It is becoming difficult to move books in and out, and the Library this spring is asking some of the professors not to return all of the books they have out on charge, as the task of fitting in all that are returned is now serious. It may be necessary to store part of our accessions in Department rooms during the coming year." Nonetheless, he chose to end on a positive note: "There is still a long way to go before we have the equipment, especially in periodicals, to be able to begin to be satisfied, but it should be recorded that for undergraduate use, in most respects, we are reasonably on the way to a satisfactory collection of books, and the habit of reading in the Library has undoubtedly taken root among the students, so that we have the foundation laid."[33]

Mr Cameron was considerably less positive in a memorandum to the incoming president regarding the inadequacy of the Library's 1928–1929 budget appropriation of $2400 for books for academic departments, despite the fact that it represented a 25 percent increase from the previous year. The substitution of the $5 student library fee for the traditional allocation of $5000 had led to diminished budgets, compounded by the several new departments and faculties that were inaugurated, including Agriculture, Dentistry, Law, Medicine, and Nursing. In addition to the responsibility to support these entirely new disciplines, there were the costs of duplicates, binding, and repairs: "The Amount available has never reached what Departments expected, and our only resource has been to charge all expense, such as unexpected allowances to new departments, to the general fund. This has been persistently detrimental to the interests of the library, and the source of general irritation." Finally, resorting to the bluntest language he would allow himself, Cameron concluded: "The present money in sight for the literary departments is one half of what it used to be, and must be declared entirely inadequate. The library has been starved, and there is no use disguising that fact. It is devoutly declared that a library should be the heart of a university. Ours has been, not the heart, but the vermiform appendix, left to fester in the ill-ventilated bowels of the Arts Building."[34]

Nonetheless, Mrs Jean Lehmann (née Millar) fondly recalled her four years as a junior librarian on Mr Cameron's staff, which she joined in the autumn of 1926 at an annual salary of $1200. After six months working alone in the medical library, she transferred to the reference desk in the Arts Building, where, within six months, she replaced the Library's cataloguer, Miss Dorothy Richards, and was herself replaced on reference by Miss Carman Craig. Recalling those days, she described her cataloguing duties:

The Library Reading Room in the Arts Building.

[UAA 77–92–1]

I typed my own cards as there was no clerical help and classified the books by the Cutter system — even then acknowledged to be an outdated system....There were only the three of us: Mr Cameron, Carman, and myself, aside from a student or two who would oversee the Reading Room during the evenings and when the hours were extended around examination time.

Mr Cameron was a fine man to work for — a truly remarkable man. He had no library training but was a great scholar endowed with a phenomenal memory....He did all the administrative work and bookkeeping, kept track of each department's allotted funds, ordered all the new books and still found time to pore over antiquarian booksellers' catalogues, and make many astute purchases.

Such a small staff was scarcely sufficient to provide service coverage during the day, so they had little time for leisure:

The Library was open from eight-thirty to five during the week and on Saturday mornings from eight-thirty to one. We worked without coffee breaks in those days, but I had a weakness for bringing in cold toast from

the breakfast I never had time to eat and munching it in the course of the
morning, hoping the telltale smell would not penetrate beyond my little
office. Mr Cameron often retreated through the side door to smoke his pipe.
I can't remember Carman's vice.[35]

When illness sidelined Mr Cameron for several months in 1930, the pressure on his small staff became even more intense, as they laboured to spend a $3,000 grant awarded to the English Department by the Carnegie Corporation of New York. Especially vexing was Cameron's "habit of answering a letter by writing a note on the bottom of the original and sending it back," leaving "inexplicable gaps in the files." Ever the frugal Scot, blessed with an eidetic memory, and "Lacking any secretarial help at all, he carried the whole operation in his head."[36] Mr Cameron was appointed at a time when the heads of academic libraries were drawn from the ranks of scholars, without formal training as librarians. Approached toward the end of his career for advice about enrolling in a library school, he advised an undergraduate that, "He had not felt the need for one himself and thought the courses, 'not worth a damn except for the prestige'; if one went, one might as well go to Columbia or Chicago which he considered the most prestigious."[37] Despite Cameron's scepticism about the value of formal library training, by the 1930s "attendance at a library school for a full term is required of everyone joining the library staff either before appointment, or as soon afterward as is convenient to liberate them for this purpose." But if Cameron thought the cost excessive, it might be repaid in professional recognition and commensurate earnings/salary: "This added professional training is costly, requiring...eight months of time, and the expenditure of a sum approaching one thousand dollars. It is felt that this additional training should be distinctly recognized in the salary scale."[38]

From time to time, Mr Cameron found his budget for acquisitions distrained on higher authority. Early in his tenure, during his absence from the campus, Dr Tory approved the purchase of a set of scientific texts that absorbed that year's entire book budget, while yet another year's acquisitions budget was totally expended in the purchase of law books and reports.[39] On another occasion, however, Cameron's insistence carried the day with Dr Tory over the location of a new plant pathology laboratory. As recalled by Robert Newton, then Dean of Agriculture, that happened

*one morning early in the spring [of 1928], when two teams of horses, one
with a plow and the other with a scoop-shovel — that was before the days of
bulldozers — appeared on the building site to begin levelling and excav-
ating. The librarian, D.E. Cameron, happened along, and immediately
rushed in great excitement to Dr. Tory's office to protest that we were using
part of the site intended for the library. Actually no such purpose for this site
was shown on the master plan hanging in the president's office, and the
Rutherford library, when it came, was built elsewhere. But because of its
central location, Cameron had suggested the site that we appeared about to
preempt. Dr. Tory came out at once, and asked me to look around with him
for another place for our laboratory extension. We walked about at the energetic pace he normally used, his arms swinging vigorously, and eventually
reached a small knoll just south of Pembina Hall, a women's residence. "Put
it here," said Dr. Tory.*

The Dean's objections were for naught: "I mentioned the inconvenience of having it 200 yards away from our main laboratory, also
the questionable propriety of placing a relatively uncouth building
on the highest and most conspicuous point on the campus, but as I
could not on the spur of the moment suggest a more suitable site, the
teams, plow, and scoop-shovel were called over, and there it went."[40]

Although Tory conceded Cameron's choice for a library site,
other building priorities claimed what little capital funding was
available to the University. However, 1928 proved to be a water-
shed. In that year the University established a School of Education
and began assuming control over the training of the Province's
teachers; the Edmonton Academy of Medicine transferred its
medical library to the University, which thereby assumed responsibility for providing information services to medical practitioners
throughout Alberta; and, after serving for 20 years as president, Dr
Tory left the University to head the National Research Council in
Ottawa. Also, the Library's collection surpassed 30,000 volumes in
1928, and clearly a tipping point had been reached. At the end of that
year, Professor Cecil Burgess, the University Architect, submitted
a memorandum in which he outlined three different sets of cost
estimates for the construction of a separate library building. In
the first scenario he projected a building to accommodate 85,000
volumes, 10 classrooms, 8 seminar rooms, 16 staff offices, seating
for 200 readers, 2 meeting rooms, 2 locker rooms, a janitor's closet,
and a bindery, as well as spaces for the University's book store, post

office, Student Union, and *The Gateway*, the student newspaper, all
for a total cost of $250,000 for the building, plus $25,000 for the
furnishings. His second iteration merely added 6680 square feet
to accommodate the Extension Department, at an additional cost
of $100,000, including furnishings. A still more optimistic third
version also included space for the Extension Department, while
nearly doubling the first version's capacity for books to 166,000
volumes, as well as providing seating for 282 readers and 12 classrooms with seating for a total of 680, all for $605,000 ($575,000
for the structure, and $30,000 for furnishings and equipment).[41]

Weathering the Great Depression

President Tory's successor, Dr Robert Charles Wallace, formerly of
the University of Manitoba, assumed the presidency in Fall Term,
1928, and was immediately confronted by a critical shortage of space,
most particularly in the Library, a deficiency highlighted by Donald
Cameron in his annual reports. Professor W.H. Alexander, one of
Tory's first faculty appointees, summarized the situation thus:

> The university is literally outgrowing its clothes; where are students to be put
> if the present rate of increase is maintained? Graduates who have not seen
> students sitting on the floor or in embrasures of class-room windows, or even
> standing, can hardly realize how pressing is this situation alone. A glance
> during term into what serves at present as a library is bound to be
> informing, and if one says that it has hardly the "air" of a library, there will
> be many to understand the pun. During the ten years of the "new order" the
> laboratory has had the inside track on the library; obviously the time has
> arrived to redress the balance. A library building is "indicated," as the doctors
> say and, of course, a library building without books is about as useful as a
> watch-case without works inside. The very thing on which so much emphasis
> has been laid during the last decade, research, is seriously hampered by the
> constant impossibility of finding out what has already been done.

The new president agreed that a library building must be the
University's number one capital building priority, and in his 1929
report he stressed that,

> The need for a new library building...is now the more urgent in that the
> library can give only partial service to the students in its present cramped
> quarters....Relief will be obtained in all directions by...a modern library

building, and ultimately to be devoted wholly to that end. The position
which it is planned that the new building occupy — facing west on the
main University thoroughfare between the Arts building and the residences
— is a central position among the University buildings, and all depart-
mental libraries may be consolidated in the building without inconvenience,
and with a relief of space to the departments concerned.[42]

The following year, President Wallace returned to the same theme,
to urge:

The library building asked for last year is an urgent necessity. Not only is
the library much overcrowded and quite inadequate for the needs of the
University as it now is, but relief will be obtained in the library building for
the Extension department, now very unsatisfactorily housed, and for the
Applied Sciences courses....It is unnecessary to elaborate a situation which
is critical.

Critical to the University it was indeed, but the global economic
depression was unrelenting, and Wallace was compelled the
following year to report that, "The Government did not feel justified,
in view of the economic conditions, in voting capital in whole or in
part for the library building. It has been necessary to endeavour to
carry on."[43] Upon hearing this, Cameron responded in a letter
to Wallace:

I do not find myself this morning quite as staunch a stoic as I tried to be
yesterday, and feel somewhat as a man does who has been running around
for a bit without knowing that he has been shot. However, I know that my
part of the disappointment is much smaller than yours must be....Please
accept the warm assurances of the library staff that we shall do all in our
[power] to lessen the inconvenience that the delay in getting the new
building is bound to cause in the general work of the University.

Nonetheless, Cameron, undaunted, undertook a tour in the summer
of 1931 to visit, "many of the larger libraries in the eastern States
and in eastern Canada, and studied the latest developments in
buildings and administration. Full information was collected
for our own guidance in future developments, and continued
study is being given to the decisions that must be reached when
building becomes possible." Although "annual whisperings of

Alberta's new library" were regularly reported, students and faculty must have felt twinges of envy later that same year to read *The Gateway*'s account of the University of Manitoba's imminent move to an entirely new campus, then under construction.[44]

While he continued to press the case for a proper building to house the University Library, Cameron also cherished a wider view regarding the entire Province's need for library service. In February 1930, he joined forces with professional colleagues from the Edmonton Public and Alberta Provincial Libraries to invite librarians and board members from 22 academic, public, and special libraries across Alberta to a conference the following December, "to consider whether steps should not now be taken towards the formation of an association for the promotion of library service within the Province.... [and] give thought to the best way in which to meet the increased demand for library facilities, which is now making itself felt, and which will do so increasingly in the near future." When the two-day conference was held on 9 and 10 December 1930, the University provided a venue, hospitality, and a welcoming address by President Wallace, while the Provincial government supplied a small grant to cover delegates' travel costs. Mr Cameron delivered the opening and keynote presentation, a "Survey of Existing Library Facilities and Suggested Projects for Extensions." He stressed the obsolescence of the concept of the self-contained and self-sufficient library, and instead urged the need to establish a centrally administered network of branches that would provide for the needs of everyone in Alberta, no matter how geographically isolated. He expressed confidence in both the interest of the government and the desire of the public for such a system, and ended by declaring that, "Knowledge of good books and love of them are not to be regarded as accessories to the good life...[rather] they are in themselves for us, part of the good life that we desire."[45] Subsequent speakers addressed such things as "Suggested Constitution and Aims" for the proposed provincial library association, and the role of library services in "Education and Training in Industry." Delegates passed nine separate resolutions, and deemed the conference a success in promoting what grew to become a vibrant and influential provincial library association.

In the same issue in which *The Gateway* reported on the library conference in some detail, the editors urged the government of Alberta to solicit money from the Carnegie Corporation, from whose largesse Acadia, Dalhousie, and the University of Saskatchewan were already benefiting. The editorial suggested that Carnegie funding could become, "a step to securing our long-awaited and much-needed university library." Alternatively, a Carnegie grant might be sought, "to found a School of the Fine Arts, for which there is now specific need," to satisfy "a marked increase of interest in music and painting, for example...." Even funding directed at Alberta's public school libraries would mean "new life sent pulsing through that system [that] will in turn stimulate the University."[46] The University administration was scarcely averse to such private funding initiatives, as the earlier Rockefeller Foundation grant in support of the medical faculty demonstrated. Indeed, the Carnegie Foundation had already provided the University with a $50,000 grant in 1929 "for the advancement of teaching," and in 1932 a $15,000 grant enabled the Library to sustain its book acquisitions. In 1933, the Extension Department received a $30,000, three-year Carnegie grant, "to stimulate the cultivation of the drama and the appreciation of music and art in the rural districts of the province," efforts which "led not only to a broad program of extension activity in these fields but to the summer program in Banff which culminated in the Banff School of Fine Arts and Centre for Continuing Education."[47]

In November 1933, the University received an offer from the Carnegie Corporation of a grant of $50,000 for "some single project of value." Too small a sum to finance the desired library building perhaps, but President Wallace hoped he might use it to secure supplementary, perhaps even matching, funding from the federal government:

> After careful consideration had been given to the matter, it was decided that if by means of the grant impetus could be given to the plan of erecting a library building, a service of first importance would be rendered to the whole institution in relieving the greatly congested quarters which now serve for stack and reading-room purposes. The possibility was explored of utilising part of the relief funds which the federal authorities were to grant to the province for building purposes to aid in the erection of the library building, and of using the $50,000 grant to assist in the project. A decision was reached at Ottawa, however, that this fund would not be applied in any province to university buildings. As no provincial funds were available, it was necessary, though with reluctance, to abandon the plan of a library building in connection with the grant, and to consider other productive channels into which the grant could be turned.[48]

At the end of 1929, the prescient author of a satirical chronology published in *The Gateway*, accurately predicted that no library would be built for many years to come:

1930 *Government promises new library building.*

1933 *Government considers plans for new library....*

1935 *Foundations for new Library commenced....*

1936 *Plans for New Library Building altered....*

1939 *Plans for new Library Building revised....*

1943 *Government says library will be ready next year....*

1946 *Government says library will be ready next year....*

1948 *...Government says library will be ready next year....*

1950 *...Work on library building suspended.*

The author of a satirical article published fourteen months later was even more cynical:

FLASH.— *Plans for the construction of a library at the University of Alberta will be drawn up in the near future.*

Edmonton, Alta., Canada, Earth, Feb. 13, 4931.— The authorities at the University here today gave out the following statement for publication: "It is estimated that inside of ten years, the plans for the new library at the University of Alberta will be completed. This has been a long felt need, and we feel that at last we are going to have this much-needed building.

Records show that ever since the founding of the University in 1908, far back in the 20th century, practically every year fresh attempts were made to solve the problem of the library building, and at last, it would seem that definite action was going to be taken. And so, the students of the University of Alberta may rest assured that inside the next hundred years they will have a building that would do credit to any organization in the Universe....[49]

The author of an article published in *The Gateway* in 1933, who contrasted the University of Alberta with its younger rival in Vancouver, could neither suppress, nor conceal envy of the buildings on the University of British Columbia's Point Grey campus, which opened in 1925: "On the whole, I would say that the U. of A. buildings are larger and more numerous than those at the far western metropolis, but they lack the beauty of the buildings of the latter institution.... The Library is...a magnificent and massive structure...of B.C. granite."

Nor were its contents numerically deficient, at "82,500 volumes, about 10,000 pamphlets, receiving regularly about 550 magazines and serial publications...," with study space for "around 300 students." Indeed, "Comparing these figures with those available regarding U. of A.'s library shows a distinct advantage in favour of the first."[50] The author perhaps felt no need to note that Alberta was considerably less prosperous than its western neighbour.

In the autumn of 1934, an editorial in *The Gateway* offered a more positive view:

> *The students of this University are exceptionally fortunate in the libraries which are at their disposal. Although there are a few queer creatures who boast they have never been within the University Library proper, yet the majority not only have spent many grievous hours working at its long tables and hard chairs, but they have enjoyed many leisure hours meandering through its stacks. Then there still remains the Parliamentary, the Extension, and the Public libraries, if you find your own is not sufficient. We can not boast of the number of volumes we have access to or the variety, but for those who do not specialize the facilities are quite satisfactory.*[51]

Two years later, at the end of 1936, *Gateway* reporter Murray Bolton presented a less charitable view, noting,

> *it is singular indeed that the mention of library to the majority of the students does not suggest such a haven of learning. The word "library" rather means that stuffy room in the Arts Building where the few fortunate attempt to do some work. It's hot, it's close, it's crowded. Does that inspire work? Does that encourage a student to put his odd hours in study rather than in Tuck? A ventilation system supplying only forty per cent enough air cannot be expected to help matters either.*

The solution, Bolton added, obviously lay in

> *the construction of a separate library building. This at present is impossible but a most beneficial compromise could be arranged at a moderate expense by the extension of a wing of one of the present structures. The main point, however, is that, since a university is intended as a place of study, its library should be the principal rock upon which the institution rests. If this rock should falter in its duty, then what of its dependent?*

After giving voice to widespread student frustration with the Library's inadequate facilities, Bolton ended with a thankful acknowledgement:

> The patient, helpful assistance which anyone of Mr. Cameron's co-workers is so ready to give is appreciated by all, faculty and students, alike. Even the freshman with his sincere but dumb inquiries, receives a polite reply. Mrs. Race, Miss Hamilton, Miss Barber, Miss Ennis, Miss Conroy, in the Arts; Miss Dixon in the Med. And Mr. Appelton [sic] in the Ag., are all fired with the purpose of their leader, Mr. Cameron, as they strive constantly to assist in the seeking on Quaecomque [sic] Vera.[52]

The cramped conditions experienced during the mid-1930s by the University's 2000 students, both on the campus generally, and in the 80-seat Library in particular, were recalled in later years by a commerce graduate, class of 1936, with some exaggeration: "The Library was in the Arts Building too. It was the only place to study. There was no other place to sit around and do anything." However, a contemporary classmate observed in a letter to the editor of *The Gateway* that alternative study space was readily available elsewhere:

> The lower [men's common] room is the...study room for many an unfortunate male who cannot find a vacancy in the library.
>
> The only comment that can be made concerning the Upper Common Room is that it is grossly underutilized....
>
> Our suggestion at this time is this...have all tables clear in the upper common room to accommodate the male overflow from the main library.[53]

During the summer of 1937, though, the Men's Common Room in the Arts Building was made to provide not only study space, but space for books:

> Book-space doubles itself in ten years, explained Mr. Cameron. Many university libraries over thirty years old have to be rebuilt or extended in a fashion of which the original architects never dreamed. In the case of our own library, last summer there were 840 feet of bookshelves. Yet in the early part of the summer additions had to be made to include 200 feet more. During Summer School, when the Arts library was the only one open, shelving had to be put in the Men's Common Room to accommodate the

necessary books and to provide the reading-room space for the students. Our
library has expanded to such a degree that we have only about one-quarter
of the necessary space.

This shortage of space had been deemed "temporary" for more
than two decades, and as a result the Library's collections, Main,
Law, Medicine, Chemistry, Agriculture, and Education, were
"distributed over most of the buildings on the campus." That
same autumn, *The Gateway* reported that the Library was, "filled
to the doors almost every day since registration," and offered
by way of explanation that, "Since the depression students have
been spending progressively more time over their books, and as
a result the library facilities have become more and more taxed
to meet the demand for books and space in which to study."[54]

In reviewing the University's "Three Decades of Progress" by
the end of 1937, *The Gateway*'s editors endeavoured to sound positive about an institution just emerging from its "period of infancy
and adolescence" and "now embarking upon a promising maturity."
But they nonetheless felt compelled to echo Murray Bolton's
sentiments from the previous December's end-of-term issue:

> *Perhaps the most pressing problem that, at the moment, confronts the*
> *University is the necessity to provide for the growth of the library. In the*
> *opinion of many people, the development of the library has not kept pace*
> *with the advance of other University facilities. Stack room space is prac-*
> *tically exhausted, the sitting room at various hours of the day no longer*
> *offers adequate seating accommodation, while the [de-]centralization of the*
> *library units must necessarily result in a loss, both of time and of books.*[55]

The absence of a proper library building may have been keenly
felt by students, faculty, and administrators, but the lack of a proper
athletic building and student union building were also serious issues
at mid-decade.

> *Dr. Wallace stated that for several years he had felt that a Students' Union*
> *Building would be a great asset to the University. He believed that the neces-*
> *sity for it was unquestionable. However, he was convinced that the need for*
> *a University Library building was even greater. He pointed out that if the*
> *Government decided to give the U. of A. a grant they would undoubtedly give*
> *the building of a library their first consideration.*

Nonetheless, President Wallace expressed hope of building both a gymnasium, complete with swimming pool, *and* a student union, but reminded *The Gateway*'s reporter that the cost of constructing the University's ice rink had taken seven years to amortize. Since the projected cost of the gymnasium and pool was a then-unobtainable $150,000, Wallace suggested that the students establish a fund, seek public subscriptions, and ask the government for a loan toward the cost of a student union building. He noted that the Student Council had already established a fund for general purposes, and "stated definitely that he was confident that the University of Alberta would be equipped with a Students' Union building in the not too distant future. We hope, nay, rather we believe, that he is right."[56]

Although overcrowding in the Library was the most chronic source of complaint, and was regularly highlighted in the annual reports of the President and the University Librarian, other matters also drew criticism from the student body, ranging from professors in 1934 monopolizing current issues of periodicals, "until they are only of use for reference," to a far more anguished outcry over the decision taken at the beginning of 1936 to close the Library's book stacks to all undergraduates, except those reading for honours. *The Gateway*'s editors argued that, although the new rule meant "less wear and tear on the books, a smaller number are lost, and the stacks are undoubtedly tidier," the sacrifice was too great to bear, for,

> *A great many of us come from homes and schools where books are very few. Outside of the few classics included in the English courses in high school, we have had little or no opportunity of becoming acquainted with good books. We have come to University anxious to read anything, everything. But we don't know the names of the books or the names of the authors. We could find them if we were allowed the freedom of hunting through the bookshelves ourselves, of taking down one book after another, spending an hour or two with one we find interesting. Of course we have a card index system, efficient and neat, with all the titles typewritten in black, the name of the authors in red, and a row of mysterious letters and figures — and all as cold and forbidding as a steel vault.*

Was it fair or democratic, the editorial continued, when all students paid the $5 library fee, "if the sheep must be divided from the goats, why should the goats pay the same fee?" In a biblically rhetorical flourish, the editorial concluded with the hope that students, "will not have cause to say, 'We asked ye for books and ye gave us a filing system'." The editorial elicited support from another student several days later, who wrote, "The authorities no doubt thought the present restrictions as necessary, but — and here lies the unfairness — why should almost the entire student body be penalized because a few students broke some of the rules?...It is our sincere hope that the authorities will before next term remove the restrictions which in fact counteract the very thing for which a university is supposed to be striving, mainly the cultivation of the mind." In his report the previous year, Cameron had noted that overcrowding in the reading room was driving students to seek study space in the stacks room below, making it "difficult to keep a satisfactory measure of control." But the subsequent restriction of access to the stacks was primarily driven by the need to add more shelving to the stack room at the expense of study space.[57]

Despite space problems, Mr Cameron regularly sought to augment the Library's collections by obtaining donations of useful titles from both individuals and institutions. In 1928, Professors Owen and Coar of the Modern Languages Department began making substantial donations of German-language books; McGill University Library was a reliable supplier of various medical journals. Upon learning that McGill had accumulated 40,000 duplicate titles, Cameron wrote to President Wallace, who was then about to depart on a trip east, asking him to "investigate what they have with a view to securing some of them." This was valuable because, pressured by declining revenue as the worldwide depression deepened and beggared prairie farmers, the Provincial Government cut the University's annual operating budget over a two-year period from $588,388 to $375, 000. Thankfully, the $5 student library fee kept the book budget relatively constant, so that by 1932 the collection had grown to 45,085 volumes, including a number of complete runs of periodicals purchased with special grants provided by the University's administration. Then, in 1932, when the fortunes of both the University and the Library appeared bleakest, the Carnegie Corporation provided a grant of $15,000 over three years for book purchases. Mr Cameron could barely restrain his excitement:

> *An outstanding event of the year was the visit of Mr. Hugh C. Gourlay*
> *representing the Carnegie Corporation of New York, in the early part of the*
> *summer. Mr. Gourlay spent a few days with us and following on his report,*

the Canadian Advisory Committee of Carnegie Corporation recommended that we be awarded a portion of the grant being made to College Libraries. In December the University received the first installment of a sum of $15,000 to be paid in three yearly parts, for the purchase of books to reinforce the Library, with particular attention to the work of the Arts College. This munificent gift has greatly stimulated the Library, and will be of greatest value to us.[58]

When interviewed by a student reporter several years later, Mr Cameron credited the student library fee and the generosity of the Carnegie Corporation for the Library collections' continued growth to 55,000 volumes and 500 periodicals: "'Books are being bought continually,' stated the librarian. 'In one month 530 new books were catalogued....Books come from all over the world to the U. of A. library...'." Cameron went on to praise the "co-operative habits" of libraries in providing inter-library loans (ILL) to smaller institutions, and to describe the exciting new technology of microfilm photography. Asked by the reporter about career opportunities in librarianship, Cameron observed that "'As for the qualifications necessary for librarians, no one can describe them — in fact, anything short of tap-dancing. An all-around live interest is the important thing, on the top of a generous education'." While noting a shortage of male librarians, he dismissed the notion of creating a library school at the University: "'The constituency is too small. The number of students taking library work annually in Canada is about fifty, and McGill and Toronto adequately cover those'."[59]

A year later, *Gateway* reporter Murray Bolton praised the library staff for their responsiveness:

A request for a book by a department or a number of students receives prompt attention and, if the suggestion is a good one, the particular copy is ordered immediately....

Numbers do mean a great deal, extent and capacity of the library is of importance, but more important is the fact that the library is strictly a utilitarian organization. There is no dead wood there. Every book given a place in that library must have some specific use; every volume must be of service or it is not kept. Its aim is strictly academic....

Indeed, limited budgets as well as limited space compelled the Library to take a brutally pragmatic approach to collection development. The reporter faithfully reflected Mr Cameron's firmly held collections policy, as Cameron had explained it earlier: "We need books to use. A good reproduction of Shakespeare's 'First Folio' is as good to us as the original itself. Of course, many of our books are worth more now than the price we paid for them."[60]

Returning to the same subject two years later, Mr Cameron conceded that, "Although there are many extremely valuable books included in the University collection, there are really no rare books. The reason is obvious. In a library such as this a rarity would have no place, except possibly as a curiosity. After all, the aim of the library is to collect and maintain a modern and complete set of educational books, and not to make a collection of rarities." Such "curiosities" as the Library did possess, Cameron demonstrated, were acquired more by fluke than by design: "As regards old books, it might be of interest to the reader to read the oldest book in the library, which Mr. Cameron was kind enough to show to the reporter. Although published in 1589, the volume is not of much value except as an interesting curiosity. It is one volume from a set of eleven, on the works of Paracelsis [sic], and was found in an empty log shack near Drumheller."[61] While such a pragmatic and utilitarian approach precluded any systematic collection of rarities, the small number of such volumes acquired could be confined to, and preserved in a locked cabinet. Indeed, a separate "special collections department" or "Rare Book Room" was not established at the University until the inauguration of a second library building in 1964 made space available for this by-then rapidly-expanding sub-collection.

While donated books might be described as "a gift that goes on giving," properly invested endowments of cash donations may be made to do the same. In 1939, Colonel J.H. Woods of Calgary, Honorary President of the University of Alberta Men's Faculty Club, donated $1000 "to go towards the building up of an authoritative collection of books" in the field of Canadian-American relations. This sizeable donation was administered by Mr Cameron, assisted by a committee of four faculty members; seven decades later, it still exists as one of the Library's numerous trust funds. Mr Cameron also urged students that

> no matter how wonderful your own library may be, there is great joy to be found...in haunting any good or even goodish secondhand bookshops

*within reach of your legs. Nothing the university or its professors can do can
take the place in your education of poking around old bookshops. A lot of
education can be absorbed by the eyes and by the finger-tips of the happy
ones who find something of unending fascination in turning over the
miscellaneous assortment to be found in a good secondhand shop. It is not
the buying that counts, but the tasting, the touching, and the handling.*[62]

In a sparsely populated and impoverished prairie province, the
University Library, for all its deficiencies, offered its students a pass-
port to the wider world. One such wide-eyed student, Robert H.
Blackburn, who matriculated in 1936, found the Library's collections to be, "a revelation of riches." Seven decades later, and following
a long and distinguished career as director of the University
of Toronto Library, Blackburn recalled in vivid detail how,

*My inability to buy more than a few of the books I needed led me almost
immediately to the Library, the first I had ever seen apart from our glass-
covered bookcase on the farm, and the small box of University Extension
books that hung beside the wicket in the Lavoy post office. The University
Library, it was said, then had about 50,000 books, more than any person
could hope to read in a lifetime, but a mere fraction of today's additions. The
Library visible to junior students at the time was a long paneled reading
room, entered through an imposing doorway on the left as one entered the
lobby of the Arts Building. The five long tables on each side of the centre aisle,
eight chairs to a table, were usually fully occupied by mid-morning. At the
south end, in a large alcove, were the card catalogue, a big dictionary stand,
some journals and a counter where one could apply for other books to be
brought up from mysterious regions below. The near end of the loan counter
was blocked by a dumb-waiter with shelves holding a few books waiting to
be sent below. And on the near side of the dumb-waiter was the entrance to a
narrow metal stairway leading downward. The entrance had no sign beside
it, but it was known to be forbidden ground to anyone below fourth year.
Opposite the stairway entrance was an office desk from which Dorothy
Hamilton directed operations, dispensed information, and kept a sharp eye
on the stairs. At the beginning of my fourth year I entered the stairway
bravely, but was called back by Miss Hamilton to show my credentials. There
were no fines for overdue books, but none was needed; one did not keep
anything overdue again after being spoken to by Miss Hamilton on the
first offence.*

But once young Blackburn was admitted to those "mysterious regions," he recalled,

> Downstairs in the basement, at the south end, there was an alcove containing the collection of English literature, in Cutter classification. Under the window was a large table for the use of fourth-year and graduate students, though there were not many graduate students in the whole university — I think Alberta had yet to grant a PHD in any subject. Those of us who worked sometimes in the English stacks were vaguely aware of other libraries on campus: one in the law school on the second floor above us, a medical library in the Medical Building, a few books and journals in the Agriculture Laboratory, but we had no occasion to visit them. Several times I made the trek southward to the Normal School to borrow from the Extension Library that was housed there, and once or twice I looked in at the Edmonton Public Library. In principle the topics for MA theses had to be chosen to fit within the limited scope of the collection in the Arts Building.[63]

During the decade of the 1930s, thanks to the annual $5 library fee levied on all students and the generosity of the Carnegie Corporation, and despite the fiscal stringency of the Province and the University, approximately 25,000 more volumes were added to the Library's collections. Cameron had already noted at the beginning of the decade that, "the pressure on our shelf space requires that we should use storage space for the less used books and journal files, and this policy is being resorted to." The 2360 feet of additional shelving in this new "storage space" were obtained by installing an eight-foot-high ceiling over a ventilation chamber to leave a four-foot, overhead clearance for air ducts, thus creating an underground passage known as "the wind tunnel," where the books "became impregnated with grit and sand."[64]

Cecil Burgess, the University Architect, undeterred by the deepening economic morass of the Great Depression, went on refining his earlier plans for a separate library building. In memoranda revised at the beginning of 1934, he noted that because building costs had declined from 50 cents per square foot in 1928 to 45 cents, his "Total cube as designed 1,431,836 ft. cost at 45¢ [is less than] $650,000," although three potential reductions to the plan might reduce total costs to only $400,000. Even this lower sum, however, lay well beyond the reach of the University or Provincial Government. To compensate for this, the removal of a partition provided 24 additional seats in the Arts Library Reading Room and a classroom was annexed to the law students' reading room during the 1933–1934 academic session. Two years later the Arts Common Room was co-opted as supplementary reading space. By 1939, accessions totalled 67,082, and Cameron speculated that it could be "necessary soon to invite departments to scan their shelves with a view to discarding the older and less useful material. The effort to maintain as much reading space as possible holds the shelves in an uncomfortable state of congestion and makes the tasks of the staff more difficult."[65] Greater difficulties, however, were soon to follow.

Surviving Another War, 1939–1945

The outbreak of war in September 1939 did not result in a precipitous drop in enrolment, unlike the 30 percent decline experienced during the 1914–1918 conflict. Instead of encouraging students to rally to the colours, the government encouraged them, particularly those in fields with a high demand for graduates, to complete their course of studies prior to enlisting in the war effort. Even later, under the conscription act, students enrolled in all programs other than Arts and Law were exempted until graduation, and those in the upper half of the Arts and Law faculties were also protected. Some chose to enlist nonetheless, but during the first two years of the war, enrolment fell by only 12 percent from its pre-war level. These numbers were easily made up after the summer of 1942 by the arrival on campus of the Royal Canadian Air Force's University Air Training Corps Number 8 (part of the British Commonwealth Air Training Program), soon followed by a University Naval Training Division, both of which provided training paralleling that of the Canadian Officers' Training Corps that had existed on campus for decades. In addition to the hundreds of officer candidates in training, the University also provided technical training courses for large numbers of servicemen in the enlisted ranks.

The military commandeered the three residence halls — Assiniboia, Athabasca, and Pembina, half of the University's major building stock — which exacerbated the perennial crowding on campus. The influx of Canadian, Commonwealth, and later, American military personnel helped create a housing shortage in the Edmonton area. However, the RCAF soon erected on campus a drill hall, a cafeteria, an infirmary, and army huts to provide additional classrooms and student housing; many of these 'temporary' buildings continued to serve the University for years after the war ended.[66]

The University was soon operating on a year-round basis, with double-shift instruction, so class periods ran from early morning till 10 P.M.; the Library provided up to 14 hours of daily service. The inauguration of accelerated programs in the Dentistry and Medical Faculties to speed graduation of dentists and physicians compounded demand for the Library's resources and services, and increased pressure on Cameron's staff. The Library's staff ranks were also thinned when some members answered the call to the colours. Thus Cameron wrote the President, "As Miss O'Connor has been asked to accept a position with one of the British Government Services, may leave be granted to her please, as from September 1st...for the duration of the war, or for such shorter time as her services may be required in this position? The position I understand is a confidential one, not named in public."[67] The next member of Cameron's staff to go to war was Miss Doreen Fraser, who reported for naval service the following March; she was replaced in the medical library by Miss Blanche Giffen.[68]

On top of the Library's perennial problems, the war also compli-cated acquisition of European books and journals. Initially, all imports from the German Reich were suspended. In the spring of 1940, however, the government allowed German publications, "which the University can certify to be essential to the proper conduct of its work, to be imported through the National Research Council." Nonetheless, the following year Cameron reported that,

> For the first year of the war a few numbers only of German periodicals were received, but now no journal arrives from any German-occupied country, the only surviving journal from continental Europe being one from Sweden. Books bought in the United States suffer from a price enhanced by approxi-mately 25%, and books from Great Britain are greatly delayed in delivery. We are, however, able to maintain our connection to a remarkable degree, and the London book trade is making heroic efforts to meet the emergency.

Not surprisingly, Cameron noted that, "Long delays occur and corres-pondence has often to be duplicated." But amazingly, in view of the carnage wreaked on the North Atlantic by German U-boats, "so far, no single book coming to us from London has to our knowledge been lost at sea; one only returned by us to London is reported as damaged by sea water, and useless."[69]

The toll taken on British publishers by the Luftwaffe's bombing campaign against London also disrupted library acquisitions, as Cameron noted in his report the next year:

> Under war conditions many difficulties have to be met. Deliveries are slower everywhere, and in the case of British books there is often a long delay, and as a result an unusually large proportion of orders placed during the year remain unfulfilled. In some cases publishers lost their stock of books in print, and both stock and records of our London agents were destroyed. This loss in particular has involved an exceptional dislocation of the flow of books to us, and made necessary the repetition, after long delays, of missing orders, and the restoration by us from our records of all details lost in London....
>
> Restrictions continue in effect regarding books and journals from enemy-occupied countries, but arrangements are being made by libraries on this continent to restore our holdings of these, at least as far as they can later be made available in microfilm reproduction. In this service the Rockefeller Foundation is playing a leading part.[70]

Throughout the war, as indeed in the years prior, inter-library loans, many of them from American lenders, played a major role in supplementing the University Library's resources, especially for medical books and journals, which in turn encouraged the wider application of microfilm technology in fulfilling ILL requests, and prompted the Library to acquire its first microfilm reader. Before the war, the Dominion Government had lowered by half the book rate for materials posted between libraries to five cents for the first pound, and one cent for every subsequent pound, which was a boon for ILL services, but this special postal rate only applied to domestic shipments.

In his report for 1942–1943, Mr Cameron noted shortages of other materiel: "As it is impossible to obtain equipment urgently required, particularly for filing catalogue and other cards, temporary provision only can be made." And, by then predictably, "Unusual delays occur in the delivery of books, so that we still await many that have been long on order." Annoying as this was, their absence was not unwelcome in another sense, since, "The lack of space imposes on us the necessity of tedious and time-consuming moves and temporary shifts, which always seem to have already passed the tolerable limit. The Library owes much to the patience and willingness of its staff." With a hopeful view to the end of hostilities, Cameron also reported that, "The Universities of the Allied Nations are preparing, by collecting useful material, chiefly duplicate journals, to aid in re-establishing damaged libraries after the war. Our Library is joining in this useful movement, and will presently ask the aid of members of the staff who may have books and journals of use in University work to contribute for this purpose."[71]

The war years also witnessed a major change in the University's governing structure through the work of a University Survey Committee, whose recommendations were embodied in a new University Act passed by the Provincial Legislature in the spring of 1942. Under the terms of the new Act, the University assumed control of the training of primary school teachers in the Provincial Normal Schools, which had been one of President Tory's long-term goals, and the University's School of Education was raised to the status of a full faculty. This amalgamation brought into the Library system 13,000 volumes, 3000 of them uncatalogued, located in Edmonton, and a further 8000 volumes located in the Calgary Normal School. The addition of elementary education to the Education Faculty's mandate also led the University, perhaps belatedly, to establish a Department of Fine Arts, to formalize scholarship and teaching of music and the visual arts.

In the spring of 1945, in his final Librarian's report, Mr Cameron noted, somewhat gloomily, that,

> The difficulties of administration have...been more serious than in any of the earlier war years. Miss Giffen has fortunately continued to serve in the Medical Library, and for some months we had the services of a trained cataloguer, [but] in January we lost three full-time assistants, owing to war conditions, within three weeks....Miss Hamilton and Mr Appelt have borne the brunt of the present situation with great cheerfulness, but relief in regard to trained staff is urgent.

The unavailability of trained replacements, Cameron noted, led him to rely more heavily on student assistants, at a time when,

> The condition of the retail and wholesale book trade has been very difficult.... Our agents have had to inform us that they can handle only a portion of our orders — in some cases about a third — as publishers cannot deliver and

they cannot collect. An appeal to another large house received the reply that no new account could be received, as staff was recently reduced by a further 10 percent. The result has been that we have a very large backlog of unfilled orders, which we hope soon to be able to correct. Correspondence has been proportionally heavy, and fruitless.

In journals there has been printing of short editions, and resultant missed copies, but it is hoped that this will soon end with the relaxation of controls on paper. Altogether this has been our worst year in these respects.

After so many years of frustration over the Library's physical inadequacies, Cameron failed to sound optimistic, even as he announced that, "During the year the Librarian had a first conference with Mr. Mather [sic], the Architect, and the Library is ready to submit its suggestions when the time comes for the consideration of details affecting the proposed plan."[72] The plan to which Cameron referred was proposed by the Toronto architectural firm of Mathers and Haldenby, which had been commissioned to survey the University's building needs. The building program recommended included new wings for the Medical Building and the long-deferred library building, which, "Mathers proposed...be built south-east of the Arts Building and facing north on the 112 Street Mall. The first stage would include a reading room to seat nearly three hundred students, with tiers of stacks for one hundred and seventy five thousand books, expandable to accommodate three hundred and fifty thousand."[73]

A capital budget proposal for new buildings, drawn up in July 1944, had earmarked $390,000 (later raised to $400,000) for the new library building. The following January, in a letter to Premier Ernest Manning, President Robert Newton "pointed out that no permanent building had been constructed on the campus in twenty years although the student population had doubled. No more than ten percent of the students could find accommodation in the library reading room at one time. Many books could not be used because they could not be made accessible in the library stacks." President Newton struck a far more positive note in his report to the Board of Governors: "V-Day in Europe was really D-Day in Canada. Now we must put in motion our plans for rehabilitating returned veterans and building a better world. The presence in our midst this year of 34 returned student veterans has given us a useful preview of their needs. We may easily have ten or twenty times their number next year." Newton went on to announce that, "Mr.

D.E. Cameron will shortly be relieved of his duties in order that he may devote full time to advisory work with student veterans."[74]

Prior to the recruitment of a new University Librarian, President Newton conferred with Cameron, who observed that converting the Library's catalogue from the outdated Cutter System to that of the Library of Congress, "Might cost 15 to 20,000," mainly in clerical work. Cameron noted his staffing difficulties, made worse by the continuance of war, such as the continued absence of Miss Fraser and Miss O'Connor, whom he doubted would return, and recommended that the Library have four permanent, academic posts. These he enumerated as "1. Cataloguer (Mr. Appelt), 2. Ref & Circulation (Miss Hamilton), 3. Fac. of Educ. (Miss Clever?), 4. Med. & Dent. Library (Miss Fraser?)." After declaring these preferences, Cameron promised to make only "temporary arrangements, so as not to put anyone in the way of filling the above posts with the proper people."[75]

Mr Cameron's resignation as University Librarian was effective as of 1 September. In addition to his duties as Librarian, he had been serving as Director of the Extension Department since 1936–1937, and he was appointed in 1942 to head the University's Rehabilitation Committee, established to provide counselling to returning war veterans. That role naturally drew upon the experience of his former pastoral career in the Presbyterian Church, and as a wise and avuncular figure on campus for 25 years. His retirement from the Library was intended to free him to devote more time to advising veterans. Alas, this role was destined to be brief, for in April 1946, overwork and deteriorating health prompted him to retire to Victoria, British Columbia. At that time his successor as University Librarian wrote:

> In September the resignation of Mr. D.E. Cameron brought to a close a long period of scholarly administration, notable for the wise and careful building-up of the book collection from its early beginnings to its present well-balanced state. Mr. Cameron will be greatly missed, by the students, by his colleagues of the faculty, and by the general public throughout the province. His wide scholarship and intimate knowledge of books, and his immense kindliness and interest in people made him counsellor and friend as well as Librarian, and his departure from the Library leaves a gap which can never be wholly filled.[76]

On 19 October 1946, at the age of 67, Mr Cameron succumbed to a brain tumour, following unsuccessful surgery at the University of Alberta Hospital. *The Gateway*'s obituary noted that,

> *It has been said that Mr. Cameron did more for our university than any*
> *other man, with the exception of Dr. Tory, who founded this institution. His*
> *influence is felt all over this campus. As Librarian he did a never-to-be-*
> *forgotten job. He was extremely well-informed, and his discernment and*
> *skill in choosing books has made our library worth twice as much as any*
> *other one with the same number of books.*[77]

WITH THE IMPENDING RETIREMENT of Mr Cameron, after a quarter century of service, nearly all of it in the capacity of University Librarian, President Newton conducted the search for a successor with meticulous care, in stark contrast to the relatively casual and informal hiring practices of Dr Tory. Indeed, an international search was mounted; early in 1945 the following advertisement, designed to reach expatriate Canadians, wherever they might be, was placed as far afield as the British scientific journal *Nature*:

UNIVERSITY LIBRARIAN

The University of Alberta invites applications for the post of University Librarian; duties to begin Sept. 1, 1945; initial salary $3500 to $4000, according to qualifications. Applications, stating age, nationality, and other personal information, particulars of academic and technical qualifications and experience (including teaching experience, if any) and names and addresses of referees, should be sent before April 1 to President, University of Alberta, Edmonton, Canada.

Alexander Calhoun, the long-serving director of the Calgary Public Library, responded to an advance copy of the ad in a letter to President Newton: "I have no very definite recommendations or suggestions. I can think of no Canadian male librarian whom I would suggest for the position." Nonetheless, Calhoun continued: "I venture to suggest you consider Miss Marjorie Sherlock for this position. As you know, she is head cataloguer at Queen's University. I know you have her in mind for another position but all her training and background have prepared her for a university librarianship." He concluded by offering to make enquiries about

3

Marjorie Sherlock and a Decade of Recovery, 1945–1955

Marjorie Sherlock.
[UAA 69–90–218]

potential candidates at the next Canadian Library Council meeting
in Ottawa, urged Newton to consider American candidates, and
declared that "An able University librarian can make an invaluable
contribution to the whole library movement in this Province."[78]

More than three weeks later, Newton, who had been travelling in the East, replied to Calhoun, and reported that he had seen
Miss Sherlock at Queen's, and that she was still interested in
succeeding Miss Montgomery as Alberta's Extension Librarian,

> *but that naturally she would prefer to be considered for the senior post of*
> *University Librarian. I remember that when you and I discussed this matter*
> *last summer you expressed the opinion that it might be advantageous to get*
> *a man for the University post, since he might be able to play a more influen-*
> *tial part in...the development of library work throughout the Province.*
> *However, I formed a very high opinion of Miss Sherlock's qualifications and*
> *should expect that our advisory selection committee would give her very*
> *serious consideration.*

Newton ended by noting that Calhoun's own employee, Miss Flora
McLeod, had been suggested by Mr Cameron as a potential candi-

date for Extension Librarian, and by inviting Calhoun to serve on the selection committee for University Librarian. Two days later Calhoun wrote to accept Newton's invitation to serve, said he had discussed the Extension post with Miss McLeod, who was thinking it over, and offered this revised opinion:

> While I still think it would seem desirable from many angles that a man should be appointed University Librarian, I think it quite possible that no Canadian may apply who would be as well qualified as Miss Sherlock or other woman for that matter, in which event my vote would be for the woman. In the existing climate of opinion, a man's weight may count more but we are moving into an era when this will be less true.[79]

The widely advertised search elicited 14 applications (and 1 late entry) — 8 from Canadians and 6 from Americans, 12 men and 2 women — whose average age was 40. It was an impressively well-qualified field of applicants, 4 of whom held master's degrees in subjects other than librarianship, 1 held a law degree, 4 others had earned doctorates, while 4 had experience as heads of academic libraries, and another 4 as public library directors.[80] Of the three applicants who received the closest consideration by the advisory selection committee, Miss Sherlock proved to be their unanimous choice, although she "has not yet had opportunity to demonstrate executive experience."[81] While not the 'safest' choice, her appointment would prove to be an inspired one. Cameron's successor, Marjorie Sherlock (1903–1982), was born in Lethbridge, Alberta. After graduating with highest honours in English at the University of Alberta in 1927, she studied and took further degrees at Oxford (BA and MA as an IODE Empire Overseas Memorial Scholar) and Toronto (DIPLS, 1932; MLS, 1940). After serving successively as Chief Cataloguer at the University of Saskatchewan (1933–1941) and Queen's University (1941–1945), she returned to her alma mater as Chief Librarian. In an interview with a *Gateway* reporter she declared that, "As a westerner, who has lived in the East for five years, I am happy to be here, while as an Albertan who has been away for 15 Years, I am even happier."[82]

Miss Sherlock's homecoming to Alberta was far from singular, though, for that year 450 returning war veterans helped swell the University's enrolment to a record total of 4811, an increase of 2,132 over the previous year; two-thirds of these new students were veterans receiving government "rehabilitation" benefits. The following year the University anticipated that an additional 2400 veterans would seek to enrol, 500 of whom would be married. To cope, the University had, since VE-Day, hired an additional 60 full-time and 40 part-time instructors. These sheer numbers created a student and staff housing crisis that President Newton described as the University's own "Battle of the Bulge," citing the example of the Chemistry Department, serving students in several other disciplines, with laboratories equipped for 800 students that had been forced during the previous term to accommodate 2000.[83]

What was true of Chemistry, was more than doubly true of the Library, with its paltry 285 reading room seats. In her first annual report, in the spring of 1946, Miss Sherlock addressed the all-too-obvious need for a proper, new library building, as a preface to the challenge presented by,

> The taking-over by the University of the teacher-training work of the province [which] involved the inclusion in the University Library system of the former Normal School libraries in Edmonton and Calgary. These had been in temporary quarters during the war, with many of their books in storage, and the move back into their own buildings involved the packing and unpacking, the moving and shelving of thousands of volumes in the short period between the end of Summer School and the beginning of Fall term on September 18.

To meet the demands of the increased enrolment, additional 50-seat reading rooms were opened in both the Arts and Education Buildings, study tables were added in the Men's and Women's Common Rooms, and 30 seats were added in the law library at the expense of moving 3000 books into a storeroom beneath Convocation Hall. More significantly, Miss Sherlock announced that, "A series of conferences was held in October with Mr. A.S. Mathers, consulting architect for the University, and plans were drawn up and completed for a new library building, which will also house the Medical and Extension Libraries."[84]

In her annual report the following year, Miss Sherlock recorded the first of her most lasting and significant achievements: "In March 1946 a revised salary schedule for the Library was approved by the Board of Governors. Members of the Library staff now have academic status and their salaries are graded accordingly. This is a reform long needed, and one in which this University is leading the way for other Canadian universities."[85] In addition to presenting the Administration with a wide survey of librarian salary schedules at university and public libraries across Canada, as well as in both federal and provincial civil service structures, Miss Sherlock pressed the University Administration to grant professional recognition for librarians, fought for annual merit pay increases, and succeeded in obtaining both. The rationale for such changes she summarized in a later publication:

> Librarians today are professional workers, trained in the principles and techniques of a highly specialized field, who have added one or more degrees in library science to their academic degree. To be able to appraise the objectives of the University's program, to study the needs of the various courses, and to translate this knowledge into effective service, calls for qualifications in the professional library staff equal to those of the teaching staff.[86]

A grateful Miss Sherlock reiterated the significance of these changes in a letter to President Newton:

> The members of the Library staff wish me to express to you their appreciation of this action of the Board. I feel that in giving its professional librarians academic standing and salaries in accordance with their qualifications, the University is leading the way for other Canadian universities. The result, I am sure, will be an increased loyalty and interest on the part of staff, and will enable us to secure and retain really good people in our Library.[87]

At the same time, the University of Saskatchewan's president opposed any such recognition for librarians, who, as a result, joined the support staff union, and thus failed to keep pace with salary advances elsewhere. Qualified librarians were in very short supply during the ensuing decades, and Saskatchewan's intransigence, Bruce Peel later recalled, "condemned the U. of S. Library to mediocrity in staff for about 20 to 25 years...until the mid-1960s before the librarians left the union."[88] More than two decades passed before other Canadian universities followed the example of Alberta, which was among the relatively few universities in North America to accord academic status to its librarians.[89]

Curiously, although her second annual report was replete with details and statistics of library operations, Miss Sherlock made no further mention of the primary task with which President Newton had charged her, namely the detailed design of the long-delayed library building, which had finally been approved for funding by the Provincial Government in 1947, in which year the University's capital budget rose to a breathtaking $741,000. Over her assigned task of designing, building, and equipping the new library Miss Sherlock took the greatest pains. After touring some major American university libraries, she,

> was able to persuade the University Governors and the Provincial Government that only the best quality materials and furnishing should go into the new building. While many people on campus participated in the planning, none contributed more than Professor H.G. Glyde, head of the Art Department, through advice on colour schemes and furnishings throughout. He also designed and painted the historical mural in the great reading room.[90]

Years later, Bruce Peel recalled that,

> The pastel colors in the library were beautiful and you can't get the same sense of them now [1987]. Professor Glyde...worked with the interior decorator and apparently quarrelled with [her] — a lady who thought she knew her business. But she'd hold up a paint chip and say "Now this is the color for this room," and Glyde would say "No, that looks fine on the chip, but if you have it in the big reading room it will be too deep a tint," and so on. So the tints, the shades, were just perfect.

While Miss Sherlock deferred to Professor Glyde on such aesthetic matters, she took a more direct hand in the new building's design and physical appointments.[91]

After many years of enforced dispersal of books across the campus in branch libraries, departmental offices, and sub-standard storage spaces, and endless lobbying for a proper building by successive generations of students, faculty, and administrators, the looming prospect of centralizing the Library's collections was greeted in some quarters with something less than delight. Confronted by the prospect of surrendering the specialized, subject collections they had housed, in some cases for many years, a cabal of department heads sought exemption from the new facility. Dr Sinclair, the Dean of Agriculture, went so far as to demand additional space and the appointment of a dedicated librarian for his local collection.

Miss Sherlock, however, fought this attempt to undermine the many advantages offered by centralization. As President Newton recorded in his minutes of a meeting with Miss Sherlock and his assistant, Dr Walter Johns:

> Miss Sherlock reminded me of continuous pressure from depts. to retain branch libraries. She is strongly opposed, but agreeable to Dean Macdonald's suggestion that [the] question be reviewed after two years' experience with [a] centralized library. I am against Branch libraries because:
>
> (1) We made a firm decision, after consultation with deans, and based our request to gov't for library building partly on saving of space in teaching buildings.
> (2) Branch libraries [are] expensive to maintain: duplication of books & services.
> (3) Students using branch libraries rarely visit central library, hence many graduate with good professional training, but little education. At least they are deprived of some educational opportunities we should encourage them to use.[92]

The following year Miss Sherlock also took a stand against the suggestion that the Library begin lending gramophone records and pictures, which would have entailed considerable additional staff work, but acceded to President Newton's proposal that the third floor of the new library building might house a temporary art gallery, without prejudice to the Library's future need for the space. She reminded the President that,

> the Gallery is space that we originally thought would be used...for an Archivist....There is little doubt that there is need for an Archives collection, and of a trained Archivist. Our graduate students in History and Economics are already encountering difficulty in securing the original Alberta material they need for their research. The Provincial Library was never intended for this purpose, and is not geared for such service....
>
> Much of the valuable early material of the province is disappearing for lack of a trained investigator to track it down, collect, and record it. I know that the members of the Departments of History and Economics feel as I do, that the appointment of an Archivist within the next few years is very greatly to be desired. Saskatchewan took the step about ten years ago, and as a result much valuable local material has been saved....[93]

As laudable as this goal must have appeared, the University Administration was mindful of the additional expense, apart from initial capital building costs, that would be imposed by the new library building. These were expected to total approximately $60,000 a year, plus a one-time cost of $2000 to pay for moving into the building.[94]

Elsewhere on campus, objections to the project were gathering steam. Only two years after winning the first round of what might be called the Library's "consolidation wars," Miss Sherlock was reminded that ultimate victory is rarely secured by a single battle. In June 1950, President Newton warned the Board of Governors that,

> Certain vested departmental interests are threatening to fight consolidation, and the University Librarian had appealed for support, pointing out that her plans developed over several years would be seriously disrupted at this stage, and that the cost of supervisory and other administrative service, as well as of books duplicated, would be substantially increased. To make any exceptions, beyond those already approved for the Faculty of Education libraries here and in Calgary, would start an avalanche of requests. Departments having branch libraries prize their convenience, but do not stop to consider the inconvenience to members of borderline departments, like biochemistry, agriculture, etc., who now have to visit as many as five libraries to get access to all the books they need on one subject.

The President reminded members of the Board that consolidation was also intended to free space in existing buildings for classrooms and labs, on which basis the Provincial Government was persuaded to fund the new library building, and, finally, that consolidation, "is educationally as well as economically sound; students should not be segregated by narrow fields and exposed only to books in their own specialties. Failure to consolidate would nullify to a considerable extent our efforts to promote the general education of students." Newton's strong presentation of the case for consolidation elicited a unanimous resolution to reaffirm its policy of consolidating all except the education branch libraries in the new structure then under construction.[95]

A change of regime later that year, with the resignation of President Newton, and his replacement by Andrew Stewart, an economist who headed the University's Commerce Faculty, and had more recently served as the Dean of Business Affairs, offered opponents a further round in which to contest library consolidation. A meeting of the Library Committee was set for late December to settle the consolidation issue, barely five months prior to the opening of the new library building. Heads of all departments with branch or deposit libraries were invited to attend. Miss Sherlock provided the new President with a seven-page background document in which she surveyed the history and policies surrounding the several branch libraries, summarized the arguments for and against consolidation, and indicated where some compromise was possible or even desirable. In addition to the barrier to access presented by the physical dispersal of the collections, hours of access to them were limited and varied widely, especially in the case of books housed in professors' own offices; reference assistance was generally not available to readers; and supervision and security for these collections was too often nonexistent, so that books were neither traceable nor recallable, and losses were common. Miss Sherlock noted that the Deans, and most of the heads of those departments directly affected, in fact supported consolidation. The policy had been laid down by the Board of Governors in 1945, before detailed planning for the new library began, to incorporate "divisional" reading rooms devoted to Medical Sciences, Applied Sciences, and Law, alongside the general collection devoted to the humanities and social sciences. While cautioning against the unrestricted duplication of titles paid for from faculty budgets, Miss Sherlock concluded by recommending that the President stress several points at the forthcoming meeting: that the Library would duplicate material where necessary, such as "'lab manuals' and other works required as adjuncts to lab courses," that some selected titles might continue to be retained within departments, and that titles not required for students to read might be kept by faculty members "for a term or for the academic year, subject to recall at urgent need."[96]

When this enlarged session of the Library Committee, augmented by numerous departmental representatives, met late on the afternoon of 20 December 1950, President Stewart "opened the discussion by reminding those present that there was no possibility of altering the decision to consolidate small libraries and reading rooms in the central library, a decision which he fully endorsed. He had call[ed] together the members of the present committee...to arrive at the most effective means of bringing the consolidation about, and of giving faculties, schools, and departments concerned an opportunity to register their views on the move."[97] Subsequently, departments were invited by President Stewart to submit lists of titles proposed for retention on site for the Library Committee's consideration. This compromise may have appeared to have settled matters, but nine months later the head of the Chemistry Department sent the President a newly published survey of policies at American universities in support of his renewed claim that his department required its own library.[98] Arguments for decentralization would continue to arise and vex future generations of chief librarians.

Excavation for the new library building had begun in the summer of 1947, and a progress report on its construction in *The Gateway* was almost anticlimactic: "Slowly, but, after twenty years of rumour, surely, it's coming. Clanking concrete mixers and gangs of workmen are now at work on the new library building which will house all the library facilities at present scattered throughout the University." On 25 November 1948 the Hon. John Campbell Bowen, Lieutenant-Governor of Alberta, laid the cornerstone of the new library, fittingly named for the late A.C. Rutherford, former Premier of Alberta, and long-serving Chancellor of the University, The ceremony was almost upset by some engineering students, who absconded with the corner-stone beforehand. A wooden facsimile was commissioned in haste, and covered in fast-drying cement to simulate the original. Before their prank got out of hand, however, an hour before the sched-uled ceremony the culprits telephoned anonymously to reveal the stone's hiding place. "Years later a solid citizen of Calgary gleefully narrated to the Librarian the inside story of the cornerstone caper."[99]

But further progress was slow because of post-war shortages of structural steel and delays in receiving and installing hardwood. The target for completion was pushed first to the summer of 1950, and then to December of that year. Work was at last completed in the late winter of 1951; over the course of eight days in April and May 1951, a crew of "25 library staff members, 25 graduating students, 20 janitors, and 2 movers trucks and drivers" moved 150,000 books from libraries and offices across campus. One staff participant later recounted memories of "dust, hard work, laughter, good fellowship, rain, and more dust [as] Books and unbound journals that had not seen the light of day for 20 years were unearthed amid clouds of dust, and moved to new quar-ters." The work was hard, but the task was exhilarating, because,

Hon. J.C. Bowen lays
the Rutherford Library
cornerstone.
[UAA 69–97–291]

*no single word...can possibly describe the sensations of wonder and relief we
feel at the space and facilities that are now ours. After the crowded rooms
and packed shelves of the old quarters, it gives us a feeling of astonished
delight to contemplate the spacious reading rooms and book-stacks, and to
find ourselves after so many years able to seat our readers in comfort and
actually to shelve our books....For the first time in our history we can bring
out from the vault and cupboard, the library's treasures of rare books, old
pictures and maps...and display them....it is a great advantage to have the
small reading rooms, formerly scattered over the campus, united under one
roof. It enables us for the first time to provide trained reference staff for all,
and to give much more efficient service and longer hours....After the dark,
stuffy and crowded workrooms of the past the library staff can hardly as yet
realize their good fortune....Those of the staff who have lived through the old
days almost pinch themselves at times to realize that at long last the dream
has come true.*

Top: *The Rutherford Library (now Rutherford South).*

[UAA 69–97–302]

Bottom: *U of A Library staff in front of Rutherford Library main entrance, May 1951.*

[UAA 90–36–3]

Or as *The Gateway* enthusiastically reported: "It is difficult to over-esti-
mate the importance of this new Library Building, which will be one
of the finest in Canada. For the first time in its history, the University
will be able to provide good study facilities for its students and to
bring together its book collections."[100]

On 15 May 1951, 600 guests and faculty members crowded into
the general reading room for the opening ceremony, at which Dr
R.C. Wallace, Principal of Queen's University and former University
of Alberta President, delivered the main address. Over the next
three days, more than 5000 visitors attended a public open house,
and toured the new building. Most went away impressed with
the new structure, which featured such exotic interior finishes
as blond oak imported from China, white oak from Japan, orna-
mental bronze balustrades and hand railings in staircases lined in
Italian marble, and a foyer lined with Tyndall limestone quarried in
Manitoba.[101] Reviews by those on campus were mixed, however, with

President Stewart (left)
with former Presidents
Wallace (second left)
and Newton (right) and
Premier Manning at the
opening of the
Rutherford Library.
[UAA 71–147–87]

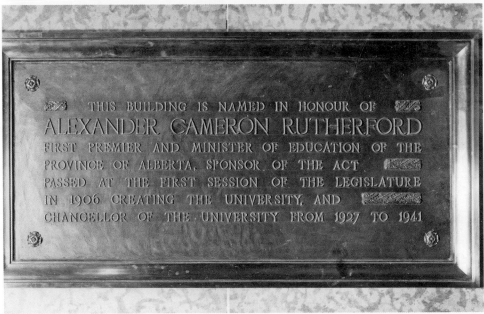

THIS BUILDING IS NAMED IN HONOUR OF
ALEXANDER CAMERON RUTHERFORD
FIRST PREMIER AND MINISTER OF EDUCATION OF THE
PROVINCE OF ALBERTA, SPONSOR OF THE ACT
PASSED AT THE FIRST SESSION OF THE LEGISLATURE
IN 1906 CREATING THE UNIVERSITY, AND
CHANCELLOR OF THE UNIVERSITY FROM 1927 TO 1941

Top: *Unveiling the Glyde mural.* [UAA 79-101-5] Bottom: *The Dedication Plaque.* [UAA 69-97-301]

the greatest dissatisfaction expressed by the law students, whose issues were more administrative than architectural. The editors of *The Gateway* thought the new building provided more reading space than would *ever* be required, little realizing that within seven years library space would once again become a pressing concern.

After waiting more than 40 years for a proper library, the University's 5093 registered students and 731 academic staff members were anything but slow to avail themselves of it. Reading room use the next year shot up by 75 percent, to a total of 181,000, and in the following year, 1952–1953, 268,000 readers' visits were recorded. According to Miss Sherlock:

> In its new central building...and with a well-qualified staff, the Library is at last beginning to play its proper part in the work of the University.
>
> The Rutherford Library has become literally the centre of the campus....
>
> The Rutherford Library is a beautiful building and one of which every member of the University and every citizen of the province may well feel proud. But the true measure of its worth is its capacity to provide for the first time in the history of the University, a standard of library service worthy of the University's program of teaching and research, and second to none in Canadian Universities.[102]

New Organization Within the New Library

Within the new Rutherford building, four distinct, senior units were established: Orders, Cataloguing, Circulation, and Reference, divided for the first time into separate departments. The selection, ordering, and renewal of books and periodicals was shared between the Reference and Order Departments until a separate Periodicals Department was created a decade later. Centralizing the Library within the new Rutherford building also brought together the four subject departments of Applied Science, Education, Law, and Medical Science. And the combined staff increased almost three-fold, with 17 professional and 15 associate staff for a total of 32. An additional 1.5 full-time positions comprised the staff of the Library's recently established branch in Calgary. One of the new librarians recruited by Miss Sherlock was a young cataloguer whom she had met in 1945, when visiting her former colleagues at the University of Saskatchewan on her way to be interviewed at the University of Alberta. Late in 1950 she wrote to Mr Bruce Peel, and invited him to send a letter of application. After moving

from Saskatoon to Edmonton with his bride of only a year, Mr Peel reported for work on 1 June 1951. Engaged to replace Miss Helen Farquharson, who retired that year due to ill health, he was then unaware of what administrative fate awaited him.[103]

Upon her arrival at the University, Miss Sherlock was surprised to discover that faculty participation in the University Library Committee, which had never been rigorous, had lapsed altogether during the war. Indeed, from extant minutes she was able to ascertain that the Committee had limited its work to advising on matters of general policy and the budget allocations made to the various departments, as well as to reviewing requests for new journal subscriptions. Between 1920 and 1924, the Committee met annually each spring; monthly meetings were held in 1924–1925. During the following decade, 1925–1935, yearly meetings were again the norm, with extra meetings only "as special needs required." No meetings appeared to have been held between 1935 and 1940, nor again after a single meeting in April 1940. "In 1945," Miss Sherlock wrote, "I enquired about the Committee. President said everyone [was] too busy & it would be a burden to members to revive it."

Opposite Top:
Rutherford Library
service desk.
[UAA 69-97-301]

Opposite Bottom:
Rutherford Library's
majestic lobby.
[UAA 69-97-940]

Above: Rutherford
Library main
reading room.
[UAA 69-97-935]

Although some of her successors would have reason to envy Miss Sherlock this lack of oversight by a committee of faculty, she realized that impending changes in the Library required that she have the support of a committee at her back. The strong opposition to the centralization of library collections made that abundantly clear. She continued: "In 1950, I suggested to President Stewart that the advice and support of a Library Committee would be of great assistance in dealing with problems arising from the reorganization and consolidation of the Library."[104] Thus, special meetings called in the winter and spring of 1950–1951 to adjudicate the dispute over consolidation in the new Rutherford Library led directly to the revival of the University Library Committee, its membership expanded to include all Deans. The bulk of its business, however, was conducted by a smaller Sub-Committee, which met under the chairmanship of Professor H.R. Thornton, head of Department of Dairying, who established a tradition of serving refreshments at its meetings by routinely bringing ice cream that was freshly made in his department. This helped ensure that meetings attracted a quorum.[105]

The Library Sub-Committee met for the first time on 12 July 1951, to consider the titles requested for retention in teaching departments. But first they considered their somewhat vague mandate from the President that the Sub-Committee "be advisory to Miss Sherlock." Dr Walter Johns, Assistant to the President, urged that the Sub-Committee should exercise an executive role in the affairs of the Library, which he categorized thus:

1. *Matters of routine administration, which were the Librarian's responsibility.*
2. *Matters of minor policy and the applications of certain general policies already laid down by the Library Committee, which should be dealt with by the Librarian, and the Sub-Committee.*
3. *The establishing of general principles and overall policy, which should be dealt with by the full Library Committee.*

Miss Sherlock, acting as secretary, concurred, and all present agreed "that the function of the Sub-Committee was to act for the Library Committee, except where it feels a matter should be referred to the Library Committee."[106] Thus armed with the authority and support of a faculty committee, Miss Sherlock proceeded to implement some long-needed reforms, beginning with the issue of retention versus collection consolidation. She then succeeded in ending a long-standing tradition by fining students for overdue books. Although initially applied only to those titles on the reserve shelves for short-term loans, this break with the past provoked criticism from students.[107]

Miss Sherlock also needed to deal with the Cutter System, which had long been a cumbersome anachronism; its official schedules had not been revised since before World War I. Worse, only an abbreviated version had been adopted at a time when no one imagined the size to which the University Library's collection would eventually grow. The Library Sub-Committee passed a resolution on 31 March 1952 authorizing reclassification of the collection to the Library of Congress system, adding the following compliment: "this Committee appreciates the very able manner in which this matter has been presented." That able presentation took the form of an eleven-page memorandum which Miss Sherlock forwarded to the President, along with the Sub-Committee's resolution and request that the matter be laid before the Board of Governors without delay. Miss Sherlock argued that,

> We are hampered with an inadequate and outmoded classification which is difficult to administer and frustrating to both library users and the cataloguing and reference staffs.
>
> Each year our annual acquisitions by gift or purchase are greater than the previous year. These are now being classified by Cutter that means that just as many more volumes will need to be reclassified when it is decided to do so (and we are convinced this will have to be, sooner or later)....Every passing year will aggravate the situation.
>
> Twenty years ago Mr. D.E. Cameron, urged on by various trained cataloguers on his staff, considered reclassifying. He decided it was too expensive and would take too long. Twenty years ago we had 1/4 number of volumes we have now (40,000 in 1933). The Library is growing very rapidly now with between 8000 and 10,000 volumes being added annually. We shudder to think of the chaotic condition of the collection in another 20 years, and the labor and cost involved in reclassifying then. We consider reclassification inevitable. For the first time in some years we have the physical space and facilities to undertake this. Every year's delay will add to the difficulty and cost of the process.
>
> This is an undertaking the necessity of which has been long recognized. When I became Librarian in 1945, I submitted a survey to Dr. Newton in

Rutherford Library
Technical Services
Department in early,
halcyon days.
[UAA 69–97–933]

which I dealt with the necessity for reclassification at the earliest possible
opportunity. Such an opportunity has not occurred until now. With the
move to the new library, space and facilities are now available to undertake
the work. Both Mr. Peel and I are convinced that it is inevitable and therefore
the sooner it is undertaken the greater will be the eventual saving in time
and expense.[108]

Miss Sherlock's dire projections, which stopped just short of the
apocalyptic, proved persuasive.

Bruce Peel was intimately familiar with the Library of Congress
classification system from his experience at the University of
Saskatchewan, where Miss Sherlock had directed a similar reclassification twenty years earlier; this must have greatly influenced her
when she sought to recruit him. Indeed, Peel recalled that one of his
first tasks upon arriving the previous June was to begin planning
for the reclassification project. With only two junior cataloguers and
two typists to provide assistance, however, he calculated that additional funding would be required to engage an additional cataloguer,
a cataloguing clerk, and a number of part-time student workers
for at least four years. Armed with Miss Sherlock's memorandum,

including Peel's budget for additional staff, it took the President only two weeks to secure the approval of the Board of Governors for a grant of $28,175 to be spread over four years.[109] On 8 April 1952 the Cutter system was discontinued for new accessions, and the conversion to the Library of Congress system begun. A complete inventory of the collection was taken, made possible for the first time in many years by the consolidation of the collection. "During the process much out-worn and outdated material was discarded, with the advice of members of the teaching staff, preparatory to the reclassification." Sixteen months later, a story in the *Edmonton Journal* described the reclassification project and the reasons for it in great detail, featured a photograph of Mr Peel and other project staff at work, and reported that 26,123 volumes were reclassified during its first year. Still later that year, a report in *The Gateway* praised the project for the way in which students, some of whom were employed in the task, experienced very little inconvenience when seeking books in the Library. By the spring of 1954, Miss Sherlock was able to report that half the collection had been reclassified in the first two years of the project. A decade later, the LC reclassification was extended to the Library's medical books, hitherto classified by the system employed at the National Library of Medicine in the United States.[110] The reclassification of the collections was the third major and lasting achievement of Miss Sherlock's administration.

Developing those collections was also important. War-time and post-war dislocations in the publishing industry and the book trade left a large, reserve surplus in the Library's book fund. This enabled the Library's collections to support the large increases in enrolment that were propelled by the returning veterans. But post-war price inflation, which saw the cost of books rise by 90 percent between 1939 and 1952, proved a drain on the reserve funds. At the same time, student enrolment more than doubled, from 2327 in 1939–1940, to 5093 in 1951–1952, and academic staff (including clinical and part-time faculty) rose from 279 to 731 in the same period. While only 16 departments featured graduate programs in 1939, 25 offered them by 1952, two of which had introduced PHD programs. Moreover, 170 new or enlarged courses had been added, as well as three new departments — Fine Arts, Physical Education, and Chemical and Petroleum Engineering — with a fourth, Geography, waiting in the wings. The assumption of teacher training at the former Normal Schools in both Edmonton and Calgary, and the addition of lower division liberal arts courses at the latter, added a further burden in the form of necessary duplication of titles, at a time when the Library was also playing catch-up binding its backlog of unbound materials, renewing subscriptions that had earlier been cancelled for lack of adequate funds, and seeking to fill in the consequent gaps in its holdings. While all this expansion in the University's teaching and research was continuing unabated, the Library's purchasing power had declined by 41 percent on a student per capita basis since 1939.

Confronted with such a stark picture, the Library Sub-Committee on 22 January 1953 petitioned the Board of Governors to approve an increase in funding, and suggested that the University's central administrative budget assume responsibility for the funding of current periodicals. Miss Sherlock was asked to appear before the Board of Governors on 10 April to make the case for additional funding. Once again, she had done her homework thoroughly. In a twelve-page survey and analysis, based on the standards of the American Library Association, she concluded that the Library's annual budget for books, periodicals, and binding should be $49,884, whereas in 1951–1952 it stood at only $31,792.42, an $18,000 short-fall. She went on to propose that the difference might be made up by adding $8000 to the budget and by raising the student library fee from $5 to $8. The Board of Governors was not persuaded to grant the $8000 recommended increase, but resolved to consider increases for binding and periodicals in the next year's budget deliberations. It did, however, approve the proposed increase in the annual student library fee, unchanged since it was first estab-lished in 1922, from $5 to $8, and from $2 to $3 for summer school students. Collected with minimal complaint, this revenue stream continued to provide a significant portion of the book budget until 1959, when it was abolished as a separate levy on top of tuition fees.[111]

University Librarians confront a perennial challenge in allo-cating budget resources among many subject disciplines, a particular challenge when confronted with an expanding insti-tutional curriculum. Miss Sherlock provided special budgetary allocations for new programs, and, even before gaining the support and added authority of the revived Library Sub-Committee, she proved generally adroit in her management of faculty requests, and sought a just balance in the development of the Library's collec-tions. As she noted in a letter to President Newton in 1947:

It is my endeavor to see that our collection is well rounded, to restrain certain departments which are inclined to be greedy, and to encourage some of the others (which have not been well-bought in the past) to build up the fields in which they are poorly provided. I have also been filling in gaps in our periodicals and reference collection as opportunity offered. I hope to have more time to devote to this aspect of the library, when we are not quite so pressed with the demands of reorganization and service.

For a still-struggling provincial university, with a primary focus upon teaching, it was sufficient challenge merely to fill basic gaps in the Library's collections, while keeping up with a flood of new publications. But Miss Sherlock was mindful of the growing importance of research at her institution. When Professor William Rowan, the distinguished head of the Zoology Department, sought to sell his valuable ornithology collection, Miss Sherlock wrote a lengthy letter recommending the purchase of "only those works which are of real use and value from a research point of view," for,

I feel very strongly that this University's future standing in graduate work will depend to a great degree upon the building up of research materials in the Library. Up to now our collection has been largely based upon the needs of our undergraduate teaching work. But from now on, as finances permit, we should set ourselves to acquire original source materials, and the classic and authoritative publications to which the research student must turn for original work.[112]

As the University continued to expand its enrolment, its curriculum, and its faculty, the Library's acquisitions budget could never fulfill all the fondest wishes of the professoriate. The need to divide the budget by subject and department into allocations that were equitable and defendable, by a process that was transparent and without apparent bias, was a challenge well-suited to the Library Sub-Committee. In preparing the budget for 1955–1956, the Sub-Committee worked with Miss Sherlock to develop an allocation formula for "Apportioning Book Funds Based on Evidence of Book Need and Cost of Materials." The formula weighed a number of quantifiable factors to generate departmental allocations, that the Sub-Committee's report admitted, *may appear somewhat arbitrary in some places, but it is not whimsical. It required a great deal of thought and work to prepare. The result, inevitably, is not as objective or scientifically accurate as the term "formula" would indicate. To a considerable extent, the techniques used involve personal opinion and pooled judgments. Nevertheless, we feel that the attempt to reduce as far as possible the degree of subjectivity in the process of appor-tionment has given us a sounder and fairer basis for allocation, and should safeguard the Library against possible charges of favoritism.*[113]

The degree to which it shielded the Library (and the Librarian) from such criticism was the best measure of the project's success. As an experienced librarian, Miss Sherlock would have real-ized that all allocation formulae, however well intentioned, are in the end the fruit of tradition laced with political compromise. In subsequent periods of budgetary stress, the quest for the perfect allocation formula retained its seductive appeal.

Perhaps the greatest retrospective acquisition during Miss Sherlock's tenure was the splendid library of the late Premier A.C. Rutherford. Negotiations began in 1938, when Rutherford, who had originally intended to donate his books, but had suffered finan-cial reverses in the Great Depression, offered them for $25,000, a sum the University could not afford and the Provincial Government refused to provide. At the suggestion of the Board of Governors, President W.A.R. Kerr sought support from former Prime Minister R.B. Bennett of Calgary. Bennett responded favourably, but felt the price excessive. Bennett proposed donating the books to the University if Rutherford would accept a cash offer of $15,000. Perhaps remembering their days as political adversaries, who clashed over the location of the University, among other things, Rutherford responded peevishly by suggesting that a fairer price would be $27,000. When apprised of this, Bennett expressed his regret, but requested of President Kerr that, "If anything transpires about the library, you might advise me." To which Kerr replied,

In the end the old gentleman — really to the distress of his family — declines to accept less than $25,000, more than his own immediate relatives think — times and conditions considered — the collection to be worth.

Of course, Dr. Rutherford is now a very old man and obviously failing. Might I venture to suggest that meantime the whole matter be left in abey-ance. I should like you, however, to feel that the University authorities are

deeply appreciative of the kindly and liberal-spirited attitude which you
have taken throughout this whole affair.[114]

Upon Rutherford's death in 1941, and the sale of his home on
Saskatchewan Drive to the Delta Upsilon fraternity, the University
agreed to pack and store the cream of the collection — 1000
volumes selected by Mr Cameron — pending negotiation for
their purchase. There the matter rested until 1947, when President
Newton informed Miss Sherlock that Rutherford's two chil-
dren wished to come to an agreement. Hazel Rutherford McCuaig
wished to donate her share of the collection, while her brother, Cecil
Rutherford, sought cash for his half interest in the books. In the
summer of 1949, an appraisal of $9100 was obtained from a profes-
sional bookseller, but this failed to satisfy Cecil Rutherford. At a
meeting in January 1950 he cited a pre-war estimate of $26,000,
insisted that he could find a buyer for $20,000, and therefore should
receive no less than $10,000 for his share. In the end, he settled
for $7000, a compromise that preserved the integrity of the collec-
tion and retained many fine books for the university which Premier
Rutherford had been instrumental in creating. While a handsome sum at the time, the cost of acquiring Rutherford's books
proved a brilliant investment, for to replace those 1000 volumes
today would prove difficult and cost well in excess of $1 million.[115]

Several years later maps became important to the Library. In
1953, the Library began building its collection of maps and atlases to
support the new geography curriculum introduced that year under
the direction of Professor William C. Wonders. The rapid expansion of the map collection, and a growing shortage of space, led to
its relocation within the Geography Department itself. After three
decades of exile, in 1995 it was moved once again, back into the
University Library. Today the William C. Wonders Map Library ranks
as the second-largest map collection in Canada, and the third largest
among North American research libraries. Also in 1953, a major
effort to collect government documents began with the purchase
of a complete backfile of all United Nations publications, and an
archival collection established of university calendars, exam papers,
theses, staff publications, and files of *The Gateway* and *New Trail*.

The administrative workload in the Library, paralleling the
large increases in the size of the staff and the acquisitions budget,
had greatly increased since Donald Cameron's time. Miss Sherlock

had, for some years, contemplated appointing an associate, or, "Assistant University Librarian" in the usage then current. Indeed, such a position had its own budget line before the new Rutherford Library was even completed. However, she delayed making an appointment from the need to find a suitable candidate, and from sensitivity to questions of long service, seniority, and succession. When Robert H. Blackburn, the University of Toronto's newly appointed Chief Librarian, invited Bruce Peel to apply for appointment as his second-in-command, Miss Sherlock encouraged Mr Peel to go to Toronto for an interview, but to make no commitments. When he was offered the Toronto post, Miss Sherlock sought the support of the Library Sub-Committee in promoting him to the position of Assistant University Librarian. The Sub-Committee members concurred in her endorsement of Mr Peel; they not only considered his qualifications to be excellent, but the fact that he was just then considering the offer of a similar position at the University of Toronto proved decisive. Several colleagues rushed to congratulate him, but, not surprisingly, at least two librarians with more seniority were left unhappy. One of them, the most senior, sought out Miss Sherlock, and, after objecting "with hammer and tongs," took her case directly to the President. Dr Stewart sought to mollify her feelings by adding a three-month leave to her regular holidays, thus allowing her to achieve reconciliation while touring Egypt.[116]

By the spring of 1955, Miss Sherlock was herself in need of an extended holiday, after a decade of the most intensive, if also satisfyingly rewarding, work as University Librarian: bringing to fruition the Library's first dedicated building, overseeing the re-cataloguing of the collection, and achieving academic status for her librarians. Accordingly, she departed for a lengthy stay on British Columbia's west coast, leaving Mr Peel in charge. As he later remembered, "on her return from summer vacation, Miss Sherlock called me into her office and surprised me by saying, 'I am going to be married in six weeks. You will find yourself librarian *pro tem*. The first thing you must do is prepare a library budget, for it is due about the time of my wedding'." In August 1955, Miss Sherlock resigned to marry Dr H. Grayson-Smith, then head of the Department of Physics, and went on to enjoy nearly three full decades of life in retirement. Years later, Peel recalled that,

Miss Sherlock was a most attractive woman...with personality plus. She sparkled and she had drive, [and] excellent ideas. The organizational pattern and the principles that she established when she first came here endured for several years after her departure.... She knew everyone on campus on a first name basis. Of course, she came when there were still only about 200-250 staff members. She was a hard act to follow. In fact, I never did follow it in the sense of having her outgoing personality and her ability to slap every university staff member on the shoulder.

Indeed, "As Chief Librarian she had developed high staff morale and maintained excellent library public relations on the campus. She was recognized as an outstanding library administrator. The beautiful Rutherford Library stands as a monument to her planning."[117]

BRUCE BRADEN PEEL (1916–1998) was born and raised on a prairie farm near Ferland, in southern Saskatchewan. After teaching in rural Saskatchewan schools, and war service in Ontario, he studied history at the University of Saskatchewan (BA, MA) and earned a library degree at the University of Toronto. After five years at the University of Saskatchewan Library, where he began work on his groundbreaking prairie bibliography, he joined the University of Alberta Library in 1951. By 1956, the year of Mr Peel's permanent appointment as "Librarian to the University," the Library, with holdings of almost 160,000 volumes and subscriptions to over 1600 periodicals, was acquiring an average of 9000 volumes a year, and had just achieved an annual rate of 207,101 items circulated and 412,198 "student days" of reading room use. And a new dimension was added to library service that year when the Alberta College of Physicians and Surgeons donated a Remington-Rand Transcopy, the Library's first photocopying machine; it was to allow journal articles to be copied and sent to medical practitioners who lacked ready access to the University Library.[118]

Within the Library, Mr Peel and his regular staff of 30, plus 50 part-time student assistants, provided service in a building described in *The Gateway* as, "one of the most modern and best equipped in Canada, [that] plays a vital part in scholastic activity on the campus." That scholastic activity was increasing at a dizzying rate, as total student enrolment tripled between 1957 and 1970. The steady growth in enrolment, particularly of graduate students, whose numbers increased more than six-fold — from a mere 334 to 2098 — in the decade following the promotion of the School of Graduate Studies to the status of a full faculty in 1957, required that the Library step

4

Bruce Peel and the Years of Exponential Growth, 1955–1970

up acquisitions well beyond the requirements of undergraduate programs.[119] While not unwelcome, this rate of growth over-taxed the Library's study space of 900 reading-room seats and 70 study carrels in the stack tiers, the latter available only to graduate students and honours undergraduates. It also prompted serious consideration of further library expansion. In the late autumn of 1956, the Library Sub-Committee held a series of six meetings devoted to studying, estimating, and making recommendations for the Library's space needs for the next decade. Various strategies were considered and rejected, including greater reliance on microfilm, storage of low-demand books, and other forms of decentralization, including perhaps moving the Extension Library out of Rutherford. Extension, then acquiring about 3000 volumes a year, was cramped for space. Thought was even being given, within the Government of Alberta, to 'adopting' the Extension Library as part of its own expanding library services, a prospect the Sub-Committee members feared would deprive the University of many valuable contacts in rural Alberta. The Sub-Committee's preferred solution, which Dr Johns agreed to present to President Stewart and the Board of Governors, was to add, within the next five years, several more stack tiers atop the Rutherford Library. The members also resolved that, "the Rutherford Library should not become a patchwork, [and] that the Library was so essential to the functioning of the University that the building must be extended as required."[120]

The Sub-Committee then turned to more long-range planning. Their subsequent report, "The Library: Its Problems and Its Future," predicted that in ten years the Library's collection would increase by at least 100,000 volumes and student enrolment rise to 6500. In fact, it took only five years to achieve those numbers. Over the next two years the space issue occupied the agendas of the monthly meetings of the Library Sub-Committee, as well as the annual meetings of the larger Library Committee. The Sub-Committee's proposed short-term solution of multiplying the stack tiers upward was deemed structurally untenable, so a more modest addition to the building was proposed. Mr Peel suggested that a west-facing wing might be added to the southwest corner of Rutherford Library to double its capacity for collections; his proposal was endorsed by the Library Committee at the end of October 1958. At the same meeting, Vice-President Johns revealed that $750,000 had been notionally allocated for library expansion.

When Andrew Stewart resigned in 1959 to become head of the Board
of Broadcast Governors (later the Canadian Radio-television and
Telecommunications Commission), he was succeeded as President
by Walter Johns. That same year, the proposed "modest addition"
to Rutherford Library was firmly rejected by the newly appointed
Vice-President, Lawrence Cragg, who now chaired the Library
Committee; Cragg urged immediate planning for a more major
expansion. It was Hobson's choice, for not only had the Library's
holdings doubled over the preceding decade, to 200,000 volumes,
but the burgeoning rate of acquisition had pushed the ordering of
books to an average of 2500 a month, so that the Library anticipated
receiving a minimum of 22,000 volumes during the current year.[121]

At the beginning of March 1960, an ad hoc committee, that
included the former Librarian, Marjorie Grayson-Smith (née
Sherlock), and the Superintendent of Buildings, B.W. Brooker, met
to discuss expansion of the Rutherford Library. They urged that any
addition harmonize with the exterior of the existing building; that
it be built to the maximum size the site would allow; and that space
not immediately required by the Library be given for temporary occupancy, probably as classrooms. One proposal that received serious
consideration was to 'twin' the Rutherford building, doubling it by

erecting its mirror image on the south side of the existing building, to create a core of book stacks surrounded by reading rooms and offices. Mr Peel shared with the Sub-Committee his reservations about the inherent operational limitations of such a scheme, and the members accepted his proposal that they secure the consulting services of the leading authority on academic library design. So in August 1960, Dr Keyes D. Metcalf, Librarian Emeritus of Harvard University, spent "three days reconnoitering and evaluating the situation." Dr Metcalf believed that, "an addition of something over 100,000 square feet (is needed) just as soon as possible; and I can assure you... that the need is very great at present....A second and perhaps a third addition will be needed sometime after 1975." Metcalf's recommendations were based on an extrapolated projection of 1 million volumes and 10,000 students by 1980. As *The Gateway* report stated:

> *Dr. Metcalf figured that the one new addition would cost $2,500,000 and the needed changes to Rutherford for ventilation, proper connections between wings, and extended elevator services would amount to around $500,000, a figure confirmed by the Public Works Department.*

The report went on to say:

> *Dr. Metcalf was very decidedly in favor of construction of a new library rather than adding to Rutherford....*

> *...although it would cost $2,500,000 to replace Rutherfords [sic] gross space with another library of the new style, because of Rutherford's monumental character and waste space, the building is worth only $1,500,000 to the University unless beauty can be considered an asset that can be evaluated in terms of dollars.*

> *Dr. Metcalf claims that if Rutherford were added to, because of additions, alterations to the present building, and extra cost needed to make the addition resemble Rutherford in beauty, the value of Rutherford would drop to a value from nothing to $200,000.*[122]

Metcalf's hard-headed cost-benefit analysis convinced the Board of Governors, and persuaded them to accept his vision for the new building, as described in the same series of front-page articles in *The Gateway*:

The proposed new library, if it is built will have emphasis on advanced study and research leaving Rutherford for the use of undergraduates, a Fine Arts building or for use of a Law School.

The type of construction favored is sometimes referred to as a "supermarket style".

Once a student is in a library of this style, he has access to all the books and materials contained in it. All the stacks are placed openly within his grasp.

The design is much simpler with open floors strong enough to carry stacks placed at any desirable position....

The proposed building might be five storeys high because of the ceilings being lower than in Rutherford.

Perhaps unwittingly, Donald Cameron's once-preferred location was confirmed:

Dr. Metcalf's favored position for a site is behind the Arts building between the North and South Labs.

He thinks the first unit could be constructed there and at later dates the labs could be demolished leaving enough open space to take care of demands more or less indefinitely.

Obviously pleased by the acceptance of the Metcalf report, Mr Peel nonetheless "stressed the urgency of...beginning construction...since the Rutherford Library is adding to its collection at such a rate that book storage after September will be a serious problem [and] that the problem of space might retard the Library's development, and thus the progress of graduate studies on the campus." In a subsequent discussion of the Library Sub-Committee's proposal to increase the acquisitions budget for the following year to $300,000, a member of the full Committee reiterated, "that if the University was to continue to develop its graduate program it must continue to increase its book stock *and the problem of storage should only be of secondary importance.*"[123]

Meanwhile, some space relief was achieved through the decentralization of collections, something the Rutherford Library was originally designed to end. First, the maps had been transferred to

Beginning construction of the new "Research Library" west of Convocation Hall.

[UAA 79–51–325–2]

the Department of Geography. Then, early in 1960, the Departments of Chemistry, Mathematics, and Physics sought to keep their periodicals in a reading room in their own newly-completed building complex. The Library Sub-Committee studied the request, heard from interested parties, and reported to the full Committee on what would be required, but recommended neither for nor against such a move. When the full Committee came to consider the proposal, Vice-President Cragg "said it was not a question of whether or not there would be a library in the Physical Sciences building, but the type of library that would be established [and] ruled that this was the question before the meeting." Other members objected that the principle of establishing any such library had not been agreed upon. Engineering professor James Parr suggested deferring any vote until the full Committee could reconvene, four members having left the meeting early. However, Cragg, who chaired the Committee, and who was himself a chemist, insisted on proceeding; when the members' votes divided evenly, he cast a tie-breaking vote in favour. The Chemistry Department's decade-long battle to win a separate library thus ended in victory for the Department; the Physical Sciences Reading Room was opened in the fall of 1961.[124]

In 1961, while the University awaited approval and funding for the proposed new library building, *The Gateway* reported that the Library anticipated receiving almost 30,000 books during 1961, and that an additional 1000 students were expected to matriculate in the next academic year. As if to reinforce in the public mind the pressing need for more library space, at the end of 1961 Mr Peel took the then-drastic step of closing the Library's smoking rooms to secure more storage space: "'I strongly believe that students should have a place for relaxation and smoking in a library, but this is a necessary and a temporary measure,' he said. 'The only other alternative is to stop ordering books'." Smoking restrictions in the Library had been eliciting protests since Rutherford Library first opened.[125]

Excavation for the new $2,500,000 research library, designed to hold 550,000 volumes and named in honour of Donald Ewing Cameron, began at last in August 1962. Construction was completed in September of the following year; by the third week in November 1963, the building was ready for occupancy. The moving of offices and 343,500 books was completed on 9 December. On 28 May 1964, Cameron Library was officially opened in a ceremony at which Mr Cameron's widow, Winnie Fletcher Cameron, accompanied by her son, Dr Donald Cameron, cut the ribbon.[126] Reactions to the new building, designed by D.L.G. MacDonald and W. Wood, were highly mixed. Its style contrasted starkly with the surrounding structures, both the older buildings slated for eventual replacement, as well as the newly opened Math-Physics and Chemistry buildings. Student Union Secretary-Treasurer Iain Macdonald was rudely dismissive.

> Asked if the building [s u b] would fit into the array of architecture already on the campus, Macdonald said, "The new graduate research library is a vulgar trifle.
>
> We will do our best to make the new s u b the first architecturally pleasing building on the Edmonton campus."

No less dismissive was Professor Pocklington of the Political Science Department, who declared that the library, "looks like hell from the outside." Mr Peel agreed that "Squeezed between the ancient remains of the North and South Labs the Cameron Library does look a bit odd," but Peel explained "that the library was built with the understanding 'that these two labs would be torn down'." This led one *Gateway* writer to suggest that,

Above and right:
The Donald Cameron
Research Library.
Above: [UAA 79-51-325-1];
and right
[UAA 88-77-64-250-14].

To mitigate this glaring contrast between the two styles, we would modestly propose that very luxuriant window boxes be hung from each window in the Math-Physics and Chemistry Buildings.

Not only would the buildings then appear less austere, but whole new fields of endeavor would be opened to the university as well. The horticulture and botany departments, for example, could develop a golden geranium to match the new library. We would then rival the Hanging Gardens of Babylon in splendor.

A *Gateway* survey of campus opinion recorded that,

But the main complaint was its generally oriental look. "It adds a little of the orient to the campus," was a common criticism.

One humorist thought that while this is supposed to be a cosmopolitan university Chinese architecture was going a bit too far.

But at least one student was found who defended the building. He thought "it is more important for buildings to look modern, exciting and functional than to have them all looking the same." Perhaps stung by all of the criticism, Dr B.E. Riedel, head of the Campus Planning Committee, assured readers of *The Gateway* that while a plan for the aesthetics of campus architecture did, indeed, exist, "'there are no definite plans to make a uniform campus. Changing standards require changing designs,' he said. 'We want to have a good looking campus, but we have to consider the costs. In planning new buildings, the functional aspect is important'."[127]

Another example of a purely functional structure was completed at about the same time. The new Education Library opened as part of a large, new education complex in the fall term of 1963. While austerely modern in design, it failed to elicit much comment or criticism, perhaps because the Cameron Library was too tempting as a target, and therefore distracting. In 1968 a third floor was added, that provided the Education Library with an additional 14,000 square feet of space. In 1979 the building was named for Herbert T. Coutts, the previous Dean of Education.

Cameron Library, designated for graduate research collections, while the Rutherford Library continued to house the undergraduate and reserve collections, as well as the Law and Extension Libraries, not only set the University of Alberta Library on the road to further decentralization, but the differential split between a graduate level

*Right: Original entrance
to Cameron's
"Bronze Pagoda."*
[UAA 88–77–68–2288–8]

*Below: The Cameron
Library featured open-
plan work spaces.*
[UAA 88–77–68–3325–20]

"research" library and an undergraduate collection did not escape criticism. The head of the Zoology Department observed that the new Cameron Library was already excessively crowded, while the Rutherford Library appeared to be providing only study space, and added that, "Maybe we should reconsider the division...into 'undergraduate' and 'research' sections and look again at other types of division, e.g., Humanities and Social Sciences and the Natural Sciences." This suggestion anticipated by a decade the division of collections undertaken when Rutherford Library was expanded. In responding, Mr Peel countered the implication that study space was space wasted, by noting that North American standards called for 20 to 50 percent of a library to be devoted to study space, and adding rhetorically, "Where would you suggest they go? They cannot all stand around in corridors, or crowd into the tuck shop, so that the logical place for the well-organized student to go is to the Library."[128]

The Cameron Library's open-stacks plan required staffing of a bag-check station at the exit to ensure that all books were properly charged out at the Circulation Desk. Students were also issued library identity cards for the first time. As well, the traditional honour system of not imposing fines on students for overdue books, other than those placed on reserve, was ended, albeit reluctantly, to ensure that borrowers would return books in a timely manner. This measure was initially met with fierce criticism by students, which Mr Peel addressed in a letter to *The Gateway*, in which he noted that overdue books inconvenienced other readers, and consumed considerable staff time and expense in sending overdue and recall notices for 10 percent of all books loaned. It also meant faculty members were led to request that more and more books be placed on reserve, or designated as "non-circulating." Imposing a daily fine of 25 cents for each overdue book reduced overdue notices by 41.6 percent, from 48,351 to only 28,216. However, under pressure from the Student Union, the daily fine was reduced to 20 cents, with the result that the following year overdue notices climbed by 40 percent, back up to 40,158. The need for greater control was clear enough, generally accepted, and eventually the public grumbling subsided.[129] Open stacks also meant that older and more expensive books had to be identified, and segregated from the main collection. The Library's holdings of rare books, many already kept under lock and key, were thus considerably augmented and moved into a Rare Book Room established in January 1964, under the curatorship of Miss Dorothy Hamilton, formerly the long-serving head of the Reference Department. A separate Government Documents Section was also created within the enlarged Reference Department.

Additional staff were required not only to run the public service departments of a second, large library on campus, but also to deal with the ever-increasing intake of new acquisitions. In 1965, the Library also took over responsibility for staffing and operating the John W. Scott Reading Room in University Hospital. A much enlarged staff complement led to the creation of several new administrative posts, beginning with an Assistant University Librarian for Public Services and another for Technical Services.[130] Dealing with a growing avalanche of new acquisitions was only half of the challenge of developing the Library's collections. The pressing need to evaluate holdings, draft and revise collections policies, and provide liaison with faculty, prompted a search for a Collections Librarian in 1963. When all of the prospective candidates for the post declined to apply, Mr Peel observed in a letter to Vice-President H.A. Armstrong that, "this is confirmation...that people with this specialized knowledge are extremely scarce, and when they have built up this knowledge through experience they are then firmly rooted in the institution where they have built up the collection. I agree...that the best prospect is to grow our own species." More than a year later, early in 1965, Dr Gustave Hermansen was appointed for one year to establish the Collections (later "Selections") Department to direct retrospective collection development in consultation with the teaching departments. In June 1966, Hermansen returned to the Classics Department, and was succeeded by Miss Lillian Leversedge. A survey conducted in 1969–1970 led to the appointment of a Coordinator of Circulation Services.[131]

As student enrolment and book acquisition numbers continued to climb, space in the new Cameron Library reached a critical stage within two years, rendering more imperative the architect's planned doubling of the building by adding two additional wings of 50,000 square feet each. However, by January 1966 it was clear that a two-year delay would be unavoidable to allow for relocation of the Dairy Science laboratories from the adjacent North and South Labs buildings. In addition to accommodating an anticipated 100,000 new volumes, the Library was recruiting staff to fill 30 to 40 new positions for which working space would be required. Mr Peel therefore raised the possibility in *The Gateway* of storing books in a de facto, if temporary, return to closed stacks. The following year he even raised with the Library Committee the question of building a temporary storage structure for books. The University's expansion plans envisaged further development on the eastern side of the campus, in the North Garneau neighbourhood, as a future home for humanities and social sciences departments. Building an adjacent library facility in North Garneau was already under consideration by University planners. Thus, when the Library Committee submitted its own development plan, pressing for speedy completion of both North and South Wing additions to the Cameron building, it raised the question of whether to proceed with the first 50,000 square foot addition to Cameron, or switch to a North Garneau site, and erect the first phase of a new Humanities and Social Sciences Library. These issues were discussed at some length at a meeting of the Academic Development Committee in March 1968, where it was made clear that since a 200,000 square foot facility would be required for the humanities and social sciences collections, on a sheer cost basis, the first Cameron expansion of 50,000 square feet was the more affordable option. Professor (later President) Harry Gunning took the opportunity to remind the Committee that "If money is allotted to the Library, to allow it to expand as much as it desires, then this will be money that will not be available to other departments on campus. He felt that the Library was no more important than other departments and should not necessarily get preferential treatment when money is allotted for expansion." The following day the expansion question was laid before the University Planning Committee, where the Library's urgent need for space more-or-less settled the issue.[132]

Construction of the Cameron North Wing began later that year, following demolition of the North Labs building. When completed in November 1969, the North Wing added 47,500 square feet of space, which would take, at most, three years to fill at the then current rate of book acquisition. Therefore, planning continued for construction of a North Garneau Library. Despite a pleasant surprise when the Cameron expansion project came in at $441,321 less than its $1.4 million budget, other budget shortfalls and protests prevented the planned demolition of the South Labs building, so the original design for the Cameron Library remains unfulfilled to this day.[133] Well before ground was even broken for the new North Wing of Cameron, it was clear that it would prove to be too little space, arriving too late. In March 1966,

Top: Cameron North Wing expansion takes shape. [UAA 88–77–69–5162–2]

Bottom: Cameron North Wing complete. [UAA 88–77–69–7174–44]

the chairman of the Campus Planning Committee, pharmacy professor B.E. Riedel, appeared before the Library Committee, and

> suggested that the Committee should prepare a concise, documented statement on the timing of future library construction, indicating what the needs of the Library were, and that this statement be submitted to the Campus Planning Committee. Dr. Riedel also suggested that the Committee should consider making a start on the planning for a new library building east of the Arts Building, or for the first unit of such a building.

The Committee lost little time in complying, and had such a document ready for consideration at its 5 April meeting, in which it urged that planning for a new Humanities and Social Sciences Library commence without delay, "since there is no possibility of the addition of a South Wing to the Cameron Library for occupation before the Spring of 1970." Faced with the immediate need to create space for the influx of 175,000 books that the proposed 50 percent spending increase would yield in 1967–1968, as well as for the 50 to 60 additional staff who must be hired to process and catalogue them all, the Library Committee proposed that the Extension Library be moved out of the Rutherford Library and into rented quarters no later than 1 April 1967.[134]

The Library had a particularly strong argument for additional staffing, for it was already living with a backlog of 40,000 volumes awaiting cataloguing, retrieving them by means of an accessions file; this backlog was projected to grow to 100,000 volumes by 1969. As if to reassure President Johns, as he was confronted by these requests for enormous budget increases, Mr Peel sent him the 1966–1967 budget figures for twenty Canadian university libraries. These showed the University of Alberta trailing its nearest rival, British Columbia, in both library salaries and acquisitions budgets.[135] The University of Alberta had evolved in the post-war decades from a small, provincial school focused upon teaching, into a full-service, research-intensive institution with a full complement of graduate programs, that increasingly aspired to earn national as well as international recognition and respect. Masters degrees and the occasional doctorate had been granted from the University's earliest days, under the aegis of the Committee on Graduate Studies (GS), established in 1915. Three doctoral students were admitted, in Biochemistry and Agriculture, as early as 1951, by which time the GS

Committee was known as the School of Graduate Studies, that was formally established as a Faculty of Graduate Studies in 1957, under the leadership of the dynamic plant physiologist and former Dean of Agriculture, Arthur Gilbert McCalla. That same year witnessed the hiring of the equally dynamic Harry Gunning as the new head of the Chemistry Department. In the words of the University's official historian, Rod Macleod, "Other departments in the university took note of the changes that launched Chemistry within half a dozen years from a sleepy scientific backwater to one of the leaders in North America. Chemistry provided the model for the rest of the university in the massive expansion of the 1960s."[136]

The physicists soon emulated their neighbours, the chemists, in seeking enhanced support to reinvent their department. English Professor Henry Kreisel soon expressed to his colleagues on the Library Committee his concern "about the future development of the Humanities at the university — that the sciences were moving rapidly ahead and that it would be disastrous if the Humanities should fall back and our university become a one-sided institution." Dean McCalla replied that, "at present we have a one-sided university," and cited the number of graduate students enrolled in the sciences as proof. Undeterred, Kreisel urged, "that unless the level of book purchases in the field of the Humanities was strengthened the ratio will increase." Although the science 'tail' had, indeed, begun to wag the University 'dog,' eventually even scientists such as Vice-President Cragg had to acknowledge the role of superior library holdings in attracting graduate students, when he urged his fellow members of the Library Committee to, "direct our attention to building up the humanities and social sciences collections at Alberta." The Library's acquisitions budget grew by leaps and bounds, until by 1964–1965 it stood at over $400,000, of which $50,000 was a special allocation earmarked for the Department of History, which "has been designated as a department which is to expand rapidly, so that the Library now has a directive with regard to this particular department."[137]

The phenomenal growth of the University, and its transformation from a minor provincial institution to an academic powerhouse, were certain to lead to changes in its governance. Upon assuming the presidency in 1959, Walter Johns commissioned a review of the University Act, as revised in 1942. Succeeding years witnessed growing demands for wider faculty participation in the University's governing structure, a broadening of representation on the General Faculties Council (GFC), and autonomy for the University's Calgary division. By 1965, these trends led to the of birth of the University of Calgary as an independent entity, more democratic and representative university governance, and a restructured system of committees reporting to GFC as the principal forum for originating, developing, and endorsing academic policies, subject only to the administrative blessing of the Board of Governors.[138] From the Library's perspective, however, not all of these developments were equally successful, and one, in particular, proved a notable failure.

Administration by Committee

In 1963, the annual meeting of the full Library Committee was postponed because of the move to the new Cameron building. When the Committee met at last on 27 February 1964, Mr Peel described the new procedures in place in the Cameron, Rutherford, and Education Libraries, and Assistant Librarian Donald Baird announced that the Library's collection had grown to 352,108 volumes, with over 4900 journal subscriptions (1000 of them free), and distributed a table showing growth since 1959 compared to the libraries at UBC and Toronto. Later that same day, outgoing Library Sub-Committee chairman James Parr, who had just been appointed Dean of Applied Science at Windsor, wrote to the President to urge that, in future, the Library Sub-Committee, the policy-making body, should report to GFC directly, or to GFC through Deans' Council, and that the larger Library Committee, which included the Deans, be abolished because, "the present arrangement isn't working well: it is clumsy; it does not assist the Librarian in the way it should; it does not serve the University effectively." This was true enough, and a reasonable proposal. Parr then went on to urge:

> The body that we know at present as the library sub-committee must have as its chairman a senior administrator....For at the very core of the sub-committee's business is the budget: and a chairman from Faculty simply does not enjoy...a proximity to budget matters that enables him to guide his sub-committee, nor to forcefully put the sub-committee's recommendations. In short, the chairman of the sub-committee has to be the Vice-President....To summarize my suggestions: the library committee as it is now constituted should be dissolved. The library sub-committee (constituted in much the same way it is just now — that is, properly representative) continue its

present duties under the Chairmanship of the Vice-President, and also take over the responsibilities for suggesting policy. Regular reports, including policy recommendations and other general matters of interest (budget, allocations), be brought before gfc through Deans' Council.

President Johns replied to say that he saw merit in Parr's proposal, but hesitated to impose the task of chairing the Sub-Committee on Vice-President Armstrong without first consulting him, Mr Peel, and other members. Johns expressed his regret at having delegated the role upon assuming the presidency because,

I have a very keen interest in the Library Sub-Committee for I was responsible for setting it up in the first place, when Marjorie Sherlock was the Librarian. The purpose in doing so was to have a number of faculty members keenly interested in the Library and its problems, work closely with the Librarian, and help her with day to day policy decisions that had to be made between annual meetings of the Library Committee itself. One other object of it was to protect the Librarian from the abuse that was often visited on her head by staff members who disagreed with her policies (often on the basis of inadequate understanding of the problems of the Library). I still think it works reasonably well, bearing in mind the original purpose it was designed to fulfill. All this is not to say that an improvement might not result if we adopt your suggestion.[139]

Although Mr Peel saw merit in the role played by the larger committee, which at least acquainted a wider audience with the Library and its issues, as well as lending weight to policy decisions, he agreed that its annual meetings were ineffective in dealing with daily operating issues. He agreed to survey practices at other Canadian universities, and submit a reorganization proposal. Meanwhile, Vice-President Armstrong wrote the President in support of dissolving the larger Library Committee, and offering to chair a reorganized Library Sub-Committee. The following month, adopting Professor Parr's suggestions that the larger Library Committee be abolished, and that the former Sub-Committee, one advisory to the Chief Librarian, report directly to GFC, Peel prepared and submitted a two-page document summarizing the proposed terms of reference for the reconstituted Committee. President Johns replied to express his agreement in general, and to suggest that annual reports to the GFC at its March or April meetings could, when approved, "become part of the Librarian's Annual Report to the President and the Board of Governors."[140]

Unfortunately for the Library, events did not unfold so simply. In September GFC appointed a committee to study the matter, and make its own recommendations. Losing no time, the committee, chaired by Graduate Studies Dean McCalla, held several meetings, and within the month tendered its report. It began ominously with a declaration:

> It has been obvious for some time that members of the academic staff have been dissatisfied with the operation and administration of the Library, particularly in respect to major policy decisions related to the needs of research and graduate programs. This is shown by the submissions made to the President by a number of staff members and by at least one departmental committee.

The committee then recommended that the old Library Committee,

> be replaced by a new Library Committee organized more or less along the lines of the present sub-committee, but with much more authority. That this committee determine policy for the library and develop procedures in keeping with the rapidly changing nature of the University and the increasing emphasis being placed on research and graduate studies [and] that the Librarian be directly responsible to the Library Committee.

The report went on to propose names of nine faculty members to serve initial terms under the chairmanship of Professor of Economics Eric Hanson, Associate Dean of the School of Graduate Studies. Two months later, after the report and all its recommendations were approved by GFC, Dean of Law Wilbur Bowker reviewed the University Act, and gave his assurance that these changes were well within the powers and authority of GFC under Section 61(3)(k) "to make rules and regulation for the management and conduct of the library."[141] In the eyes of Chairman Hanson, to whom the Librarian now reported, instead of directly to the President, the Library Committee's authority was no longer merely advisory, but had become absolute.

This radical change was brought about by a growing groundswell of faculty frustration largely, but not exclusively, confined to the sciences, where discontent over library policies lingered, despite the recent victory over creation of a separate Physical Sciences

Library. The expanded acquisitions program, that resulted in massive increases in the number of books received, as well as delays by publishers and booksellers in filling orders, left the Library's technical services staff scrambling to keep up. And while the Library sought to expand the number of staff to deal with the increases, recruiting and training new staff was time-consuming and frustrating for the Chief Librarian. All of these adjustments were compounded by the unavoidable dislocation created by the move to the new Cameron Library building. For the faculty, the rapid expansion of the Library's collections and services was key to boosting the University into the upper ranks among Canadian universities. For Graduate School Dean McCalla and his Associate Dean, Eric Hanson, any obstacle to the goal was intolerable. Overlooking the space and staffing issues that had hobbled the Library's more rapid expansion, even when vast new budget allocations were made available for a new building, the purchase of more books and journals, and the hiring of more staff, they placed the blame on the Chief Librarian.

The announcement that the Library would, as before, close daily at 5:00 P.M. during the summer proved to be a trigger. Dean McCalla forwarded a letter of protest signed by 30 staff members and graduate students to Mr Peel, and added, "I wish to record my unconditional support of the...protests from graduate students. A research library cannot be operated effectively on a schedule that closes it at 5:00 P.M. every day." Professor Henry Kreisel, head of the English Department, wrote President Johns to report similar protests by his faculty, including a colleague enraged "because a janitor just turned off the light and asked him to leave, literally in mid-sentence....something must be done to change this situation." Kreisel added, "We are now spending a great deal of money on Inter-Session Bursaries and on research in general, and I think the practices which were good enough when this was primarily an undergraduate institution are now completely out of date." The President took almost two weeks to reply to Kreisel.

> *I certainly have some sympathy for your colleague but I also have some sympathy for the people who have been on duty in the library for eight hours already and who may have other appointments or responsibilities awaiting them at the end of their day's work. I have always tried, personally, to respect the rights of others as I hope they will respect mine.*

The regulations governing the hours during which the library is open may require review but if they call for the library to be closed at 5 o'clock, I think we should not insist that our non-academic colleagues await our convenience.[142]

President Johns, by the tone of his reply, betrayed a degree of irritation, perhaps because he had just received two still-more-disturbing letters of complaint, and was contemplating how best to reply to them. On 27 May, Dean McCalla wrote to the President, "You have known for some time that I consider that Mr. Bruce Peel lacks the basic qualifications needed by the Librarian of a University like Alberta. There has been ample new proof of this recently. You also know that I base my opinion not only on performance but also on the qualifications demanded by Universities elsewhere. I have referred to Uppsala University in Sweden." The Dean then went on to list the qualifications cited by a colleague at the Wageningen Agricultural University in the Netherlands:

First, scholarship, preferably a scholar in the humanities with at least a Ph.D. degree. He must be aware of the needs of scholars and keep in close touch with the developments in the various academic and research fields.

Second, the librarian must have the assistance of competent scholars in other disciplines.

Third, of course there must be staff qualified in library techniques and administration, but these must certainly be at the second level.

In my opinion we are trying to operate with a librarian in this third category, and it is seriously handicapping the work of the University of Alberta. The undergraduate philosophy of the Rutherford Library has apparently been transferred to the Cameron Library along with the staff. I should like to go on record renewing my opposition to this and urging that drastic steps be taken to correct the situation. I feel sure that those staff members concerned with research and graduate students will virtually unanimously support this position.

Two days later, McCalla's Associate Dean, Eric Hanson, wrote to the President to renew the attack on the Library and Mr Peel.

An immediate problem faces us as far as library facilities and services are concerned. Furthermore, this affects all faculties which have graduate and research programs. I have heard many complaints by staff members in the past, but in recent weeks these have been compounded. I was horrified when I found out that the Rutherford staff was moving to the Cameron Library; I thought we were going to get a Librarian with vision and depth of under-standing essential in a research and graduate library. As matters stand, I do not see how it will be possible for the Humanities and Social Sciences to develop adequate research and graduate programs, unless the log jam in the library is cleared up. We will be losing our most promising young staff members if nothing is done.

Hanson then promised Johns that he would "provide you with a memorandum on the library situation. *Among other things, we need to revise the present procedure of having library staff lay down regulations for the academic staff. It is time the latter made the regulations.*" He then concluded by expressing a "wish to support strongly the propositions put in Dean McCalla's recent letter to you on the library problem."[143]

In a succinct reply to Dean McCalla, the President wrote:

I am aware of the point of view of a number of universities on the role and function of the Chief Librarian, and I realize that there are serious reserva-tions we all have about our present incumbent. I think we should bear in mind, however, that the ideal librarian in the English-speaking world is a very rare person indeed and very hard to find. Those who are particularly desirable nearly all have positions which they would be reluctant to leave and they would be almost unobtainable.

After dismissing the notion of recruiting a paragon scholar-librarian, the President conceded, "I think the solution here may be to revise the terms of reference of the Library Committee and see whether this would not provide the answer we seek." As the President grasped for the means to quell faculty discontent, he fell back upon the tried-and-true solution of passing the problem along to a committee, in this case the redesigned Library Committee. In his reply to Eric Hanson, he summarized his own view thus:

I had thought that when we first set up the Library Sub-Committee a number of years ago we would have a group of faculty members who would take a position of leadership and responsibility in directing the affairs of the Library and in ensuring that matters of University-wide policy were discussed in the annual meeting of the Library Committee as a whole, while the Sub-Committee dealt with policy in greater detail and with the routine problems of staffing and operation of our Libraries. Somehow this leadership has failed to materialize, perhaps because the Committee did not have the terms of reference they required.

I hope that we can change the policy and structure of the Library Committee by enlarging the Sub-Committee, making it responsible to General Faculty Council, and doing away with the Library Committee. If this is supplemented by giving the Library Committee, as reconstituted, responsibility for such matters as staffing and general operation, we have done the best we can to ensure that this operation is effective.

To his credit, President Johns was also at pains to defend the Library and Mr Peel by questioning the vagueness of the criticism levelled:

So far as the Librarian himself is concerned, I know there has been some criticism but it has not been expressed to me in terms sufficiently specific for me to grapple with them personally. You refer to "the log jam in the library." Does this mean that the books are not being accessioned quickly enough or is there something wrong with the cataloguing? I should also like to know in what way the library facilities are inadequate. I realize, of course, that very few libraries can keep up with all the current literature except by subscribing to the best journals and ensuring that reports and other documentary material comes in promptly, but apart from this I wonder where our library service falls down.[144]

After the President expressed his pleasure, "to note that you will be preparing a memorandum on the subject," Dr Hanson, doubtless with the full approval of Dean McCalla, seized the occasion to prepare a five-page manifesto for the virtual academic rebirth of the University and its Library, beginning with a reiteration of his vision of the role of the Library.

My primary concern is with the development of graduate work and research in the Humanities and Social Sciences, but library operations are also of great importance to all other faculties on [sic] the University....I would like to stress the point that the library is a major research centre. It is the equivalent of the laboratories in the sciences, as well as our major centre for the communication and analysis of information and ideas. Staff and graduate students need ample space and ready access to books and documents in the writing of theses, books, reports and articles, as well as for the preparation of lectures. It has to be recognized that the writing of a thesis or books in the Humanities and Social Sciences involves the use of hundreds, and some-times thousands, of books, manuscripts, and documents. A university library is not merely a lending library; its functions go far beyond this. The library should acquire a large collection of books and documents for permanent and temporary uses, promote working conditions conducive to scholarship and encourage scholars generally to perform the difficult and intricate tasks of research, writing, and teaching.

While he must have been well aware that this was all so much gratuitous rhetoric addressed to a classical scholar such as President Johns, Hanson then laid out a program for the Library that included immediate expansion of the Cameron Library; building the collec-tions to 1 million volumes by substantially increasing acquisitions budgets and by hiring "an experienced, topnotch Acquisitions Librarian," with the international connections to obtain material from around the world; appointing a documents librarian as well as a rare books specialist; reviewing library utilization and extending summer hours; improving the micro-materials collection and reading facilities; simplifying circulation and inter-library loan procedures; immediately reordering lost books; and — not surpris-ingly — allowing academic departments to purchase and house "basic reference works for use in their offices." Because the need was urgent, in Hanson's view, sweeping steps were in order: "An admin-istrative reorganization of library affairs needs to be undertaken at once. In doing this we must proceed far beyond the one-sided and simplistic approach and philosophy of the past. The university library must perform many functions, some of which are exceedingly complex. The procedure of having library staff at any level laying down regulations should be reversed. The academic staff should, and must, work out the procedures for operating the library."[145]

Hanson then turned to the alleged deficiencies of the Chief Librarian.

There is a general consensus among academic staff that the present Chief Librarian is not providing adequate leadership in developing the library, that he is not sensitive to the needs and requirements of a rapidly growing university, and that he has not established close and continuous liaison and consultation with academic departments regarding library matters. My conclusion, and many concur, is that as long as he is in charge of the library services we shall never make a mark in graduate and research work in a major way in the Humanities and Social Sciences, as well as in other fields in which library research is basic. We will also lose promising young scholars who are presently handicapped by existing facilities and regulations.

Therefore, in addition to placing the reconstituted Library Committee in direct control of all aspects of library management, Hanson urged the President to:

Appoint a Director of Library Services to serve as the executive officer of the committee. He would be responsible for the operation and development of university library facilities. He should be an academic, and a senior scholar in his own right; such a person would have an appreciation of research and teaching problems which is required to produce harmonious and effective relationships between the library and academic staff, and he should have a perspective of our potential future growth and needs. If possible, he should have some administrative experience. Trained librarians would be responsible for different aspects of library operations; they would essentially carry out the policies determined by the Director, in consultation with the Library Committee. For example, the present Chief Librarian might be given responsibility for cataloguing, which is his specialty.

The Director of Libraries should know what research is going on in the University, and he should be responsible for taking steps to secure the major materials necessary for the research. He must be in constant, intimate touch with all departments in the university. He must make himself familiar with their needs, and it is essential that he have world-wide contacts.

Some funds will be required for the travel expenses involved in recruiting such a person. These would be used by someone travelling from here to interview candidates, and to enable us to bring in candidates for the position for interviews on this campus.

Admitting that finding a qualified candidate would not be easy, Hanson proposed that an executive committee of the Library Committee "would need to meet weekly to deal with library operations directly. Librarians in charge of departments would report to the executive committee. In short, the executive committee, assisted by the whole committee, would perform the functions of the Director of Library Services, until he is appointed."[146]

The Graduate Faculties Council, meeting at the end of November 1964, gave its blessing to all of the recommendations of the draft report of Dean McCalla's Committee on the Administration of the Library. Eric Hanson, installed to chair the revamped Library Committee, having made his agenda clear enough, lost little time in the new year scheduling weekly meetings of the ten-member Committee. Soon all members of staff and student representatives received an announcement of the Committee's review of all library policies, with a request for feedback. In November 1965, the Committee issued *Library Requirements in the Decade Ahead*, a report prepared, in Mr Peel's words, by "a poet with imagination and an economist accustomed to the astronomical figures in government financing," in which the Library Committee recommended two major policies for adoption: "that the library appropriation for the fiscal year 1966-67 be increased very substantially; [and] that we build up our library holdings to the equivalent of three million volumes as rapidly as possible." At weekly meetings during Dr Hanson's two-year tenure as the head of the Library Committee, Mr Peel was kept waiting, and only invited into the room after the previous week's minutes were read and approved, and then only to answer questions put to him by Committee members.

> Eric would say, "Well now, today we would like to know about such and such a subject."...So I would drone on for an hour, and with some questions asked. But I think my explanation was usually full enough that there was very little said. It was very depressing to sit there...[and] just not really get much reaction. And I would leave and that would be it....And so I suppose [in] cross-examining me, the purpose was to see how the library operated and the Library Committee was going to run the library, not the librarian.
> It was like the Star Chamber court; it was really a terrible experience.

Mr Peel was so depressed by this turn of affairs that, "I started to keep a diary for the same reason as Samuel Pepys kept his second diary."[147]

Far from blaming President Johns for this demotion in his authority, in later years Mr Peel reflected that neither he, nor Johns was fully in control of the situation, for, "at that stage there was this agitation to take control away from the President — he was under fire and many of his officials. And it was known, of course, that I reported to him....I think if you studied what was going on all across Canada, you would find that it was not unique to this campus." Indeed, it was not, and only the year before, in 1964, the librarian in charge of the

Calgary branch was driven to resign on a point of principle. Mr Peel referred to that unfortunate episode in a letter to President Johns at the end of April, 1965:

> I am enclosing a copy of the terms of reference of the Library Committee in Calgary as recently approved by the General Faculty Council. The emphasis on the advisory nature of the Committee is significant in view of the recent history of the Library Committee on that campus. About a year and a half ago, during the illness of the librarian, the Committee assumed control of the Library. The executive role assumed by the Committee led to external and internal confusion since neither faculty nor library staff knew who was responsible for what. After this unsatisfactory experiment, it is interesting to see the Library Committee going back to the normal role of library committees at universities on the North American continent.[148]

In his letter to the President, Mr Peel stopped just short of saying that he himself had now been forced into the same administrative trap by some senior faculty members intent upon micromanaging the daily administration of the University Library.

Despite having achieved effective control of the affairs of the Library, and usurped the authority of the Chief Librarian, Hanson and McCalla had not abandoned the rest of their project. When McGill University replaced its Chief Librarian at the recommendation of a library consultant's report on the deficiencies of its library, including having clung to the Cutter cataloguing system for far too long, Dr Hanson forwarded a copy of the McGill Library Report to President Johns in the spring of 1965, and urged that the University of Alberta should also commission an external review of the Library. In his reply, the President was unimpressed.

> I have studied this whole problem carefully and I feel that we have been fortunate in avoiding most if not all of the problems that McGill has faced recently. We have been able to raise the amount of money made available for the library very substantially, we have introduced a good system of cataloguing, we have a good scale of payment for the staff, and have introduced a system of student and staff familiarization with the library that may not be perfect but has a good deal to commend it.
>
> In short, I think it would be wrong to say that our library is in the same position as McGill's library was three years ago and in desperate need of a survey.

*This is not to say that a survey might not be useful but I cannot believe
that it is urgently required.*

But the President's was not the last word on this subject. The Board
of Governors was persuaded, and by December an external review of
the Library by two consultants — Stephen A. McCarthy and Richard
H. Logsdon, Library Directors of Cornell and Columbia University
libraries, respectively — was commissioned.[149] Meanwhile, an opportunity brought Mr Peel some welcome time away from the University
in succeeding months. In January 1966 he received an invitation from
the Association of Universities and Colleges of Canada (AUCC) to
serve on a team to study "library resources, administration, financial
support , and automation, and provide guidelines for the development of academic libraries for the next 15 years." Peel accepted the
invitation with President Johns' encouragement and blessing, and
from March 1966 through June 1967, he devoted considerable time
and travel to the work of this commission.[150] After the unfair criticism
to which the Library had been very publicly subjected, and, although
unbeknownst to him, the very unfair criticism directed at him
personally, his participation in the AUCC survey was a prestigious
honour, and a mark of the generally high regard in which he was held
by his peers in the library profession.

Messrs McCarthy and Logsdon visited the University between 9
and 12 January 1966, prior to which they had received a brief from the
University's professional librarians' group, formulated as a response
to the Library Committee's August 1965 report, *Library Requirements
for the Decade Ahead*. The librarians' five-page brief included
complaints that the Chief Librarian was excluded from the Library
Committee, which reported to GFC, a body on which librarians lacked
representation; that by "becoming involved in library management
for the first time in 1965, GFC has extended its activities beyond
academic courses but has not extended to the Library the principle of
self-government by those who have expert knowledge of the matters
in which they are involved"; and that to attain a total of 3 million
volumes by 1975–1976 would require adding 250,000 volumes a
year, as well as the provision of adequate staff and building space.
The librarians' brief went on to urge that librarians be given more
authority for collection development; that a blanket order system be
introduced with funds allocated by subject instead of by department,
with a general fund for acquisitions to be drawn upon continuously;

and that the Library be consulted prior to the establishment of new programs. Finally, the librarians declared that while a local library school might ease the shortage of qualified librarians, a revised salary scale, merit increases, and provision for leaves were also required to attract and retain staff. Years later Mr Peel recalled the consultants' visit: "They were here on a Sunday Afternoon and there was a general meeting. The Library Committee and I met with them and had a very general chat. And then I was out of it." After two more days of meetings with the Committee, Library staff, and others,

> I think it was on the Tuesday afternoon that McCarthy and Logsdon came into my office. And Stephen McCarthy said "Now tell us, how did this all happen?"... It was very apparent to them that the Library Committee thought it was running the library and that the librarian was about like the caretaker who sweeps the floor....They said they had already told Eric Hanson privately that he could not operate a library in this fashion — that committee administration was just not possible. Remember that Eric had the library committee meeting weekly.[151]

When the consultants delivered their 62-page draft report, with its lengthy preamble and 44 recommendations, the Library Committee's reaction might have been predicted. The report was so strongly, albeit ever so politely, critical of the Committee, that Mr Peel later recalled that a motion was raised to reject it outright. The consultants' wide-ranging recommendations covered internal organization, developing collection resources, technical services, reader services, staffing, budget and finance, buildings, automation, and the case for establishing a local library school. But the sharp end of the consultants' comments lay in their remarks on administrative relationships:

> while the usual forces of conflict and accommodation are at work in the University of Alberta campus environment, they have in recent months seemingly developed in breadth and intensity somewhat more on the conflict than on the accommodation side. Faculty judgments with respect to library resources have outpaced the capacity of the library. Senior members of staff had become so involved in managing the internal affairs of the Libraries that serious breaches developed in communications with the faculties.

And, as if that were not pointed enough, the consultants added that,

*the library committee cannot successfully administer the library and should
not attempt to do so. The principal library officer is the administrator
charged with the duties of administering and directing the library and he is
responsible to the president for the satisfactory discharge of the duties
involved. This is in keeping with the University Act and with experience and
good practice in other institutions.*

*In an institution such as the University of Alberta in which a major
library development program is underway and substantial further expansion is envisaged, the opportunity for the library committee to render service
to the institution and its library is very great. This opportunity can be best
realized, however, if the committee conceives its role in the broad context of
formulating major goals, assisting in the explanation and defense of these
objectives and participating appropriately in the efforts to achieve them.*

The consultants also addressed

*the qualifications to be sought in the principal library officer of a university.
As has been observed elsewhere, the time has passed when a professor who
has tired of the calssroom [sic] or has proved ineffective as a teacher can be
expected to assume the principal library position in a university and make a
success of it. The experience of many institutions shows that the administration of a large university library system is a complex and difficult task
requiring broad professional knowledge and administrative competence of
a high order....A university will serve its own best interests if it recognizes
that the principal library post is that of a high level administrative officer
who should be expected to have the appropriate professional library preparation and experience and those personal qualities essential to the
maintenance of effective relationships with members of the university
community.[152]*

The initial draft of the McCarthy-Logsdon Report was reviewed at
Library Committee meetings in March, at which one member "criticized severely the generality and tone of many of the comments in the
first ten pages of the report." However, the draft report was approved
in April with "minor reservations regarding wording," and returned
to the consultants for further revision. Chairman Eric Hanson
and his fellow Committee members may well have felt personally
stung by the consultants' remarks, but they too praised it, once the
consultants had 'cosmeticized' some of their blunter criticism of the

Committee, and after President Johns not only gave the report his stamp of approval, but declared that "this seems to have been another example of the excellent way in which we have been served by library consultants. They seem to be the most expert of any consultants we have had in special fields in recent years." The consultants' revised report was given a page-by-page review by the Library Committee later that summer. "Although reservations were expressed at some points," principally, one may surmise, about "administrative relationships," there was general assent to the recommendations dealing with collection development, technical and public services, budget and finance, staffing, and automation. Indeed, the recommendations of the McCarthy-Logsdon Report provided wise counsel and a reliable guide for the University of Alberta Library's development and expansion over the coming decade. Among the recommendations soon implemented were an expansion of the Library's administrative staff with the appointment of an Associate University Librarian, charged with supervising the Assistant University Librarians for Public and Technical Services, as well as the establishment of the Library's first "blanket order" contracts for new books. The Richard Abel Company was contracted to supply American scholarly publications, while Blackwell's of Oxford was engaged to supply British imprints.[153]

During the late summer or early autumn of 1966, Mr Peel composed a five-page review of the history of the Library Committee, in which he made recommendations regarding its terms of reference, size and composition, agendas, and reporting structure, stating the reasoning behind each recommendation. For example, "The Committee should be advisory to the Librarian as otherwise the administrative responsibility and initiative of the latter is [sic] undermined. In practice it would seldom happen that the Librarian would disregard the advice of the committee." Nonetheless, the question of the administrative relationship between the University Librarian, the Library Committee, and GFC was neither quickly, nor easily settled, including a future role for the incumbent University Librarian. In December 1966, the Library Committee was considering appropriate qualifications to chair the Committee, and "there was much in favor of having the Associate Dean of Graduate Studies serve in this capacity, *at least until a Director of Library Services was appointed*, at which time the situation could be reviewed. Professor Walker and Mr Peel expressed reservations in regard to this principal [*sic*], and it was agreed that the matter required further discussion...." Almost three months later the Committee was still parsing its own terms of reference.[154]

The McCarthy-Logsdon Report afforded Mr Peel a considerable degree of vindication, but until its recommendations were implemented, his continuing lack of authority to administer, let alone the implied threat to his own career, gave no cause for pleasure, nor, indeed, much time for leisure, because the coming year was a very busy one for him. His continued participation in the AUCC survey required him to request and receive a three-month, paid leave-of-absence, which, while scarcely a holiday, was at least a change in his accustomed routine. In a note sent to President Johns regarding his leave, he noted that "over the years since I have been in administration I have missed out on some of my annual holiday nearly every year. A person who does not take all his vacation is a fool, but when there are important decisions to be made or where organizational problems arise which must be settled a person in a position of responsibility cannot always get away for a large block of time." At the end of his leave, Mr Peel still confronted the challenge presented by the University's ambitious program for the rapid expansion of the Library's collections. When President Johns met with the Library Committee to consider the consultants' report, he asked whether the target of a 3-million-volume collection was a realistic one, and whether the count was intended to include microform editions, or only printed ones. "The Chairman stressed that the Committee's objective was three million volumes *or their equivalent*. The President agreed that this qualifying phrase made the objective more realistic in terms of required building space."[155]

McCarthy and Logsdon urged that "efficient and effective use of the substantially increased book funds for the graduate and research program of the University can only be achieved through an orderly process of growth and development, and one in which librarians and members of the faculty must work cooperatively, especially if the goal of the Library Committee report — 3,000,000 volumes in 1976 — is to be reached." To raise the Library's holdings from 500,000 to 3 million in ten years, they calculated, would require boosting the budget for materials from $900,000 to $5.2 million by 1975–1976, and the overall Library budget from $2.3 million to around $13 million during the same period. The consultants then cautioned that, while the goal might be reasonable and worthy,

(1) No university library to our knowledge, has ever attempted so rapid an expansion. (2) The achievement of [holdings] anything like those projected... will require profound changes in the organizational structure of the University Library system and of its interrelationships with departments of instruction, faculties, and central administration. (3) We would counsel for a shift of emphasis from pure numbers to goals related more specifically to actual needs as judged by members of the faculty who will be responsible for guiding graduate education and research at the University of Alberta.[156]

Drawing upon his recent work as part of the AUCC survey of Canadian academic library resources, Mr Peel analyzed statistical trends in the volume of scholarly publishing, population demographics, and information technologies, and produced a prescient report on the potential growth of the Library's holdings over the following three decades. In his report he accurately predicted the scale of collection growth, which argued implicitly for the need to expand library buildings, as well as an increasing reliance on both "electronic developments" and library cooperation in the sharing of resources as potential means of curbing unrestricted collection growth. But he cautioned that "the primary purpose of co-operative programmes is not economy, but the enrichment of resources and the improvement of library services. The limitations of library co-operation, as well as its values, ought to be recognized." While Mr Peel supported library resource sharing, he was realistic about its limited potential. Earlier that year, when the western Canadian university presidents' Inter-Provincial Committee on University Rationalization proposed the creation of a regional catalogue of library resources, Peel reminded President Johns that libraries had been at work on this concept for several decades, with projects such as the Northwest Pacific Bibliographic Center, located in Seattle, and that telex communications had greatly facilitated inter-library lending. But he also cautioned that "Libraries will undoubtedly be linked together by computers in a few years, but there is a lot of experimental work to be done yet. Our [AUCC] study team hope to come up with some suggestions." Resource sharing, Peel advised, must transcend regional boundaries, hence the significance of the National Library of Canada's National Union Catalogue. In closing, he boldly suggested some bigger game than library collections as ripe targets for the Inter-Provincial Committee's pursuit of rationalization:

I am afraid when university administrators worry about finance and probable duplication of resources they pick on the library. The prevention of unnecessary duplication of specialized and professional faculties and course offerings should be considered first. The duplication of teaching effort is probably far greater than that to be found in the library which takes up only 5% to 10% of an institution's total budget. No one would expect every resident on a street to read the same evening newspaper to save duplication of expenditure, yet some suggestions for interlibrary co-operation envisage university students on various campuses trying to read the same book.[157]

"Speaking truth to power" in this way merely reflected the cordial and collegial relationship Mr Peel shared with the man with whom he had worked closely for so long. The President replied to say that he concurred with Peel's views, and indicated that duplication of faculties and programs should and would also come under review. Further evidence of President Johns' high regard came in his acknowledgement of Peel's annual report for 1966–1967:

I do not normally acknowledge receipt of annual reports but the report you sent me on July 26...was so interesting that I could not fail to comment on it.

The growth in library holdings and activity is, I think, the most striking of any area in the University. Your report is so well written and so interesting that it will provide a serious challenge to the editors of the University's own annual report. Somehow or other the text will have to be reduced but it will be a difficult task.

I should like to congratulate you and your colleagues on the way in which you have managed to cope with the enormous increase in book accessions, cataloguing, and circulation. I think the whole unit deserves a special citation.[158]

That same year, in conjunction with a review and revision of the University Act, which was prompted in part by the devolution of the Calgary campus into an independent university, the growth of the University and concomitant administrative work led to the creation of two additional vice-presidential posts. President Johns afterwards sent some most welcome news to his Chief Librarian: "We have been going over our administrative organization in the light of the appointment of two new Vice-Presidents this summer and a few changes have been made. One of them is designed to make the Librarian responsible directly to the Vice-President (Academic) with respect to library matters generally and library salary scales in particular." Furthermore, "The Board of Governors feel that the Library Committee should have a purely advisory role which is very important and very necessary but has no administrative elements in it." In closing, the President stressed that, "I hope this will not mean that you and I cannot sit together and talk about library matters from time to time, since my interest in the Library and the new School of Library Science will remain high as long as I am around."[159] In a handwritten reply to President Johns, Mr Peel revealed some of the frustration the now-terminated experiment in rule-by-committee had engendered.

Needless to say I was pleased to receive your letter on policy with respect to the relationship between the Librarian and the Library Committee. The members of the re-constituted Committee at first took the view that the Committee was administering the Library, and that the role of the Librarian should be that of a glorified caretaker. Looking back this phase has a dream-like quality; I still find it strange that Committee members could be so lacking in understanding of administrative processes. Anyway it was an interesting experiment with the Librarian being present at meetings solely for the purpose of answering questions. If I ever write my memoirs, it will form an interesting chapter, but more likely some student in the field of administration in need of a thesis topic will undertake a study of the working of the Library Committee. The chairman at his last meeting with the Committee said he had learned a lot about libraries and a lot about people. What intrigued me was whether "people" referred to librarians or to professorial types who on occasion can make surprising demands on a library.

I'm glad to know that my contact with the University Administration will again be direct rather than through a committee chairman. I am sorry that the growing size and complexity of the University tends to lessen personal contacts, but I shall always be aware of your personal interest in the Library.[160]

Outgrowing the Centre
As the University continued to grow and develop in enrolment, curriculum, and physical plant, with the addition of numerous new buildings built, building, or planned, centrifugal pressures would inexorably lead to decentralization of library facilities. The first wedge in undermining Marjorie Sherlock's hard-fought, albeit only partial,

victory in centralizing collections within the Rutherford building came with the creation of the Physical Sciences Library in 1961. In the spring of 1966, the Mathematics Department was preparing for a temporary relocation to the Campus Towers Building, located on the edge of the campus, and proposed removing 5800 volumes from the Physical Sciences Library to take with them. The Library Committee, which had not been consulted beforehand, proposed instead that the mathematics collection be relocated in the Cameron Library. Not for the last time, the mathematicians proved adamant, and, because they made the moving of the collection a condition of their willingness to move at all, the Library Committee was overruled.

Writing on behalf of the Library Committee, Chairman Eric Hanson expressed their chagrin at this unilateral decision on the part of the Space Allocations Committee, just when "We are trying to hammer out a long-run policy regarding the decentralization of library facilities." Therefore, Hanson continued, the Library Committee sought to obtain representation on the University's Academic Planning, Campus Planning, and Space Allocations Committees. Two days later, President Johns acknowledged Hanson's letter, and noted that he was passing the recommendations to the Executive Committee of GFC. In the event, the GFC Executive denied the Library Committee's request for cross representation on committees with different functions, but promised that in future the Librarian and the Library Committee would at least be consulted about proposed moves to decentralize library facilities and collections. The "policy regarding decentralization," to which Chairman Hanson referred in his letter to the President, made it clear that small "collections of books ranging in number from a couple of hundred to a couple of thousand, obtained by gift, from research grants, or on departmental loan from the library" were not at issue. But where "a department asks the Campus Space Allocations Committee for special space, or if the department is servicing the collection by the provision of full-time staff and therefore operating a library service desk, then such a collection should come under review by the Library Committee....The staff should be an integral part of the library staff, and the library should be under the library administration." The policy statement outlined the factors to be considered when dealing with requests regarding branch libraries, including campus geography; quantity of books and their use in teaching; impact of block removals on the central collection; inconvenience to faculty and students in related disciplines; cost of duplication; and long-term impacts on service.[161]

That policy was soon tested. Success breeds imitation, and no sooner had the dispute over the relocation of the mathematics collection played out, than the Dean of Medicine approached the Library Committee with a proposal to relocate the medical library within the campus' health sciences zone, south of 87 Avenue. The Dean had a strong case, for not only was Cameron Library inconvenient for clinical practitioners working in University Hospital, but a new facility, with a putative target date for completion in 1972, would bring together several dispersed health sciences collections under one roof. These included 33,000 volumes in the Cameron Library, 2000 volumes in the John W. Scott Reading Room in University Hospital, 600 volumes on nursing and rehabilitation medicine in Corbett Hall, and the 1500-volume Hospital library in the Nurses' Residence on 114 Street. Hard on the heels of the Dean of Medicine, the Dean of the Faculty of Physical Education, Murray Van Vliet, submitted a proposal to establish a Physical Education Library. His proposal was reviewed and approved by the Library Committee, with the Librarian voting in support. After approving requests from Engineering and Computer Sciences to establish local libraries, the Library Committee rejected a similar request for one in the Biological Sciences building, then under construction, on the grounds that it would inconvenience the Medical Faculty at the opposite end of the campus. When the Mathematics Department moved into the newly finished Central Academic Building, and refused to give up its collection, the Library Committee again gave way, though members worried about possible opposition from Engineering. And, at the end of the decade, both the Faculty of Business and the newly established Library School sought permission to create and house their own specialized, local collections.[162] Thus, the policy on decentralization proved to be, at best, a mixed success, as branch libraries with staff developed from their humble "reading room" origins in a number of departments across the campus. One collection grew into a major branch, and subsequently blossomed into a university library in its own right.

The final annexing of Alberta's teacher training under the aegis of the University's Faculty of Education in 1945 brought with it responsibility for the Normal School in Calgary and its tiny library. Established in 1905, and housed since 1922 on a 123-acre campus on Calgary's North Hill, in a red-brick building that it shared until

1959 with the Southern Alberta Institute of Technology (SAIT), the newly rechristened University of Alberta Faculty of Education, Calgary branch, brought approximately 8000 volumes into the University's collective holdings. Beginning in 1948–1949 with a few arts and sciences courses offered to education students, the curriculum expanded in 1951 to offer lower division courses in formal programs leading to bachelor's degrees. The collection had grown to 20,000 volumes by 1957, when Miss Mary Isobel ("Belle") Grant departed after fifteen years as the librarian. To succeed her, Mr Peel recruited Miss Dorothy Edith Ryder, a graduate of UBC and of McGill's Library School, who had worked for four years as his colleague in Rutherford Library. Miss Ryder began in September 1957 with 2 full-time staff, 7 part-time student assistants, and a serious deficit of space. However, the City of Calgary donated a 300-acre plot in the City's northwest, as a seedbed campus on which to grow the university that had been for so long denied them, and so Miss Ryder's tasks included the design for a proper building to house the Library. Ambitious plans for expansion projected an enrolment of at least 6000 students by 1972 and a library of several hundred thousand volumes, figures that were, in the event, easily exceeded.[163]

Although Miss Ryder addressed these challenges with enthusiasm, she did express some diffidence to Dr Malcolm Taylor, University of Alberta at Calgary's (UAC) newly appointed Principal, who wrote to President Johns that,

> She indicated that she had been employed to perform a "branch librarian" job and now the assignment had grown far beyond that. She was not complaining, but she did want to make clear that she understood that the task of heading up and building a major university library was probably beyond her qualifications and that I should feel free to employ a head librarian any time I felt it necessary.
>
> I assured her of my confidence in her, indicating that I had heard nothing but good reports, and that I appreciated that she might not want the arduous responsibility of a head librarian.

This display of diffidence may be taken merely to indicate that Miss Ryder was mindful of the challenge and aware of her own limitations. President Johns' reply four days later suggested that she was being excessively modest, and makes it clear that she was not lobbying the new Principal for a raise and promotion:

> She may be right in her view that it is too much to ask of her to take on the responsibility for planning the new library in Calgary (or helping to do so) and administering it when it is in operation. However, we were influenced in part here by the fact that Marjorie Sherlock, now Mrs. H. Grayson-Smith, did a similar job for us, and did it with a degree of confidence that was amazing. We felt that Miss Ryder had shown here and in Calgary a degree of good judgement, experience, and initiative which would justify her attempting a similar task. In this connection, we have promoted her from Librarian Grade 3 to Librarian Grade 4, effective April 1st, 1960, and I have a very nice letter from her today, acknowledging the promotion, and expressing her appreciation of it. So far as I know she has never expressed to Mr. Peel or to me any hesitation at undertaking the responsibilities ahead of her, though I have referred to them in at least two letters to her recently.[164]

The original plan, approved by UAC's Library Committee, called for a five-storey-building of 170,000 to 200,000 square feet, designed to serve until 1975, and accommodate a collection of 380,000 to 400,000 volumes. The first two buildings to be erected on the new campus were to house the science departments in one, and the arts and education departments in the other. The library was to occupy 12,000 square feet in the basement of the latter, while the gap between them was to be filled with the new "Library Block." In a letter to B.W. Brooker, the Superintendent of Buildings, Mr Peel expressed his concern that the space provided between two other buildings should be adequate, not only for the next twenty years, but to allow for future expansion, which would probably require 200 to 400 feet of frontage. Brooker offered reassurance that the space allowed for the new library would meet requirements, but did not share Mr Peel's expectations of the need for future expansion. He also revealed his lack of awareness of the space shortage with which Peel was coping on the Edmonton campus: "I do not think we'll be considering a building with a 200 foot to 400 foot frontage. I think that 200 feet might be the maximum. Your present building is 150 feet across the front and it seems to have served the purpose up to this year."[165]

In mid-August 1960, thanks to Miss Ryder's careful planning, 50 high-school students and two moving vans were required for only two-and-one-half days to move 50,000 volumes to their new, albeit temporary, home in the Arts and Education Building. These temporary quarters were just large enough to permit the processing of books to be done on site, instead of in Edmonton. When, at last, on 8 November 1963, the Provincial Treasurer, the Hon. E.W. Hinman, performed the official ceremony opening the new, 60,000 square foot library building, the task of collection building could begin in earnest, for which the staff and acquisitions budget were significantly enlarged. In addition, the Province made several supplementary grants that were shared between the two campuses for the purchase of library books. Thus, between 1960 and 1964, the acquisitions budget at Calgary quadrupled, the staff expanded from 12 to 37, periodicals subscriptions increased from 613 to 7458, and the collection grew from 30,000 to nearly 78,000 volumes.[166]

Miss Ryder had been given leave by Mr Peel to make her own allocations from her acquisitions budget. However, once the Library embarked upon a major acquisitions program, tensions increased between the Librarian and members of the Library Committee over allocations. In 1963, the Committee overruled the Librarian's recommended allocations, and, with the support of the Principal, assumed direct control of the funds. The following year, in her absence, the Committee reversed another of her decisions, which prompted Miss Ryder to submit her resignation. This left her successor, Dr Thomas MacCallum Walker, to deal with a Library Committee no longer content merely to play an advisory role, and to cope with predictable faculty pressure for decentralization. Indeed, the Education Faculty, discontented with a perceived lack of support for their curriculum collection, reclaimed it from the central Library in 1964, and created a separate library, the Doucette Library of Teaching Resources. As early as December 1956, Dr Johns had suggested, as one solution to the University's perennial shortage of space, that "possibly the development of the Calgary campus should be accelerated." Later, as President, Johns came to embrace the vision of a provincial university system with largely independent units, on the model of California's university system, which he greatly admired. The path to independence for the University of Calgary, where, indeed, its Library operated with virtual independence after 1963, was clearly set. By 1965, planning had begun in Calgary to establish a separate medical school, and that year the University's Board of Governors reported in favour of full university status for the University of Alberta's eager offspring.[167]

Mr Peel's Perennial Search for Staff

Meanwhile, perhaps the greatest challenge Mr Peel and his colleagues confronted during this era of unprecedented growth in the University and its Library, was recruiting and training new staff. The increases in student enrolment, faculty positions, and library collections coincided with one of the greatest periods of sustained economic growth in modern times. A booming economy provided a boom in private-sector employment, offering salaries and wages that the University was at pains to match. During the 1960s the annual turnover rate among the Library's associate staff exceeded 50 percent in some years. The average length of service of the non-professional staff fluctuated between 19 and 21 months. At the same time, the expansion of post-secondary education in Canada led to the creation of new universities across the country, and the demand for experienced academic librarians prompted a still-greater turnover rate among those working at the University.

Although a comparison of seven western Canadian university libraries done in 1965 showed the University of Alberta's salary scales for librarians were marginally higher than at other schools, Mr Peel informed the President that the entry-level salary floor of $5800 was too low by hundreds of dollars to appeal to new graduates. "We have seventeen positions open," he added, "and expect with resignations this will rise to nineteen or twenty. We are now thinking in terms of a backlog in cataloguing of 40,000 volumes, and next year of this increasing by another 60,000 volumes. It will be years before our Library recovers from our present acute staff shortage." The situation was sufficiently critical, that when presenting the Board of Governors with the proposed salary scale for librarians for 1966–1967, President Johns felt compelled to add a note:

> In explanation...it should be pointed out that the supply of professional librarians in Canada is very short and if we are to meet the needs of the University of Alberta on both its campuses we must have a salary scale that will be sufficiently competitive not only to bring recent graduates here from library schools in Ontario and British Columbia, but keep those librarians we now have on the staff. This whole problem also underlines the importance of establishing a library school in Alberta.[168]

Such staffing woes grew critical in all Canadian libraries in those years; recruiting and training were major preoccupations as academic libraries across North America competed for professional staff. Canada's three accredited library schools at McGill, Toronto, and UBC lacked expansion space to accommodate the nearly one-third of qualified applicants they were then routinely turning away. Mr Peel pressed for the creation of a library school at the University of Alberta to provide a supply of locally-trained professionals. In May 1964, representatives of the library associations of the three prairie provinces met in Calgary to address the recruitment problem. They struck a committee, under the chairmanship of Edmonton Public Library Director Morton Coburn, to make the case for a prairie library school. The Coburn Committee's brief was completed in November, and presented at the Banff meeting of the Canadian Association of University Presidents by Walter Johns, who, despite the case made on behalf of Manitoba and Saskatchewan, won support and agreement for locating the new school at his university.[169]

In May 1965, the Board of Governors authorized the creation of a one-year Bachelor of Library Science program; in January 1967, Ms Sarah Rebecca Reed was appointed its first director. But new faculties take time to establish, so the first students did not enter the program until autumn 1968. Meanwhile, the Library resorted to advertising abroad for librarians. In December 1966, Mr Peel flew to London, where he met and interviewed three dozen applicants who responded to these advertisements. One of those who applied was Mr L.E.S. Gutteridge, a veteran of the British antiquarian book trade, who was hired after persuading Mr Peel to establish a unit within the Library to pursue and purchase out-of-print titles. In his 1966–1967 report Mr Peel noted that 11 librarians had been hired, but 9 others decamped for greener pastures. The following year's tally was somewhat better: 15 librarians were appointed and only 4 departed. The results for 1968–1969 were less successful, with 15 librarians appointed, while 11 left; fully one-third of the Library's budgeted positions for librarians sat vacant. However, in 1969, the year the first class of locally trained librarians graduated and sought employment, the Library filled 26 positions, thus increasing the professional staff by 50 percent. While not all of the new graduates hired that year lacked experience working in libraries, the greatest need was for cataloguers, who require significant amounts of additional training. Moreover, as the Library's collection grew more cosmopolitan, multilingual librarians were especially in demand. By 1968 staff linguistic skills embraced a total of 29 languages, including "at least one speaker each [of] Albanian, Cree, Swahili, Gugerati [sic], and Temne." In light of all of these challenges, it is little short of amazing that, "The total staff grew from 83 in 1963–1964 to a high of 390 in 1970–1971."[170]

In February 1968, a disgruntled young professor of Classics, in a resignation letter to the head of his department, blamed the deficiencies of the library for his decision to leave the University after only two years. Mr Peel responded to address the issues of collection deficiencies and processing delays in a lengthy and thoughtful letter. He noted that the Library, perennially short-staffed, had experienced a nearly twenty-fold increase in its annual book fund, from $66,000 in 1958–1959 to $1,225,000 in 1967–1968; the number of books acquired each year increased from 15,000 to 120,000 in the same decade. This explosive growth was bound to produce processing delays. Most of the young professor's complaints, however, were due to the system under which the faculty, through the Library Committee, controlled the allocation of the book fund, as well as the bulk of the titles selected for purchase, leaving the Library staff with very little discretionary funding for acquisitions. Departmental inefficiencies in placing orders merely compounded the problem. Nonetheless, the Classics Department's allocation for books had tripled in the past four years, and been fully expended each year.[171] As the University laid increasing emphasis upon research and publication as expectations of its faculty, responsibility for the allocation of the acquisitions budget by subject and the selection of material for purchase would gradually devolve from the faculty to the librarians, as more and more librarians with strong, academic subject backgrounds were recruited. But this was a lengthy process, and the complete transfer of acquisitions funds from the control of the teaching departments took another twenty years.

The Library Committee's 1965 report, *Library Requirements in the Decade Ahead*, recommended that by 1976 the Library's collection should grow to 3 million volumes (exclusive of government documents and microforms). Achieving this goal, which would require an acquisitions rate of as much as 350,000 volumes a year, or 1500 per working day, raised renewed scepticism among some, including the Chief Librarian, who nonetheless presented the Administration with a space needs plan that envisioned 9 million volumes by 1999. That same year, Library expenditures on books and other information resources exceeded $500,000, a far cry from the $35,000 Mr Peel had at his disposal during his first year in charge, $7000 of which was sufficient to pay for subscrip-

tions to 1400 periodicals. During that same time, annual accessions grew proportionally from an average of 9000 volumes to almost 60,000. Indeed, after 1964 a book was added to the collection at a rate of one every two minutes of every working day, a feat only made possible by the massive purchasing of large backfiles of journals and other multi-volume serials, upon which the Library was then expending about one-quarter of its acquisitions budget.[172]

In April 1966, on the occasion of the accession of the half-millionth book, a table was published to illustrate the accelerated growth of the Library's collection:

40 years	for	1st	100,000
10 years	for	2nd	100,000
3 years	for	3rd	100,000
2 years	for	4th	100,000
1.5 years	for	5th	100,000

In the four academic years following the opening of the Cameron Library, the acceleration in the annual acquisition of books was dramatic, from 51,991 volumes to 122,237 in 1967-68. Three years later, in 1970-71, the upward curve of acquisition reached its zenith, 142,717 accessioned volumes. Needless to say, with annual increases in workload of from 25% to 31% the technical services departments were under stress, with additional staff to be hired and trained in short order. It is to the credit of these departments that our backlog of unprocessed books never grew beyond manageable proportions.[173]

Bruce Peel gave much of the credit for that to Daniel Reicher who, as, head of cataloguing in the early 1960s, turned his unit into a model of efficiency. "The cataloguing staff at first didn't know what to make of him," Peel recalled.

> He used to prepare all sorts of work-flow charts...in different colours...and have these up different places on the walls.
>
> However, during the day from nine to five ...he did nothing but walk from desk to desk and, if he saw that this book had been sitting there all morning and others had moved along, he would want to know why. And he would say "Well, let's tackle it." And so the difficult book problem would be resolved right there and then.

Reicher approached his work like an industrial foreman: "After the initial surprise of the staff, they liked it because here was someone who was interested in their rather routine and sometimes dull work, and who appreciated it." In 1969, a Coordinator of Collection Development was appointed to oversee and direct this avalanche of acquisitions; that same year the University of Alberta Library was invited to join the elite ranks of the Association of Research Libraries (ARL), whose 70 members represented the largest research libraries in North America. On 26 May 1970, only four years after acquiring the half-millionth volume, the Library collection had doubled again, and the one-millionth volume was added. For this milestone occasion, the title selected to be so designated was *Notes of a Sporting Expedition in the Far West of Canada, 1847* by Sir Frederick Ulric Graham (1898), one of a privately printed edition limited to 22 copies.[174]

In the mid-1960s, the Library Committee recommended establishment of a special fund for the acquisition of large collections, sometimes described as "fleeting opportunities," which often come on the market with little warning, and require quick decisions about funding if they are to be acquired. In 1963–1964, $50,000 was provided for this purpose; at the suggestion of Dean McCalla this special fund was established on a continuing annual basis after 1965 and set at $100,000. It was thanks to the availability of this special fund that the Library was able, in subsequent years, to acquire such notable collections as the 3500-volume library of the Archbishopric of Salzburg, the 13,500-item library of the Viennese Juridisch-Politische Leseverein, the 8000-volume Robert Woods Collection of western Americana and Canadiana, the 14,000-volume Alfred Powers Collection of western Americana, the 3000-volume Orest Starchuk Collection of Slavonic Literature, the Georg Kaiser drama archive, the Viennese Theatre Playbills Collection, the archives of the Black Sparrow and Curwen Presses, and 103 rare, early editions of works by John Bunyan.[175]

The acquisition of the collection of the legendary California bibliophile Robert Woods in 1968 was a near-run thing. After the University of Alberta bid $151,000 at auction, the local probate court invited further bids of at least 10 percent higher. When it was rumoured that the University of California might, indeed, raise its bid to $166,100, the Library Committee authorized Les Gutteridge to go as high as $180,000 to bring home the prize. As Bruce Peel later recalled to a reporter from *The Gateway*, "In California, they literally wept when they heard it was leaving." Later that same year, the Alfred Powers Collection of western Americana was acquired for a more modest $35,000, because it contained fewer great rarities.[176] Another strong collection was achieved at far less cost, beginning in 1973, when the University of Alberta became a member of the Shastri Indo-Canadian Institute, whose modest annual membership fee yielded thousands of Indian books from the subcontinent. The Library was also the recipient of numerous gifts, large and small, that in the mid-1960s numbered around 2000 volumes annually. The books donated by Dr Yuichi Kurimoto, President of Nagoya University in Japan, and the University of Alberta's first Japanese alumnus, helped make possible development of the University's Asian languages and literature program.

DIMINISHING GOVERNMENT SUPPORT for universities, rising
inflation, and a shrinking Canadian dollar in the 1970s led to reductions both in staffing and in the rate of acquisitions. Enrolment in
September 1971 fell short of projections; in March 1972, the Library
Committee received word that the Library's budget must be cut by
$600,000 for the following year. That $450,000 of this would be
covered by sacrificing the accumulated reserve acquisitions fund
was small consolation. The Committee considered the option of
closing branch libraries, with Engineering, Mathematics, Physical
Sciences, and Physical Education being the most likely targets. Such
a move, however, would inconvenience students seeking study
space, infuriate the respective faculties, and worst of all, confront
Cameron Library with the challenge of accommodating all the books
in those branches. Moreover, the staffing costs of keeping those
branches open could yield only minor savings. So the Committee
opted in the first instance to reduce the departmental allocations
for the purchase of books, and cancel serials subscriptions, many of
which were duplicate copies in branch libraries and departments,
for a saving of $6000. This was obviously insufficient, and thus,
over the next year, 1235 more of the Library's 17,000 subscriptions
to journals and other serial titles were eliminated. A moratorium on
book purchases reduced acquisitions by 20,654 volumes over the
previous year. As well, the Engineering and Physical Education library
branches were closed in order to maintain hours of access in others.[177]

The budget cuts coincided with an inflationary spiral that
affected the global economy, but in no sector more than in scholarly publishing, where the cost of books and journals began rising
by an annual average of 20 percent, and in the case of German peri-

5

Mr Peel Confronts a World of New Realities, 1970–1982

odicals, by as much as 38 percent. The loss of the reserve acquisitions fund left the Library without money to cushion the blow. An appeal to the Board of Governors for a $100,000 bailout proved futile, so by the end of 1973 the blanket order program was suspended as unaffordable, though the Library Committee recommended, and the Board of Governors approved, a $60,000 transfer from the Library's salaries budget to the book fund. This sacrifice of funding for vacant positions was bloodless, but nonetheless harmful in the long run for the Library's levels of service. Paralleling the reduction in accessions, staff numbers were also allowed to shrink. Between 1971–1972 and 1975–1976, attrition reduced the number of librarian positions from 83 to 79 and support staff positions from 310 to 283. In January 1974, the Library received word of a 2.8 percent 'tax' that would reduce its operating budget for 1974–1975 by $150,000. This was partially alleviated by a $45,000 special allocation from the President's contingency fund. However, any repetition of a cut of that magnitude threatened to further reduce the operating budget for staffing. Worse was to follow, as price inflation continued through the 1970s and into the next decade, exacerbated by a steep decline in the Canadian dollar after 1976–1977, which reduced acquisitions proportionally. Mr Peel described 1973–1974 as a year "of financial trauma for the Library." He also wrote that "1974–75 has been one of quiet adjustment to the reality of world inflation and its effect on our Library's purchasing power." That year, a Senate committee appointed to study the Library's acquisitions budget concluded that, "Whatever the means, if the library collection at the University of Alberta is to maintain its standards, fiscal planning will be required, in addition to higher levels of financial support. Unless a concerted effort is made for appropriately funding the books and periodicals collections, this Committee can only restate its concern for the future quality of the University."[178]

This fiscal stringency prompted the Library Committee to reach once again for the illusory panacea of a funding allocation formula that would be seen to divide the diminished acquisitions money among faculties and departments both equitably and rationally. The failure of any and all formulae to meet, let alone satisfy, demand when funding was inadequate resulted, as always, in a series of political compromises that largely acknowledged historic precedents. In the spring of 1974, the Library Committee, wrestling with the allocation of that year's budget, considered a 25 percent levy on all

Opposite Top and Bottom: Rutherford North Library under construction.
[UAA 88–77–72–172–2–47] and
[UAA 88–77–72–417–1–1]

*Above: Architect Joe
Vaitkunas presents
Bruce Peel with the key
to Rutherford North.*
[UAA 88–77–74–6259–8]

*Opposite Top: Two
Rutherford Librairies
marrying two
architectural styles.*
[UAA 89–41–29]

*Opposite Bottom:
The Galleria connecting
the two Rutherford
buildings.
Courtesy of UofA
Creative Services.*
[4584–044]

departmental allocations, but decided to take $170,000 off the top of the entire materials budget, a measure that appeared arbitrary and satisfied few. Dissatisfaction among the faculty was also manifested when, at the urging of GFC, the Library Committee brought in a new loans policy designed to cope with delinquent borrowers. Limiting periodicals to overnight loans, reducing faculty loans to one month, and suspending borrowing privileges for non-compliance elicited such howls of protest from the faculty that the Committee was forced to back down. Although the Committee had even considered the radical step of imposing fines on delinquent faculty borrowers, a legal opinion warned that faculty could not be fined. Subsequently that changed; now academic staff are subject to fines only for non-return of short-term-loan periodicals and books recalled for other readers.[179]

Leaner university budgets were also reflected in a marked reduction in new construction on campus. Whereas 23 major buildings were constructed between 1960 and 1968, no more than a dozen were erected during the 1970s. However, the increases in student enrolment and library collections, beyond what was anticipated when Cameron Library was planned, led to demands for more library space. As a result of this increasing pressure, 202,000 square feet were added

between 1968 and 1973. A third storey was added to the Education Library in 1968; the North Wing of the Cameron Library opened in 1969; and in 1971 the Law Library moved from its long-time home on the top floor of Rutherford Library to a 40,000 square-foot facility in the new Law Centre. It was clear, however, that these additional facilities, however welcome, would only prove to be stopgaps in the face of the aggressive acquisitions program and burgeoning collections. Therefore, in October 1968, a Building Committee, chaired by Mr Peel, was struck to plan the proposed library building on a site in the North Garneau neighbourhood. In April 1969, the project architect, Mr Peel, and three other members of the Committee visited and inspected a dozen university libraries across North America. Later that year, in its annual report to GFC, the Library Committee urged that "phase two" planning for the "North Garneau library" be allowed to proceed. Plans were completed the following year, details shown to the Library Committee, and the building, given the name "Rutherford II, was scheduled for occupancy by December 1972."[180]

Plans for a large, new Humanities Centre along Saskatchewan Drive, east of Rutherford House, prompted the Arts Faculty departments to demand that a new library devoted to their disciplines be built close at hand. This proved to be the last major library building project of what Mr Peel labelled the University's seven fat years. "During the planning stage the proposed library building site perambulated up and down along the east side of that portion of 112 Street now surmounted by the [Housing Union Building, aka HUB] students' residence and mall." One design proposal had the new library straddling both the east and west sides of the HUB Mall, the two sides linked by overhead walkways. At Mr Peel's urging, this concept was dismissed as impractical, even dysfunctional. Eventually a site was selected immediately north of the Rutherford Library, where it threatened to block the view of Rutherford Library's handsome Georgian façade. To forestall the predictable protests, the architect, Joe Vaitkunas, of the firm of Minsos, Vaitkunas, & Jamieson, designed a glass-roofed galleria, that linked the two Rutherford Library buildings, and provided an airy interior space with year-round climate control. Construction of the 100,000 square foot Rutherford North Library began in 1971. Even before its completion, however, covetous eyes fell upon the spacious new edifice, but the Library Committee, much to the relief of the Arts Faculty, was able to defeat a motion to repurpose the building as a science library complex. At a ceremony in May 1973, Mr Vaitkunas presented Mr Peel with the key to the building, and Mrs S.H. McCuaig, daughter of the late Premier A.C. Rutherford, officially opened Rutherford North as the primary Humanities and Social Sciences Library. Upon completion of Rutherford North, the south building ceased being the undergraduate library, but served instead to house the periodicals collection, the Periodicals and Microforms reading rooms, the University Archives, and the Extension Library.[181]

The Year of Library Surveys

During the spring of 1976, Library Administration proposed that a major survey of the Library be undertaken. As Mr Peel explained in a letter to Library staff,

> A study is desirable in order that the Library may redefine its objectives and in some instances establish new objectives so that we can determine how best to meet the identified needs of the user. The study need is occasioned in part by the resource constraints that are now a part of the University reality and also through a desire of some users and staff who feel that the relationship of the Library to the University should be more clearly defined in terms of the total institutional objectives.

Study team members were charged with undertaking three surveys to measure user satisfaction, to analyze library tasks and prepare job descriptions for library managers, and to recommend a management structure in terms of relationships, communication, policy making, management style, and service objectives.[182]

Unstated in his letter, was that the discontent which had led faculty to demand a more participatory, or "collegial," role in university decision making for the past decade was now manifesting itself among the professional librarians. Libraries are, by nature, hierarchic organizations that have traditionally operated under a regime of "top-down" management. As the University and its Library experienced a period of explosive growth, followed by severe retrenchment, senior administrators increasingly drew criticism for their failure to find the means to cure systemic ills. Frustration was also growing among librarians over their too-limited participation on the governing bodies of the University. Only after years of petitioning, were librarians eventually allowed representation on GFC, where their numbers should have entitled them to three seats.[183]

Although Mr Peel had initially been designated the overall
Survey Director, the survey team recommended, and obtained
leave, to work for and report directly to Dr Myer Horowitz, the Vice-
President (Academic). The three survey reports, completed and
delivered in 1977, produced a total of 202 recommendations. Of the
faculty members and graduate students surveyed, an impressive
89 percent expressed themselves satisfied with the Library's reference services. This doubtless reflected the efforts made during the
1970s to hire more subject-specialist reference librarians, despite
the limited scope for further recruitment in a period of retrenchment. The Management Survey Team, however, identified numerous
endemic problems in the Library's management that ranged from a
reactive approach, bereft of long-range planning, to communication
deficiencies, excessive centralization of authority, insufficient staff
development and career advancement opportunities, and systemic
waste of resources through both excessive and inadequate coordin-
ation. As well, a "class system" separating librarians from support

staff, and a rigid classification and salary structure were found to breed "mistrust and resentment." The Library Committee also came in for criticism for "excessive involvement" in the management of the Library, as did the increasingly anomalous vesting of primary collection development decisions with the faculty, instead of with the enlarged cadre of subject specialist librarians.[184]

Although it might be tempting to dismiss much of the Management Survey Report as routine grumbling, some of the criticisms had merit, and a number of the Report's 44 recommendations were implemented, and led to meaningful changes in staff classifications, salary scales, and the role of the Library Council and professional staff. Indeed, an appeal lodged in 1975 by a librarian, with the support of the Faculty Association, had already challenged the legitimacy of the Library's classification system for librarians, and the caps on their salary scales, as inconsistent with the treatment of academic staff, as defined in the *Academic Staff Handbook.* While ultimately unsuccessful in eliminating salary caps, or in gaining the right to promotion through the ranks, this appeal case did result in the granting of a separately negotiated employment contract for librarians as academic staff, still under the aegis of the Faculty Association. However, the Management Report's core recommendations urged the radical decentralization of the Library into "six self-contained libraries," each one responsible for its own public and technical services staff, and operating semi-independently of the Chief Librarian, who would "retain overall responsibility for the management and operation of the Library system, but that the emphasis of this office be changed from day-to-day operations to broad policy and long-range planning, personnel and staff development, relations with the rest of this University and with other Universities and institutions." The day-to-day operations would become the responsibility of a new official, a Director of Library Operations, who would report to the Chief Librarian. The physical decentralization of the Library was an architectural fait accompli. Now, with some support from librarians, those who would further decentralize the University Library had picked up the lance, and aimed it at the central managers. This time, however, the University Librarian was proposed for *promotion* instead of *demotion.*[185]

Mr Peel's reaction to the Report's core recommendations was blunt, even when he was writing about it for public consumption:

Finally, in September, 1977, the recommendations of this last survey were
made public. The Management Survey proposed the decentralization of the
Library by subject areas and/or professional schools. Most persons on
campus having any knowledge of, or interest in, the welfare of the Library
considered the recommendation unacceptable. The Library Committee
reviewed the report over the winter, and rejected the notion of dismember-
ment. At the end of this present reporting year a Committee, chaired by the
Vice-President (Academic), is attempting to clean up the "fall out."

Fortunately, the newly formed Vice-President (Academic)'s Advisory
Committee on Library Surveys, which met for the first time on
31 January 1978, took a similar view, and the proposed dismantling
was never implemented.[186]

While these perennial debates between centralizers and decen-
tralizers were being rehashed, inflation in the cost of scholarly
publications continued to batter the Library's acquisitions budget. A
small group of European-based commercial publishers had become
dominant in the for-profit publication of scholarly journals, especially scientific, technical, and medical titles. The dependence of the
academic world upon their unique products — one title not being
an acceptable substitute for another in the same field — established each one as a virtual monopoly, and led to predatory pricing,
which increased annual subscription costs to libraries by more
than double, or even triple, the general rate of inflation. Yet some
stabilization in the acquisitions budget was achieved thanks to a
$250,000 bequest from the estate of Mr R.V. MacCosham, which was
matched by the province, and swollen further by earning $145,000
in interest before being fully disbursed between 1976 and 1979.
Mr Peel wrote to the MacCosham family to express his gratitude:

I believe we can honestly say that we obtained the optimum return from the
bequest by using a set amount each year and earning interest on the
remainder....The bequest was in this way parlayed from the original
$250,000 into $700,000. In a period of rapid inflation the MacCosham
bequest meant a great deal to the Library, enabling it to maintain an acqui-
sitions rate at the necessary level, which would otherwise have been
impossible.[187]

Buoyed somewhat in spirit, Mr Peel wrote that "From an administrative point of view, the year 1975–76 may be regarded with some

satisfaction, as the Library operated with a degree of stability seldom achieved in the decade of rapid expansion or the last quinquennium of monetary inflation and educational uncertainty." He could not have foreseen either the severe decline in the value of the Canadian dollar or the barbed criticism of the Management Survey Report. Thus, by 1977–1978, despite the cancelling of thousands of subscriptions, fully 80 percent of the acquisitions budget was committed to renewing serials. By 1978, the Library Committee was forced to target another $100,000 reduction in current serials, or allow the entire acquisitions budget to be devoured. Rising costs, a shrinking dollar, and the need to maintain a respectable base of journal subscriptions significantly reduced the number of new books that were purchased in those years. While faculty in the sciences were most distressed by the attrition of subscriptions, even the easily identified and targeted duplicates, members of the Faculty of Arts were frustrated to find fewer monographs purchased each year. Nor were the students immune, and in that era of increasing and outspoken student activism, they were willing not only to voice their discontent, but also to hold public demonstrations. The venerable student newspaper, *The Gateway*, was especially zealous in coverage of library issues. *Gateway* writers had not only waged a ferocious campaign against the threat of cost-saving reductions in the Library's Saturday evening and Sunday hours, but helped scuttle a proposal to spend $50,000 on the purchase of an original 12-volume set of Johann Blaeu's *Atlas Major* to represent the Library's two-millionth volume: "If we were to make such an ostentatious display...by spending $50,000 on a single work for the library, I think it quite possible we would further hamper our pleas to the provincial government and the public. Or worse, we would not be helping that part of the library which needs help most, and would instead squander our money on a showpiece."[188]

When the provincial government released budget proposals early in 1978 that would give the University $6.2 million less than requested, and would result in large tuition increases, as well as serious cuts to the budgets of the University and the Library, students at the province's three universities organized a protest march on the Legislature for 15 March. When the students stressed that the protest was not solely over tuition increases, but the province's underfunding of universities in general, they not only gained faculty support, but, in an unprecedented and controversial move, President Gunning announced that he, too, would join the march. *The Gateway* endorsed the march, and replied to the *Edmonton Journal*'s demand for "tangible evidence that the quality of education is suffering as a result of the government's spending restraints" by nominating impending cuts of $600,000 to the budget for Physical Plant and $150,000 from the Library's budget.[189] Forbidden by the government-appointed Board of Governors from participating, President Gunning drove instead of marching with the protesters, and addressed them at the beginning and the end of their march to the Legislature.

In a special issue devoted to the funding crisis, *The Gateway* high-lighted the impacts upon the Library, which Mr Peel described in an interview: "'A university is judged by its library. The library turns a university into a mecca, attracting top graduate students and the best professors'."

> *"If we don't get an infusion to make up this year's loss, and next year's inflation rate, we are definitely going to become a second-rate library operation....*
>
> *As it is, we must decrease our intake by an approximate total of 14,000 from the normal intake of 100,000....Five years ago in a similar crisis we cut 2,000 titles from some 17,000 periodicals....*
>
> *We are told we must make cuts in non-salary holdings. Supplies will be cut by $30,000. $46,000 will be taken from our casual or temporary employment. Since it is the part-time staff which gives the library its flexibility we will be forced to shorten library hours. Circulation services will be cut by one-quarter. In addition, because of a freeze on staff and because of the high turnover of support staff in the library there will be effects in such areas as reserve reading rooms."*

It remained only for the *Gateway*'s reporter to ask rhetorically: "How can a province which claims to be committed to developing itself into an important international area allow its libraries, the very life of education, to decline?"[190]

When no budgetary relief was forthcoming by the beginning of the fall term, *The Gateway* once again took up the cause of "Cutbacks in Staff Library Situation 'Critical'," and reported Mr Peel's fear of having to cancel as many as 2000 of the Library's 15,000 subscriptions to periodicals, when "other institutions of similar programme levels on the North American continent have a subscription list typically of 20,000 to 25,000 titles." He added that the potential elimination of 20 staff positions by 1 April could save as much as $240,000. In November 1978, the Government of

Alberta acknowledged the damage done by the recent, crippling fall in value of the Canadian dollar and the resulting escalation in the cost of imported academic books and journals — by 30 percent in the case of American titles, 40 percent for European titles — by awarding $9 million from the Alberta Heritage Savings Trust Fund (AHSTF) for the purchase of library materials by Alberta's board-governed, post-secondary institutions over a three-year period. Under a formula "based on the need, status and quality of current holdings, and related to actual expenditures during the previous three years," the University of Alberta received the largest share of this award, amounting to nearly one-third of the total. "'I'm very thankful we got this extra funding,' says U of A Chief Librarian Bruce Peel, 'for otherwise next year would have been very critical — we would have had to do some real slashing of book and periodical purchasing'." As Mr Olin Murray, Head of Collection Development, later observed, "Without AHSTF funding, in fact, the Library's acquisitions programmes would have crumbled in ruin....We are thus dependent on this source of funding for the sheer maintenance of our book and periodical purchasing." When GFC deliberated over the University's 1980–1981 operating budget, it unanimously passed a motion that "priority will be given to a corrective increase in the base budget of the Library to alleviate the reduction in services and purchasing power which have occurred in recent years."[191]

Long-Term Solutions: The Computer Revolution
Libraries have traditionally been labour-intensive organizations. Their main functions, namely selecting, ordering, purchasing, and circulating books and other information resources, as well as providing reference service, absorbed endless hours of work by large numbers of employees, many of whom work behind the scenes, out of sight of the typical library user. The continued operation of the Library, despite an ongoing reduction in the number of staff imposed by declining budgets in the 1970s, was feasible largely due to a revolution in the way libraries function. The application of computer technology to library operations began in the 1960s and accelerated rapidly thereafter. Library card catalogues were converted into machine-readable records in computerized databases, and computer programs were developed to track the orders and payments made by acquisitions departments as well as the circulating of books to borrowers. The Library's annual circulation figures

rose steadily by 13 percent through the early 1960s, jumped by 23 percent in 1968–1969, and reached 1 million by 1970–1971. Internal use of library materials followed a similar pattern. Manual circulation procedures for controlling such large numbers grew increasingly impractical, and made the case for automation a compelling one.

During Dr Eric Hanson's chairmanship in 1964–1967, members of the Library Committee showed great interest in the potential for automation in the Library, both in its daily operations as well as for information retrieval. As Mr Peel later recalled, "they were so naïve as to think that you could put just about everything in every book into a computer and retrieve it whenever you wanted it. [And] within three or four years that these miracles which a computer could perform would be standard." The Committee was indeed being naïve, but also ultimately prescient. Peel, however, was better aware of the challenges to be overcome, and preferred to learn from the mistakes of others: "my position, which I expressed at the time, was I didn't want to be the first into computerization, nor did I wish to be the last."[192]

In 1966, a campus committee on automation and information retrieval was struck, along with two internal library committees, one to focus on automating operations, the other to investigate information retrieval. "We decided that what we should automate first were the circulation records of the education library," Peel later recalled, "a very busy one with a high lending rate and a very rapid turnover of borrowed books." The recently formed Department of Computing Science agreed to work on the design of a circulation module as a joint project, and loaned the services of Mr Helge Hanson to the Library: "The programming and the key punching of IBM bookcards began in April 1966. The automated system went into operation in December, but as is not uncommon in the introduction of automation to libraries (since library automation is more complicated than is generally realized) our system had 'bugs'." When asked if the system couldn't be fixed on the fly, "Helge said: 'It would be like trying to repair your automobile while you're going down the road'... Even if you were going slowly it wouldn't work. So we pulled it out."[193]

The following year a second attempt was delayed by the need for dedicated telephone lines to transfer data. In September 1968, the system was re-launched, again failed in testing, and required new programming. A decision was made to internalize further development of automation, and in August of that year the Library appointed its first head of Library Systems,

Mr Noel Johnson, a computer specialist formerly employed by the United States Air Force. When these early efforts to create a program to run on the University's new IBM 360-67 mainframe computer proved unsuccessful, the Library's archetypal eccentric programmer-analyst, John Ebdon, developed a system that was quite literally home grown. Mr James Heilik, who joined the Library in 1979 as head of the Systems Division, recalled that,

> Circulation was built in the wild west days of computing by John Ebdon. It was based on punched cards. Each book had a card in it, and each student's library card had holes punched in it. When a book circulated, a terminal read the book and student cards and recorded these on a microcomputer housed in Cameron. The data was sent to a mainframe computer where each night a list of all items lent was printed.
>
> The terminals which recorded the transactions were made by Epic, and the microcomputer was an imsai running eight inch floppy disks. John tested the essentials in his home where he maintained duplicate equipment. One of my tasks was to move the circulation system of the University of Alberta out of the basement of a legally blind genius programmer. This was done by having the Library replace the imsais with a minicomputer for which a special computer room was built in Cameron. Over time the punched cards were replaced by bar codes and the printed lists by microfiche, and the microcomputer by a much larger minicomputer, but the system remained essentially the same until it was retired some 20 years later.[194]

When at last, on 15 October 1969, an automated circulation system finally went into operation, *The Gateway* heralded the system:

> U of A students will no longer be suffering from writer's cramp after taking books out of the library.
>
> The present McBee system will be replaced Wednesday by a new IBM system.
>
> It will be faster to operate, reducing the amount of staff necessary to process books, and will shorten annoying lineups.
>
> The system will be very easy for students to use, after picking up their new cards in front of the circulation desk. They merely present their card with their books which are processed by the circulation staff. No writing is involved.
>
> Also, the new circulation system will garner useful statistics which, when combined with the cataloguing statistics, will give information about a number of areas.

It will determine which sections of the library are used the most, thus helping to determine which parts will need expansion.

The system will not save much money, but will meet a crucial need for better and more efficient service.

If the *Gateway's* reporter reflected the debatable view that funding should be directed toward the subject areas most heavily circulated, he had at least grasped that while library automation seldom offered a cheaper alternative, it would greatly improve service. As Mr Peel later summarized, "Automation made possible the centralization of circulation services for the major libraries on campus. This eliminated procedural inconsistencies between the different service points, freed staff in subject areas to concentrate on information services, and held down operational costs."[195]

However, automation of circulation was just the beginning of the computerized revolution in the Library. In 1971, a computerized accounting system was put into operation, and a study of acquisitions and cataloguing methods begun with a view to automating them. On 18 September 1973, the circulation system began producing products such as catalogue cards and spine labels. In June 1973, the first computer-generated list of the Library's holdings of 26,000 active and dormant serials titles was produced. In April 1974, a computerized order and acquisitions system was up and running. James Heilik recalled that

When I arrived at the University Library in 1979, there were already three major automation systems in place. The oldest, and the longest lived, was circulation control. The others were an acquisition system for making purchase orders and maintaining financial records, and a system for printing catalogue cards. Also in the early 1970s, the Library stopped typing catalogue cards and began generating them by computer. This was a major step forward in that the computer could sort cards, thus making filing easier. A side benefit of this system was that the data entered for making the cards was kept and was later used in replacing the card catalogue. Some of Alberta's deforestation is due no doubt to the mountains of paper and card stock consumed by these three systems. The main style of computing used was called "batch processing"; one submitted a job to the computer and got results a few hours or a day or a week later. No such simplicity as typing a query into a workstation and seeing an instant reply. An operations unit co-ordinated collection of data, submission of jobs, and distribution of paper, microfiche and card products to the various library departments.[196]

When the decision to build a third major library, Rutherford North, was being considered, one challenge lay in producing a duplicate of the card catalogue to permit access to readers in all libraries. The card catalogue, in terms of cumulative labour to create and maintain, was the Library's single most valuable asset, but its greatest drawback was its stationary nature. The Library Committee was quite opposed to the notion of duplicating the card catalogue in a microform format, and insisted that the second copy must be printed on cards or in book form, so a second card catalogue was produced for the Rutherford North Library. However, the adoption of a computer-output microform (COM) catalogue became a fait accompli when the Library of Congress closed its own card catalogue in June 1981, prompting many libraries to follow suit. Those pioneering libraries that had long been producing automated records, such as the University of Alberta, already possessed large numbers of machine-readable catalogue records to facilitate this transition. This led the Library to adopt the DOBIS/LIBIS system to enable the generation of a COM fiche catalogue of the nearly 350,000 titles catalogued between 1974 and 1981. James Heilik was well acquainted with the DOBIS system from his work as head of Systems at the Canadian Institute for Scientific and Technical Information (CISTI) in Ottawa. He recalled that after his arrival,

> My major achievement was an early one: closing the card catalogue, and replacing it first with a microfiche one and then with an online one. The work moved the library from one era into the next. The effort took a few years, and it was not without opposition. The one irrefutable objection to doing this which I still can't answer is that the machine catalogue does not smell as nice as the cards. One factor which helped immensely was automation of catalogue card production which meant there was a large body of machine readable catalogue records already in existence.[197]

Early in 1977, a direct link to the University of Toronto's UTLAS database catalogue system was established to allow access to, and downloading of, catalogue records, and to provide a temporary host for the University of Alberta's records. Actual on-line cataloguing only began seriously in January 1981, and, as Mr Peel observed, it was not a smooth transition:

> *Initial enthusiasm faded quickly, as it became apparent that the utlas on-line system proved to be a less efficient processing system than had at first been promised. Down time was frequent, line problems were numerous, and slow response time some days brought production nearly to a stand-still....frequent communication with* UTLAS *representatives brought apologies but little else, and by the end of the fiscal year the situation had barely improved. Staff morale dropped visibly, since the terminal operators were accustomed to working with a very satisfactory in-house automated system (the system in use prior to utlas), where local control brought instant improvements, where down time...was at least at a tolerable level.*
>
> *To complicate matters further, the* UTLAS *system quickly became over-loaded due to greater use than anticipated, and only 135 terminal ports were made available to customers at any one time, placing clients in the western part of Canada at a distinct disadvantage. Quick shuffling and recruiting of staff from other areas assured 100% occupancy of the terminals from 8:00 A.M. to 5:15 P.M. each day. Nevertheless, where on the old system six operators could key in 6,000 records a month in less than four hours each day, such production quotas could not be met by manning six* UTLAS *terminals ten hours a day.*

Despite the early 'teething' problems, "derived" catalogue records from UTLAS, and later from the OCLC and RLN databases, greatly reduced the volume of original cataloguing required, and yielded increased accuracy as well as efficiency. Reflecting upon the Library's early automation efforts, Mr Peel felt that the Library "was pushed into automation about one or more years too early. And I have always said that we wasted at least a third of a million dollars with no results over two or three years. That may not seem like much now [1988], but I think that you should multiply that by five or six....It was just pure waste....I think that if we had waited about two more years, we would have been just as far ahead as any other library." However, bringing up one system at a time, he felt, had allowed the Library to avoid the failures of libraries elsewhere that tried to do it all at once.[198]

The other brave new realm to which automation beckoned was that of information retrieval, then still in its infancy prior to the widespread availability of the Internet, when electronic data-bases were available only through telephone dial-up access, or when locally mounted on CD-ROM players. These resources required individually mediated searches by reference staff familiar with the non-standardized searching protocols of each database. During the 1976–1977 academic year, Library staff assisted readers with 871 literature searches on bibliographic databases, that yielded 90,817 citations. This would soon become a major service in academic libraries, and prompted Mr Peel to observe that even as "increasing the automation of routine or technical tasks is looked to as a means of reducing or at least stabilizing staff costs…in the area of information retrieval, the more sophisticated services made possible by the computer generate a demand on the part of users that can very easily entail additional costs to the Library."[199]

New Solutions for Some Old Problems

As the increasing pressure on library acquisitions budgets was making abundantly clear, self-sufficiency in collections, even for the largest libraries, was an unattainable goal. The importance of resource sharing among libraries was old news to those in the profession, but was coming more and more to dominate the agenda when University Presidents, as well as University Librarians, gathered. Future progress in resource sharing would increasingly require development of computer-supported library networking. But inter-library loan document delivery, whether of books, or copies of journal articles, continued to depend upon the postal service, as, indeed, it always had. And postal rates, like virtually all other goods and services, rose sharply during the decades of the 1970s and 1980s. Because other libraries in the prairie provinces supplied 51 percent of the University of Alberta's inter-library lending needs, while other Alberta institutions were the source of one-third of all requests made to the University of Alberta, the creation in October, 1979, of the Alberta Universities Inter-Library Loan Service (AUILLS, pronounced "owls"), a delivery service subsidized by the Government of Alberta from the Alberta Heritage Savings Trust Fund, was a major milestone. Utilizing the Alberta Government Courier Delivery Service, AUILLS aimed to achieve 24- to 48-hour turn-around in deliveries across the province.

Security of the Library's collections was also a growing concern. Libraries have been subject to the ravages of fire, flood, and theft since their earliest origins. Floods due to breaks in waterlines are endemic during the coldest winter months. The Cameron Library, little more than a year old, was the scene of a series of floods from frozen pipes bursting on 26 and 27 December 1965. Although the flooding was widespread on the lower floors of the library when "The hot water from the whole of the building's heating system drained out to the floor," quick work by maintenance and care-taking staff, as well as by the fire department, kept losses to a bare minimum. This was the first such incident of flooding in Cameron Library, but it would prove to be far from the last. As for theft, the invasive, manual checking of bags and briefcases at exits was an inefficient use of staff, and caused irksome line-ups and delays. In 1975–1976 the exits of Rutherford Library were equipped with turn-stiles, 3M TattleTape® book detection sensors, and approximately 20 percent of the books on the shelves, as well as all incoming acqui-sitions and books returned by borrowers, were tagged with the system's magnetic strips. This was a major chore for the staff, but it proved its value within a few months by apprehending nearly 100 people who attempted to remove books without first checking them out properly. Therefore, the system was extended to all other library locations as quickly as possible. One *Gateway* reader, after a painful encounter with a locked turnstile, wrote to urge others to exercise greater care when exiting through the new equipment.[200]

Two Million Books, Too Little Space, and Fewer Dollars
Despite the financial difficulties and the trials of automation that characterized the 1970s, and derailed the ambitious growth fore-casts the University had projected in what Mr Peel labelled "The Golden Sixties," the Library reached another milestone. On 6 October 1979, a ceremony was held to mark the accession of the Library's two-millionth volume. The book selected for this honour was *Jumonville, Poèm* (Paris, 1759), by Antoine Léonard Thomas. An account of the death of Joseph de Jumonville, a French officer killed by militia under the command of a young George Washington, an event that sparked the Seven Years' War, it is one of only five copies held in North American libraries.[201] That the Library's collec-tions had once again doubled, and in less than a full decade, was, under the circumstances, little short of amazing, and was a testament to the hard work and innovation of both staff and administration. However, no good deed goes unpunished, and as another tumultuous decade in the Library's history drew to a close, two perennial problems still loomed: space and funding.

The phenomenal growth of the Library's collections rendered the need for more library space increasingly urgent. The Rutherford North building was too small from the outset, and its design less flexible than the Cameron building. But it was intended only as the first of four phases of library expansion. The next phase, to expand Rutherford North on the west side, was anticipated to begin construction by 1976 for occupancy by 1978, but was put on hold for lack of funding. By 1980, the Library faced an overall space deficit of 129,582 square feet in all of its branches, and, based on the annual accession rate of 100,000 volumes, Rutherford Library, North and South, would be completely full by 1983, and the entire library system would reach capacity by 1986. Furthermore, in May 1980, the *Final Report of the General Faculties Council Ad Hoc Committee on Study Space* endorsed the creation of more student study spaces in the Library, a measure not surprisingly endorsed warmly by the Students' Union. The formal *Library Space Proposal* document laid before the Provincial government later that year proposed three alternative scenarios:

1. *Construct a 70,000 sq.ft. addition on the west side of Rutherford North, followed immediately by a 45,000 sq.ft. addition to the Cameron Library on the site of the South Labs building. This preferred option would hold nearly two million volumes, afford 700 to 1000 additional study spaces, would provide space for 20 years of growth, and could later be connected by an all-weather, enclosed, elevated walkway. Or,*

2. *Construct only the 70,000 sq.ft. Rutherford North extension to provide capacity for 1.2 million volumes, 460–650 study spaces, and 12 years of growth. Or,*

3. *Construct only the 45,000 sq.ft. Cameron south wing to provide capacity for 900,000 volumes on compact, mobile shelving, 300–420 study spaces, and 10 years of growth.*[202]

In March 1981, Mr Peel wrote to the University's Facilities Development Committee to

emphasize the urgency of resolution, decision and action on the Library's looming space problems. In the Library system some areas are already experiencing a space crisis to the detriment of satisfactory service to users. One of our two central buildings, the Rutherford complex, will be critically short of space before new construction can be available under even the most favorable of circumstances....When the Rutherford North building was constructed the Library Administration considered the square footage provided inadequate, but accepted the building in return for a commitment that construction of Phase II would commence in 1976.

Mr Peel went on to suggest that the University's capital budget submission to the Province include a reference to the AHSTF grant for the purchase of books, which obviously needed to be housed somewhere, in hope of obtaining funding for preliminary architectural planning. Sixteen months later, in his last month before retirement, Mr Peel repeated the same pleas for space in a letter to President Horowitz, in which he noted that the Library must soon begin evicting professors from faculty carrels in Rutherford, which would then be dismantled to make room for additional shelving.[203]

The awarding in 1979 of the three-year Alberta Heritage Fund grant was, in Mr Peel's words, "a godsend" and one for which he gave considerable credit to President Gunning, whose term was then ending. In a press release announcing the first instalment of $898,000, received in April 1979, Mr Peel described the grant as "a timely rescue," and noted that

Without the Heritage grant there would have been a shortfall of $727,000 during the 1979-80 fiscal year....This would have meant disaster; it would have been necessary to cancel at least 6,000 periodical titles, and upwards of 12,000 new books could not have been purchased....The cost of subscribing to the same number of periodicals since 1969 has risen from $250,000 to $953,000 with no end to these increases in sight as we look at the trend for 1980 and 1981.[204]

Indeed, the trend was sufficiently worrisome, that Mr Peel wrote to President Horowitz early in 1981, to warn that the Library could anticipate at least a 20 percent increase in costs for the 1982–1983 budget year, the very time when the AHSTF grant funding ended. The President replied to express optimism that the grant might be renewed. In mid-May, Peel again wrote to the President to warn that a stable level of acquisitions had lately been maintained only because of the funding grant. Without replacement funding, a major serials cancellation would be unavoidable, a grim sequel to the cancellations of 1973 and 1978. On 6 July, Peel wrote to departmental library representatives issuing a similar warning of probable cancellations, and announcing that there would be no further disbursements of discretionary funds for book purchases, for English-language approval plans, or for new, or even previously approved, acquisitions projects. The President eventually resorted to a succinct form letter to acknowledge protest letters and eloquent pleas on behalf of the Library from heads of departments and library representatives.[205]

Mr Peel wrote the President again on 3 December, and, in a lengthy letter warning of a "state of emergency" in the funding of library acquisitions, attributed the funding dilemma to the need to acquire not merely the "common books and periodicals," but the deeper, research-level material that was not only the bedrock of graduate programs, but that provided the "information resources which are indispensable to the social, economic, and cultural health of the nation."

> As retiring Librarian to the University, I shall take the prerogative of a university employee of thirty years standing, to speak my mind on an issue of policy.... This prosaic but indispensable function is unattractive to private corporations, and so must be borne by government.
>
> The Alberta Heritage Savings Trust Fund grants provided the life blood of our research collections for 3 years; for 3 years our research collections were rescued from obsolescence and decline. Alberta government policy mean-while fosters a large research and development effort, with the establishment of industrial parks and medical research at the most sophisticated and advanced levels. I can provide you with plenty of confirmation that these kinds of projects can only be executed in the context of rich, sophisticated, and concentrated research library resources. There is no way such projects can secure access to the necessary specialized research materials without continuous special funding to update the existing research library resources.
>
> I hope you can find some means to convince the Government of Alberta that this vital funding must be restored and on a permanent basis, thereby ensuring the existence of what must come to be recognized as a priceless heritage, redounding ultimately to the benefit of all Albertans and Canadians, both now and in the indefinite future.

The next day, following a telephone call in which the Deputy Minister of Advanced Education revealed that the AHSTF grant would not be renewed, President Horowitz forwarded Peel's letter to the Minister with his own "special appeal that the decision regarding the special Heritage grant be reviewed." The Minister wrote Mr Peel soliciting further comment. In his reply, Peel emphasized the lengths to which the University had gone to provide additional funding for library acquisitions, but that it was impossible to bridge the inflationary gap over the past decade, when books had risen in price by three times, and periodicals by four times, the overall consumer price index, even before factoring in a 20 percent decline in the value of the Canadian dollar. Reno Bossetti, the Assistant Deputy Minister, told *The Gateway*, in January 1982, "that the program was designed 'to enhance library collections, not to combat inflation. That is dealt with in the block grants to institutions. This is an enhancement grant, not a replacement grant'." The Minister's final word came in a letter on 11 March 1982 in reply to the President's letter of 4 December:

> *As I indicated during the debate in the last session of the Legislative Assembly, government is sensitive to the problems faced by all of our libraries across the province. We will attempt to address the situation in a general way during our 1982/83 grant allocations. However, if our libraries have indeed adhered to the philosophy underlying the special grant, and not used it as replacement money, I feel confident that they will be able to address the shortfall from within their internal resources.*[206]

At the same time that the government was withholding sufficient operating funds, it was underwriting the World University Games, second only in size among athletic events to the summer Olympics (which had recently beggared the taxpayers of Montreal), that were scheduled to be held in Edmonton in 1983. Among the capital expenditures of the Games' $50 million budget was the Universiade Pavilion, an enormous fieldhouse subsequently dubbed the "Butterdome." Although it was to provide a permanent campus amenity, it was viewed by many as a symbol of misplaced priorities. In response to the government's parsimony, the students, who accurately anticipated a massive tuition hike, once again organized a protest march. *The Gateway* threw its support behind the demonstration, and in a special "Quest for Funds" issue, ran reminiscences of a student veteran of the protest march of 1978, as well as two articles on the "strangulation" of the Library. Greg Harris quoted Mr Peel as saying, "'I think the analogy of a dearth of funds to keep a library up to date is found in some of the mediaeval libraries, which became "fossilized" when they ceased to expand their collections'."[207]

In composing his last annual report, for 1980–1981, which included a review of the critical shortage of space, the increasing demand from government and the private sector to provide free services, and the impending need to shed 30 staff positions over the coming year, he allowed his cumulative frustrations some voice:

> In the writing of annual reports the chief officer of an organization tends to emphasize the positive in terms of achievements and growth figures, while glossing over the cracks in the edifice. Although the University Library remains sound organizationally, the unremitting buffeting of the winds of fiscal stringency are steadily eroding our informational resource strength and our high standard of service. As a matter of policy the Library Administration, when forced to make deletions in acquisitions and in service, has made these where they would be noticed least by our daily users. But our patrons are increasingly affected by staff shortages, periodical cancellations, reduced book ordering, and a space squeeze. The time has come for the Librarian to strike the tocsin.[208]

Throughout the lean years of the 1970s, the Library continued to print and distribute the University Librarian's very detailed, informative, and stylishly written annual reports to a wide audience, as it had done during the prosperous decade that preceded it. These reports were issued as 30–40-page octavo booklets, illustrated with black-and-white photos, bound in glossy, card-stock covers bearing attractive, full-colour photographs of the University's library buildings. Reacting to one of these "fancy" reports, one containing details of diminished acquisitions, the Chairman of the Department of Economics wrote to the President to complain that "if the money is going to be spent in this way some serious questions must be raised about how the Library sees its priorities." Mr Peel responded at length in a letter addressed to President Gunning.

> In my opinion, the format of an annual report tells something about the agency's image of itself. I hope that over the years this Library's report has projected the image of a department that takes pride in its annual achievement, and of a library staff who collectively want this to be a quality research university. Whatever campus opinion may be of the Library. I can say that in library and publishing circles on this continent and in Europe it is regarded as among the best. I believe that this is also true among faculty at other universities.

Years ago the Library Committee was concerned that in our isolation we would not have opportunities to bid on important research collections as these became available anywhere in the Western World. The regular distribution of copies of the Library's report to book suppliers and publishers has changed this situation. European dealers come to us who only touch down at a few libraries on this continent. The travel cost of even one dealer coming to us is reimbursement in itself for the difference in the cost between producing an attractive report as against one messily lithographed on newsprint.

Mr Peel went on to suggest that the public image projected by his reports, which were distributed to nearly 100 of the largest academic libraries across North America, played a role in the University's recruitment of prospective new faculty and graduate students. In addressing the marginal, extra cost of a quality format, he gave expression to principles and standards that he brought to his work.

A chief librarian as the custodian of mankind's achievement in printed form would not be true to his vocation if he did not respect quality printing and format in those documents for whose production he is responsible. In summary, the Library's report is a public relations document intended to indicate that this is a prestigious research library in Canada. At other institutions the report has enhanced the image of the University of Alberta as a whole.[209]

Mr Bruce Peel retired in 1982 after 31 years of service in the University of Alberta Library, 27 of them as "Librarian to the University." In a letter to President Horowitz he wrote

to express appreciation for the official actions taken by the University Administration to mark my retirement. The bestowal of the status of Librarian Emeritus was a surprise. And the naming of the Library's Special Collections area was also completely unexpected. I began librarianship in charge of a special collection of Canadian[a] so that the field of scarce, rare and valuable books has always been an interest of mine; I am very happy with the naming.[210]

Had he done nothing more than pursue his career as a library administrator, Bruce Peel would be remembered with no little envy for the timing of his career, the first 25 years of which coincided with an era of unprecedented growth in universities and their libraries.

As an administrator he guided the growth of the University of Alberta's library from a very modest size to its present rank, as one of Canada's three largest research institutions. He oversaw the creation of six new library facilities, as well as the development of the original library collection at the University of Alberta's Calgary branch. More than merely a very successful librarian, Mr Peel was a man of numerous and varied interests, and he produced a lengthy stream of historical, biographical, bibliographical, genealogical, and journalistic publications. It is, however, for *A Bibliography of the Prairie Provinces*, and his other publications on the history of early western Canadian printing and imprints, that Bruce Peel is best known as a scholar, and upon which his reputation among both bibliographers and historians rests. He spent a lifetime producing, collecting, organizing, and describing the printed word in Canada.

6

Peter Freeman Balances Progress and Poverty, 1982–1988

IN AUTUMN 1981, almost a year prior to Mr Peel's scheduled date of retirement, a search committee was struck to recruit his successor. The Library Committee recommended that the appointment be term-limited, or at least with provision for subsequent reviews, a feature that was then becoming the norm for senior university administrators. An emissary returned to the Library Committee with word that the search committee would, indeed, consider a review mechanism. The search committee's choice fell to Mr Peter Freeman, who, although then serving as Librarian of the Supreme Court in Ottawa, was no stranger to the University of Alberta. Peter Leonard Freeman was born in Manitoba in 1938, and educated at the University of Manitoba (BA, LLB). After practicing law in Winnipeg and Brandon, he joined the Faculty of Law at Manitoba in 1966; he moved to the University of Alberta Faculty of Law in 1968. When the Law Librarian, Miss Patricia Coffman, resigned in 1969, Mr Freeman recalled that "Inspiration hit me, and I said to the University administration, if you would send me to the University of Washington's program in law librarianship, I'll become your Law Librarian, and they accepted that proposition."[211]

After he returned to the University as Law Librarian in 1971, Mr Freeman was soon immersed in planning for the move of the Law Library into the splendid new Law Centre building that autumn. He nonetheless found time to work with the Acquisitions Division to devise new procedures to speed the acquisition and processing of legal material. Of his decade of service in the Law Library, he later recalled:

I don't think I was considered to be a typical unit head within the library
system at that time. I had the benefit of being a law faculty member as well
as a librarian, and that gave me a special status, so I was able to walk that
line between the Library and the Law School, which is more typical of the
way American law libraries reported within library systems. I know that
chief librarians never liked that there was some renegade unit somewhere
out there, but in terms of the so-called special libraries, there's a different
perspective, a public service orientation; they're more client-based than most
university libraries, which tend to be more inclined toward just putting
books on shelves.

    The law library was, I think, probably better off than most other units.
We did have some special funding...that helped us ease over the budget cuts.

We had established a pretty good base; we supported the Faculty; we had a pretty good collection. Depending on whom you want to listen to, we had the second best law library collection in Canada, and in terms of staffing...the most important thing, we had a good bunch of librarians who...didn't neces-sarily have to worry about the technical service aspect of librarianship. They could devote themselves to public service, and they were quite useful to both the students and the faculty.

He also recalled that, "like everything else on the campus at the time," the designers of the new Law Centre failed to anticipate the Faculty's growth, and thus, "it was built for 350 and it housed 500 when it opened." Nonetheless, "it provided reasonable study space for the students, which at that time was not very good on campus, and when we were in Rutherford, it was almost nonexistent."[212]

During what would prove to be a brief stay in Ottawa as the Librarian of the Supreme Court, Mr Freeman recalled, "I was asked to consider applying for the Chief Librarian's job at the University of Alberta. It came at a time when I was at a crossroads in Ottawa.... and so I guess in a way it was time to put my money where my mouth was." As he made preparations to move his family once again, he wrote to President Myer Horowitz, "We are looking forward to our return to Edmonton....The selection process brought the many challenges to my attention but it also disclosed a renewed interest in the library by the university community. With this support the challenges should become manageable." When he returned to Edmonton in the summer of 1982, it was with a vision and an agenda: "First, I wanted to change the institutional management culture if I could. And second, I wanted to change the emphasis from technical services and putting books on shelves to access to infor-mation." Meeting with the GFC Library Committee for the first time that September, Mr Freeman said he hoped to benefit from the Committee's advisory role, but also from their active participation with Library staff in addressing a number of problems, particularly the issue of library space. He also spoke at some length about his desire to undertake a Collection Analysis Project (CAP), a self-study developed by the Office of Management Studies of the Association of Research Libraries, which he believed could "be very supportive in terms of building space for the Library." Mr Freeman recently admitted to a further motive in undertaking the CAP self-study:

Peter Freeman.
Courtesy of the
University of Alberta
Faculty Club.

That was part of trying to change the organization. There were too many
good people within the Library system whose talents were not being used.
I'm a decentralizer anyhow, maybe by experience, and so I was of the
opinion that all decisions should not be made on the fifth floor of the
Cameron Library, so I tried to decentralize, and make use of the strengths
and talents of the people in the Library.[213]

The retirement of Associate University Librarian Geoffrey
Turner in the spring of 1983 provided Mr Freeman with an opportunity to flatten the Library's administrative hierarchy. Instead of
filling the Associate position, he chose to assign additional responsibility to unit heads Ms B.J. Busch and Ms Sieglinde Rooney; to take
upon himself the supervision of more than a dozen unit managers,
who now reported directly to him; and to introduce the title of
Area Coordinator for heads of major units. Looking back upon
this restructuring of responsibility, Mr Freeman recalled that

management experts would tell you that so flat an operation was not good.
There were too many people reporting to me, but we had to go through the
process...so I guess I was running around trying to keep everybody together,
and they did their own thing. I was not afraid of decentralization; it didn't

bother me. I think at that time, you couldn't make use of the talents of the people who were there without doing that....You could set up another hierarchy, or even a semi-hierarchy, but that would have stifled some of the people. I like to think that many of those people grew into their jobs, and grew in their knowledge and responsibility, and that was the benefit to everybody.[214]

Mr Freeman's appointment as Chief Librarian coincided with a deep and prolonged recession in Alberta's economy triggered by implementation of the National Energy Policy by the Federal Government. This caused investment and development in the Province's oil and gas industry to all but cease, sharply reduced the revenues of the Provincial Government, and led to years of painful budget reductions across the entire University. Mr Freeman's challenge was to seek new opportunities, while at the same time conducting damage control. With the ending of the three-year Heritage Trust Fund grant for the purchase of books, the Library's accessions rate went into a steep decline from which it would not recover for years, while the slow eroding of staff through attrition continued, mitigated somewhat by advances in technology.

Staffing was a problem, replacing people and positions. And, of course, as happens in all these situations...the academics start cannibalizing everybody in sight: the administration, support services, whatever, to get the money they want. So you were always fighting that off. One of my most important jobs was to try to keep...the necessary staff going, because that was the only way we were going to save ourselves.

And it was a struggle when year after year, every university unit had to find economies to meet its "tax" — a transparent euphemism for an operating budget cut. The tax cut more deeply into the budgets of support units, such as the Library, than the budgets of the academic teaching departments. Early in 1984 Mr Freeman was informed that $284,000 would be cut from the following year's budget; reductions of that magnitude meant giving up positions. The Library was required to cut $225,000 in 1985–1986, which was achieved by eliminating 1.5 vacant professional and 7 support staff positions. A successful application to the Alberta Heritage Fund for Medical Research (AHFMR) in 1985 began providing some much appreciated financial support for library resources in the health sciences.

At the beginning of 1987, the Provincial Government announced that it was cutting the University's operating budget appropriation by only 3 percent, but its capital budget would be reduced by more than 36 percent, for an overall reduction of about 10 percent in the Government's annual appropriation for the University. Once again, serials cancellations became the order of the day.[215]

It was inevitable that staff reductions would affect library services. However, Mr Freeman recalled that "We didn't get a lot of complaints from faculty. I mean there was the odd person who had his own hobbyhorse, but my recollection is that the faculty had other things on their minds. They would like to take the money from the Library, but they weren't going to complain about much other than when the whole serials thing started; that started to get them uptight." If the faculty remained largely quiescent until the spectre of massive serials cancellations reappeared, the students were far more vocal. Complaints voiced in the columns of *The Gateway* ranged from those sympathetically concerned about funding and space deficiencies — "Library Hurts Too" — to the petulantly trivial and carping — "Helpful Librarians Overdue." Some student opinion echoed the faculty's tendency to question the dollars spent on anything other than students, professors, and library books: "Where's the money, Myer?" Perhaps the most thoughtful and informed comments on the Library's fiscal plight by a student were by *Gateway* staff reviewer Gilbert Bouchard. They deserve to be quoted at some length.

> *Operating a University is more than just hiring professors and keeping classrooms heated.*
>
> *Often we forget the materials that are vital to the University's research and studies.*
>
> *While no one would begrudge a doctor his scalpel, or a plumber his wrenches, our government has seen fit to deprive the University of its most vital tool:* LIBRARY MATERIALS.
>
> *The erosion of our libraries is horrendous. In 1970/71 funding to the library system was 2.8 million dollars. In 1982/83, (including supplemental funding from the Heritage Trust Fund) was 3.5 million dollars. Taking into account inflation, the 1982/83 funding levels are only 64 per cent of the 1970/71 levels. This does not, however, take into account the devaluation of the Canadian dollar and the effect that has on acquisitions since 90 per cent of the libraries' resources come from outside the country.*

In 1970/71 the U of A libraries were ranked 4th overall in material acqui-
sitions by the Association of Research Libraries. The U of A ranked after
Harvard, Texas and Toronto, with 700,000 dollars separating the U of A
from the top.

In 1980/81 the U of A had fallen to 7th overall in material acquisitions.
Harvard ranked first, Texas ranked second but now over 4,300,000 dollars
separated the U of A from the top.

Library funding is vital to the quality of the education that the U of A can
offer. After all, how valuable is a degree program based on outdated and
inadequate materials? And how can the University of Alberta provide TOP
QUALITY *graduates on the world market if we aren't willing to maintain*
our libraries: the nerve center of the University?[216]

At the end of that year, moved perhaps by such powerful eloquence, the Students' Union Council voted to donate $100,000 to the Library in the expectation of a matching amount from the Provincial Government's matching gifts fund, and to demonstrate that "we truly care about the quality of education." Concern was expressed during the Council's brief debate that such generosity by students might betray to the government a willingness to accept higher tuition fees. Nonetheless, the decision passed by a vote of 21 to 2. This surprising donation revealed a large measure of student consensus regarding the Library's funding crisis, but it drew immediate fire in a *Gateway* editorial that criticized the Council for its haste in acting without documentary evidence, and without making any provision to make the Library accountable for the money.[217]

Among the steps taken in 1987 to absorb the impact of a 10 percent (inflation adjusted) budget cut was the closure of the Extension Library that had served rural Albertans for more than seven decades. It had come under scrutiny more than once in the past, and, two decades earlier, it survived a review of its operations when the Library Committee sought to determine whether it was "a proper func-tion of the University." Its collection of almost 100,000 volumes and accompanying database catalogue — assets with a replacement value of $5 million — were transferred to the recently created Peace River Regional Public Library Board. Mr Freeman can recall no criti-cism or outrage directed at the Library over the closure, perhaps because "people forget that in the universities of western Canada, extension work was one of the reasons they were established and one of the reasons they received public support." As the Library geared up for another round of serials cancellations, an exercise in which the Mathematics Department initially refused to participate, only to relent later under pressure, the Library Committee strongly urged Peter Meekison, the Vice-President (Academic), to declare the Library's acquisitions budget "tax-free," inasmuch as price inflation and foreign exchange on the weakened Canadian dollar caused more than enough damage. Mr Freeman, meanwhile, undertook meetings with the Development Office to discuss a donation program targeted at support for journal subscriptions and Canadiana, while Technical Services Coordinator Sieglinde Rooney and this author launched a Joint Serials Renewal Negotiation Project, that enlisted more than 50 libraries across Canada in an effort to obtain more favourable subscription rates from the eight most prominent publishers of scientific, technical, and medical journals.[218]

Space Wars: The Ghost of Rutherford West

Along with the growing insufficiency of both the operating and acquisitions budgets for the Library, Mr Freeman inherited a large, unresolved space deficit. When the Rutherford North Library building was under construction in spring 1972, its promised westward extension, known as "Rutherford II, Phase II," was removed from the University's building priorities list, and placed on indefinite hold for lack of funding. This would leave the micromaterials collections and the special collections department stranded in the Cameron building, isolated from the rest of the Humanities and Social Sciences collections. Then an ill-considered proposal was floated to redesignate the Rutherford North building as a general sciences and medical sciences library. According to the chairman of the Arts Faculty Library Committee, by rejecting this proposal, "we avoided a donnybrook which would have made Belfast appear pastoral." In an angry letter to the Dean of Arts, the chairman went on to protest that

> this faculty has been left with a well-nigh intolerable disposition of its library resources. What chemist would for long tolerate having his Bunsen burner in one building and his sink in another; what biologist his microscopes and microtome in one and his specimens in another; what mechanical engineer his hydraulic press in one and his materials to be stress tested in another?...this is no rhetorical analogy: the library is our laboratory, and we should not tire of hearing the truth. Can we expect our students,

graduate and undergraduate alike, and our scholars to undergo the extreme
hardships of such fragmentation indefinitely? Perhaps more to the point,
can we attract and keep them under such conditions?

Moreover, he continued,

The situation may appear to be solely the concern of the Faculty of Arts, and I
have already met with indifference, actual hostility, when I have broached
the matter elsewhere within this institution. There is resentment that so
much money has gone to Humanities holdings. I note for the record, as well,
that I have been told by more than one staff member, his faculty now secure
under the roof of a degree-granting institution, that our faculty has outlived
its usefulness, its very relevance to the institution, and not even lip-service to
culture is any longer necessary.

Then, moving beyond his humanist's wounded amour propre, he
warned,

Grave as this situation is, there looms behind it a consequence still more
grave, far bigger than the concern of a single faculty. If the present building
priority holds over a prolonged period the result will be devastating. Within
the next three years, even with the present series of drastic library budget
cuts, the library will intensify its weeding of collections and screening of
acquisitions requests, finally turning to open storage. Within five or six
years it will resort to warehousing its holdings.

Finally, he uttered a warning worthy of Cassandra: "It is a concern
for the provincial bodies that agreed, on behalf of their constituents, to fund such an undertaking, and whose constituents are
making greater and greater use of our library through a number
of channels, *as their only provincial library.* It ill behoves those who
have set their hands to the achievement of greatness to loose their
grasp and turn to the crass counting of drachmas and scruples."[219]
    Even in the absence of such prescient warnings, the Librarian
and the Library Committee continued to press unsuccessfully for
construction of the planned "Rutherford II, Phase II" library expansion; in January 1981 the Library Committee produced and printed
Additional Library Space, A Proposal of the GFC Library Committee,
which was distributed in April. However, the few available capital
funds were diverted to smaller library projects in 1982 and 1983.

Nonetheless, in December 1982, Mr Freeman reported that the Planning and Priorities Committee wished the planning for the Rutherford extension to proceed. The Vancouver firm Advance Planning and Research for Architecture (APRA) was commissioned to produce a planning study, which was ready early in 1984. A survey of University departments found 90 percent of them opposed to storing parts of the Library's collection in closed-stack, compact shelving, as an alternative to redevelopment of the Rutherford complex. A review of six site options led the consultants, for practical reasons, to recommend "Site A" – 21,000 square feet adjacent to the west side of the Rutherford North building, to which it would be connected by covered walkways between the upper storeys, and which might be extended to connect the Cameron Library building. Professor Fred Van De Pitte, Chairman of the Library Committee, explained that

> This recommendation has been made after extensive study of several sites, their advantages and disadvantages. It has subsequently been approved by the various bodies within the Library itself. It seems unnecessary, therefore, for this Committee to further debate the issue. Rather, I would hope that we might combine our energies in a unanimous and forceful effort, recommending General Faculties Council to adopt the recommendation, and to support it before the appropriate University committees, in order to begin immediately the process of gaining government approval for this essential project.
>
> The Library is the most vital asset of the University. Its level of operation cannot be permitted to deteriorate. I shall do everything in my power to promote the building recommendation within the University community, and elsewhere if need be. I hope that you will join me in taking this important first step.[220]

The Library Committee reviewed the consultants' recommendations at meetings over the spring and summer, and gave final approval to Site A, despite some reservations about its adequacy to house such a large structure. Vice-President (Research) Dr Gordon Kaplan added his endorsement in a letter to the chairman of the Facilities Development Committee: "Option A provides the best location for future library expansion all factors and other options considered....The pressure felt by the library now and in the immediate future will be met by Option A without interfering with faculty and student research needs, the organization of the collection and the internal functioning of the library....Option A provides an opportunity for an imaginative linking of the two main library collections." The recommendation was then considered at a meeting of the Board of Governors on 16 October 1984, where it was approved, with the usual "funding to be sought" caveat. At the end of that year, Mr Freeman was informed that "based partly on lack of funding for planning purposes," further planning work on the Rutherford West extension was being put on hold until the Planning and Priorities Committee could decide upon "global priorities," and that further information was now solicited: "We do not have sufficient funds to advance all projects so intend only to advance the top priorities. Hopefully the proposed Libraries Expansion will retain a high priority rating and planning will be resumed in the late winter/ early spring." In his reply, Mr Freeman's tone was a palpable

mixture of anger, disappointment and frustration. The Library has been in a "pre-planning" process for over 4 years and gone through the University's committee system twice only to be once again sent back to the beginning.

Last year I was advised that University priority was given to those projects "ready to come out of the ground" and for that reason we were told we had a "high priority." Now the rules appear to have changed and we seem to be losing ground after two years of consultants, planning, committee approvals. We seem to be like Sisyphus or perhaps a laboratory rat working itself through a maze only to find the exit changed to entrance just as we are about to leave it. You must forgive me if I wonder if there is another decision making process, operating outside the normal channels, which is brought into play whenever we receive a decision which is not liked. It would be helpful if we could be confronted with all the hurdles at once and had some assurance that they would not change rather than the present series of surprises.

We must be a source of amusement somewhere on campus as we complete each step, receive advice to proceed to the next, only to be told "sorry the rules have changed it's back to square 1."

In November I was advised that only a decision of the Board Building Committee on December 18th stood between us and the necessary planning to comply with the recent motions of the ADC [Academic Development Committee] and BBC [Board of Governors Building Committee]. If I understood your memo correctly we are not even that far along and all efforts to date, etc. have been wasted. If PPC [Planning and Priorities Committee] determines that we have a campus-wide priority, I wonder what new requirements will arise to prevent us from consideration for funding and some expectation that we will have adequate and functional facilities this century.

It is appropriate that we compete with other campus needs, but it is difficult not to believe that we are not even in the game.[221]

Mr Freeman was unlikely to have been mollified by a phone call and memo from the Vice-President (Finance & Administration), acting in his capacity as chairman of the Planning and Priorities Committee, who wrote reassuringly, "I can confirm that the Library proposal will be on an equal footing with Electrical Engineering, Civil Engineering, Computing Science, and perhaps Home Economics, in forthcoming priority discussions....Should the Library emerge as the first priority, it will be so designated in the submission to government respecting capital requirements for 1986/87." Nonetheless, the following month he complied with the request for more information by submitting a 12-page summary of the Rutherford North expansion project, that outlined the Library's space issues, the potential benefits, as well as the costs to the University of leaving them unresolved, and observed that "Expansion of the library will avert the disaster of putting half of the humanities and social sciences collection in remote storage within ten years." Much to Mr Freeman's relief, though, the Academic Development Committee, meeting in March 1985, seconded the Board of Governors Building Committee in endorsing the Library expansion as its number one priority; in April the Planning and Priorities Committee did likewise. Thus, given final committee approvals, the Library Committee reported that "Preliminary design and traffic flow studies are now under way to establish the aesthetic and environmental suitability of the site selected. These studies should be completed by the end of December. It will then be a matter of waiting for government funding." But the waiting dragged into the following year, and in September 1986, Mr Freeman's request for funds to continue the design work on the new building was denied by the Board of Governors' Building Committee. President Horowitz expressed his sympathy in a letter to Mr Freeman, but rationalized that "maybe in the long-run it wouldn't make sense for the University to allocate any of our normal funds because that might send the wrong message to Government regarding our ability to finance capital projects."[222]

The University was soon afterward planning to devote a multi-million dollar bequest from the Albert Timms estate to the construction of a Collections Centre to house Archives, Museums, and Collections, and to provide a public exhibition gallery. "I've always speculated," Mr Freeman recalled, "based on no facts at all, that as soon as the Timms money became available for the Timms Centre, that the Rutherford project was gone. And then, of course, the concept of putting books offsite seemed to find support. My regret was that we were going to develop a significant number of study spaces." In July 1986, the Chief Librarian invited members of the Library Committee to come inspect an architect's concept model of the proposed Rutherford West Library that was placed on display in the Cameron Library Board Room, a model which sits in storage gathering dust to this day as a mute testament to unrealized hopes.[223]

New Library Facilities in a Decade of Austerity

Despite these disappointments, the Library system continued to expand. If the University and the Provincial Government, living through the economic doldrums of the 1980s, proved unable to find the estimated $35 million for the Rutherford West expansion, other, smaller projects were realized. The amalgamation of the Collège universitaire Saint-Jean with the University, as the Faculté Saint-Jean (now Campus Saint-Jean), led on 1 September 1983 to the merger of the University Library with the Bibliothèque Saint-Jean, and added another library location and more than 100,000 volumes to the system.[224]

Meanwhile, a provincially-funded program of asbestos removal from campus buildings received renewed funding late in 1982, and Cameron Library was accorded a very high priority to undergo this complex procedure. Meetings were held to reassure staff, who were anxious about the health risk factor, and to develop plans for emptying and sealing off the building floor-by-floor, in two phases spread over 1983–1984, while causing a minimum of disruption to library operations. Mr Freeman also sought to use the opportunity afforded by the $2.6 million asbestos removal "to retain an architect to examine several areas within the building with a mandate to design a more flexible facility." In addition to staff concerns over the danger posed by asbestos, closer inspection of the building revealed another worrisome problem, described in *The Gateway*:

Above: The John W. Scott Health Sciences Library in the Mackenzie Health Sciences Centre reflects the architectural influence of the modern shopping mall.
[UAA 99–43–88–6381–38]

Right: Peter Freeman, Bruce Peel, and Special Collections Librarian John Charles at the dedication of the Bruce Peel Special Collections Library, 12 October 1984.
[UAA 99–43–85–7702–1]

While workers were removing the asbestos it was discovered that the joists (metal beams supporting the floor) couldn't handle the weight of hundreds of shelves filled with books.

The joists twisted under the overload and are now being strengthened.

"We've found other problems in terms of having to upgrade building safety, like in the lighting and ventilation," said University director Gordon Bulat. The lighting system will be made more energy efficient and the ventilation ducts will be upgraded to modern air-carrying standards....

Chief Librarian Peter Freeman said "it's been quite a challenge for staff to keep the system running smoothly" with the renovations. "Once you get going on a project like this, you can't just stop midstream," said Freeman, referring to the inconvenience to U of A students.

Years afterward, Mr Freeman recalled the project with genuine pride in

the fact that we were able to remove the asbestos, keep Cameron open, and then put back together. That, I think, was a great accomplishment by the whole staff. It was a real challenge. The fear of asbestos at that time was real, but the University initially sort of pooh poohed it, said it's nothing worse than off your car's brake linings. But that didn't matter. That may have been true, but people were very nervous at that time. Now I think that removing asbestos from a building doesn't seem to bother anybody.[225]

Conveniently, the asbestos removal and renovation project in Cameron Library coincided with the planned relocation of two of its component departments to new quarters in other buildings. The Bruce Peel Special Collections Library moved from the Cameron building to a handsomely renovated location on the lower level of the old Rutherford Library; it was officially dedicated in a ceremony on 12 October 1984. Three weeks later, on 31 October, the John W. Scott Health Sciences Library was officially opened in spacious quarters built as part of the new Walter C. Mackenzie Health Sciences Centre and University Hospital. This had proven to be a momentous month in the expansion of Library facilities and services, for already on 1 October, the Winspear Business Reading Room, named for Francis Winspear, an Edmonton philanthropist and one of the founders of the University's School of Business, opened to provide service to Business faculty and students in their newly completed building. And in that same month, the Library Committee supported, and the Board of Governors approved, the recommendation of the Music Library Planning Committee that the University Library assume administrative responsibility for the Music Resource Centre effective 1 July 1985.[226]

Advances in Library Automation

As some compensation for frustration with the deficiencies in funding for acquisitions and additional library space, gratifying progress was being made in advancing the Library's automated systems. The University administration was relatively generous in providing development funds for automation, and the Library Committee continued to make maintaining accessibility to the collection a "first priority." A major milestone was celebrated when, at 9:00 A.M. on 22 September 1986, President Horowitz officially turned on the Library's expanded On-line Public Access Catalogue (OPAC), which made available a database of 750,000 records of books catalogued since 1974, and reduced the microfiche catalogue to a mere emergency backup. Nonetheless, the 1980s were a decade of sometimes chaotic transition, that was neither orderly, nor painless. James Heilik recalls that "The transition from batch systems to an integrated, on-line one was more akin to stumbling into modernity than deftly marching into it. Several independent systems were in use for management of library operations. Sometimes they connected, but more often they did not. The main streams were purchase orders and financial control for acquisitions, various incarnations of the catalogue, and circulation control. Data from one stream was not available to the others."[227]

The cataloguing stream at first generated cards, then microfiche, and, later, on-line access. Fortuitously, the original designers chose to follow international bibliographic standards, and keep archival copies of the machine readable records. By the time the DOBIS system went on-line in September 1986, after lengthy in-house testing, the on-line cataloguing had yielded almost 1 million records on which to draw for the Library's first OPAC. Dial-up access to the database was made available to internal users in 1987, and to external users the following year. The initial battery of 65 computer terminals installed throughout the Library soon required augmenting; the system proved so popular that it was soon operating at full capacity. Then it exceeded the system's limit, which buckled under the strain. The Systems unit spent a year rewriting the DOBIS program, thus losing some ground in other local develop-

ment, but gaining popularity among the rest of the international
DOBIS user community. "The circulation system did manage to make
some connections with the on-line catalogue," Heilik observed.

> DOBIS generated upc bar-code labels for individual items on the shelves. The
> epic circulation system was based on call numbers. UPC bar-code numbers
> and call numbers were linked, and circulation was enabled to use these bar-
> code labels instead of punched cards. Going in the other direction, the EPIC
> circulation system was able to report circulation status to DOBIS, which
> could then display the latter in the OPAC. DOBIS itself was never used for
> circulation control.

Dial-up access to the OPAC was superseded by the internet, once
all the campus buildings were fully wired for connectivity.[228]

Mr Freeman recalled the benefits of the Library having its own
in-house Systems unit: "It was very useful to have, and I think Jim
Heilik and his group did a good job; I benefited from having someone
with knowledge and expertise around." In addition to building the
OPAC, the Library's Systems team had set about designing and implementing a highly sophisticated payment tracking system for serials.
This system tracked subscriptions to periodicals and continua-
tions by their frequency of publication, divided them into five "pay
types," and made it possible to anticipate fluctuations in annual
budget requirements, irrespective of price inflation. As senior
programmer Shirley Norris recalled, "Marlene Sherban, Don Hazlett
and I sat down and determined what was needed to get serials

onto a computer. I wrote the programs and we implemented an excellent system. Marlene spoke about the system at library conferences, and the UofA Library was the envy of many other university libraries. The system ran for many years before being mothballed."[229]

As part of the process of upgrading the circulation system, on 8 December 1987, Library staff began applying locally generated Universal Product Code bar-code labels, en masse, to those books for which automated records existed. These labels later aided in retiring the old circulation system that had employed the increasingly unreliable EPIC terminals and the awkward Hollerith punch-cards. The circulation system was used to identify students as well as books. Formerly, library staff manually punched holes in each student's registration card. These holes were later replaced with bar-code labels. As James Heilik recalled: "Student registration used to be a week long affair which included acquiring a Registrar identification card and a Library card. I was happy to negotiate with the Registrar the elimination of the library card. We did this by attaching a library bar code label to his card. The Registrar returned the favour years later when the Library implemented the OneCard and he got rid of his entirely. This was a nice piece of co-operative work."[230]

Mr Freeman was resolute in his determination that all staff should be equipped with, and learn to use, the most current technologies in their daily work. Therefore he aimed to provide everyone with access to a personal computer. Shirley Norris recalled that "the first PC was placed in our office for IT staff to check over. Nobody went near it for months because we all had CRT terminals on our desks. One day I sat down and discovered that Windows was built exactly the way my brain worked. I learned to use it in less than an hour and loved it." She was soon enlisted to help spread the gospel: "Once it was determined that all staff members should have a PC, I was chosen to train them all." Because one-on-one instruction soon proved too time-consuming, "We purchased video tapes with instructions for all. After teaching over 300 staff using those tapes, I would cringe every time I had to start a tape."[231]

Collection Development

The Collection Analysis Project (CAP), undertaken soon after Mr Freeman's arrival as Chief Librarian, entailed creation of five task forces devoted to the investigation of collection policies, organization of collection management, preservation and conservation of collection resources, resource sharing, and fund allocation. The aim was to provide a more focused and forward-looking approach to planning for and managing future development of the Library's collections, and thus address the challenges presented by the budget's diminishing purchasing power. The final, consolidated report of CAP was completed and submitted in December 1985; chief among its numerous recommendations were the appointment of an overall Collections Officer and that a second staff position be created for a Preservation Officer.[232] Pursuant to the recommendations of the CAP report, the author was recruited from the University of Toronto Library in 1987 to become the Coordinator of Library Collections; Humanities and Social Sciences Collections Librarian Ms Georgina Lewis was detached from Rutherford Library to serve as the Preservation Librarian. During the next year, she conducted a survey of the physical condition of the collection, drew up a detailed preservation program, and addressed a serious risk-management deficiency by preparing and distributing the Library's first disaster recovery manual. Concurrent with the CAP studies, the Library also participated in the National Collections Inventory Project (NCIP), and produced more than a dozen quantitative and qualitative analyses of specific subject areas within the Library's collections. These were added to a North American NCIP database maintained by the Association of Research Libraries. The project's most widely-publicised goal was to provide scholars with the means to ascertain which institutions possessed the strongest (or, conversely the weakest) collections in specific subject areas on a scale of 1 to 5. The particular local benefit to participating libraries lay in giving their librarians an opportunity to become much better aware of the strengths and weaknesses in their own libraries' collections.

By the late 1980s the faculty had, for some time, been steadily surrendering to the librarians responsibility for the selection of books for purchase. Nonetheless, annual allocations of discretionary acquisitions funds to academic departments still totalled almost $500,000. Some of these funds were often unspent at year's end because of the inherent inefficiencies of having two sources of requests for purchase. The Library Representative in each department received recommendations for purchase from colleagues and forwarded these to the Library. Library staff would then verify that these titles had not already been ordered, either by the Library or by another teaching department. Upwards of half of the requests from departmental Library Representatives were rejected for duplicating outstanding orders, thus leaving significant amounts in the departmental allocations unspent. This structural redundancy was inefficient, wasteful of time and labour, and unacceptable at a time when the Library was being forced to cancel subscriptions and shed staff positions. As Coordinator of Library Collections, the author met with Deans and heads of departments to persuade them of the need to give up their traditional departmental allocations, and cede total control of the acquisitions budget to the discretion of librarians, who possessed both the necessary subject expertise and the time to do the job with wisdom, fairness, and equity. The science faculties proved the most amenable, and, indeed, several departments had already allowed their discretionary allocations to be rolled in. The Arts Faculty departments, particularly those in more monograph-dependent disciplines such as history, proved a harder sell. However, the creation of an annual $50,000 fund for "Special Projects," to which Arts Faculty departments could apply to secure specific large and expensive purchases, succeeded in winning their cooperation.

A number of significant collections were acquired during the 1980s, despite the climate of austerity. Perhaps the most outstanding was the Gregory Javitch Collection of more than 2300 volumes on the indigenous peoples of the New World. Imprints ranged in date from the 16th to the 20th centuries and included many rare titles. Offered to the Library on a partial donation basis, immediately prior to the donor's death in November 1980, it was appraised at $2 million, half of which was paid from matching grants, which equalled the portion that was purchased for cash. It was received in annual shipments over the course of several years. In 1983, special funding generously provided by the Clifford E. Lee Foundation of Edmonton and the Social Sciences and Humanities Research Council of Canada enabled the Library to acquire the Curwen Press' own file collection of nearly 1000 books, as well as 2500 pieces of ephemeral printing and more than 800 periodicals produced by the Press between 1916 and 1956. This rich resource for the study of twentieth-century letterpress printing and book design is currently being digitized to provide researchers with wider access. In 1985 the Library received the 2240 audio recordings of the Moses and Frances Asch Collection of Folkways Recordings, through the good offices of their son, University of Alberta anthropology professor Michael Asch. Grants from the Alberta Cultural Heritage Foundation and the University's Special Initiatives Fund covered much of the cost of cataloguing the collection, which represented nearly the entire Folkways catalogue of recordings dating back to its founding by Moses Asch in 1947. This donation led in 2003 to the establishment of folkwaysAlive!, a partnership between the University's Canadian Centre for Ethnomusicology and Smithsonian Folkways Recordings. The project to digitize the entire Folkways oeuvre, and mount it on the internet, has been supported by Western Economic Diversification Canada and other partners.[233]

When a nascent program in East Asian Languages and Literature was approved for departmental status in 1980, Bruce Peel had expressed his concern to the Vice-President (Academic) that the new department would require a regular allocation for acquisitions, and, moreover, that "acquisition of books in languages not using the Roman alphabet creates problems in ordering and more particularly in cataloguing. Not only are books in Chinese and Japanese more laborious to process, but require persons with qualifications in those particular languages." When Japanese history specialist Professor Hazel Jones sought to reassure Peel that $2000 to $3000 a year, supplemented by "soliciting outside funds" and further gifts-in-kind from the Japan Foundation, would satisfy the needs of the new program, he was rightly sceptical. Fortunately, an outstanding collection of 11,000 volumes of Chinese literature, history, and philosophy was obtained in 1985 with the purchase of the library of a retired Harvard professor of Chinese, James Hightower. This collection, purchased with gifts from several donors, among them the *Edmonton Journal*, and matching grants, includes editions dating from the seventeenth century onward of Chinese classics, and provides a significant resource for the University's program in East Asian Studies. The Government of Alberta viewed the development of this program as a key component in developing a "Pacific Rim" trade policy. The following year, thanks in part to the lobbying work of Chinese historian Brian Evans, in his capacity as Associate Vice-President (International Affairs), the provincial government provided a $100,000 grant to support the cataloguing of Chinese-language collections, including acquisition of the appropriate computer hardware and software. As Mr Peel had predicted, however, more specialized language skills were also required to process, let alone develop the East Asian collection; in 1987 Mr Louis Chor was appointed to the position of East Asian Studies Librarian.[234]

In cooperation with the University of Calgary Library and University Microfilms International, between 1985 and 1988 the University of Alberta Library received more than 3000 titles in micro-form and equipment from U M I with a total value of $1,046,000, thanks to the provincial government's fund for matching gifts-in-kind. As these few examples attest, during the 1980s Alberta's universities benefited greatly from the provincial government's fund that provided a two-for-one match for gifts in cash, and a dollar-for-dollar match for gifts-in-kind. Reflecting upon that matching program, Mr Freeman observed that, "Everybody played it; Calgary did it better than we did. The government spent the money so fast, nobody will ever do a gifts-in-kind matching again. Now they are very gun shy of it. The universities have more money that they want to match than the income of a matching fund could generate."[235]

Austerity Promotes Resource Sharing

Although the 1980s were years of lean budgets, and forced austerity, especially for library acquisitions, Mr Freeman believes that this was, in one sense, valuable.

> *The benefit of it — I guess everything has a silver lining — is that it did force librarians and institutions to think more about networking, collection sharing, library cooperation, whatever you want to call it. It forced people into getting over their natural-born instincts against that, of protecting your collection and not letting anybody else have anything to do with it. So it forced that, and now it is almost a given that people are going to cooperate in some fashion. That's no longer an issue for institutions or I don't think to the same degree. The faculty will always be upset if they can't get something, but there were benefits, especially with the electronic, that you could share and they don't even know the difference. Austerity forced people into finding ways to share and to make more efficient use of their resources.*

Mr Freeman's commitment to resource sharing led to a formal arrangement in which the University of Regina Library provided funding for a full-time, dedicated, University of Alberta staff member, whose sole task was to fulfill Regina's inter-library loan requests on an overnight basis. This much-copied pilot program drew questions about what possible benefit it had to offer the University of Alberta.

We had the good fortune when it was developed, in the collection-building years, to have the resources to do that. I always felt it was an obligation to not build barriers, and to make it available to people as best one could without getting stabbed in the back by the people who thought it was an odd thing to do. But I also believed, though I don't think I ever convinced the government, that we had an information resource that was quite significant. It could support the decentralization and the economic diversification the province wanted.

This conviction and commitment to improved resource sharing lay behind the "Proposal for Cooperative Library Network Development" submitted to the Government of Alberta by the four Alberta University libraries at the end of 1983. The proposal called for $3.3 million to be expended over two years on the development of computer communication links between the four university libraries, and the cooperative retro-conversion of their 1.2 million manual catalogue records into electronic form, hypothetically yielding savings of $900,000.[236]

In late October 1988, Mr Freeman announced his resignation to accept an appointment as Secretary of the Law Society of Alberta. His six-year tenure as Chief Librarian, beset though it was by budgetary constraints and disappointments over such things as the failure to obtain more library space, featured advances on several fronts, including new facilities, the management of collection development, and, perhaps most notably, bringing the advantages of computerization quite literally into the hands of staff, students, and faculty. Today, he admits,

I didn't think the library was financially supported to the level I thought it should be, but that's something I think everybody could say, certainly including every dean in the university. We always had good support from the central administration, within reason since they had 20 "sharks" biting at them. In an enterprise like this, personal relationships are very important. One has to keep on the good side of the faculty, especially if you want their support in terms of how the pie is being divided. I don't remember any bad or difficult times with the Library Committee; they were quite supportive and the chairmen particularly were very supportive.

Although faculty support was never more important than in those years of fiscal stringency, Mr Freeman's focus never wavered from empowering his own staff to provide better service to that too-often-neglected clientele, the students. "I thought that it was important to give them that good experience. And I always thought that when it comes to fundraising, if you want alumni who are appreciative of the university, you have to treat them a little better, because the first day they come here is when you begin making proud alumni." Mr Freeman remains proud of his efforts to change the Library's organizational culture, because

> individuality and initiative and thinking were not encouraged by the structure; people weren't prepared to take on challenges or to rock the boat. I would like to think that what we did shook out some of that, and showed people that there are other ways of doing things. We had good staff and we were able to push some in terms of their skills and abilities. And when I left, this was underway, and if some of the change in the culture and the management structure is still there, I would like at least to say that I started it.[237]

MR PETER FREEMAN'S DEPARTURE from the University at the end of 1988 coincided with the announcement of the appointment of Dr Paul Davenport of McGill University as the University's tenth president. Dr Davenport's arrival coincided with a decision by the government of Alberta to rein in spending and take much closer control of the administration of its universities, and thus began one of the most troubled periods in the history of government-university relations. Dr Davenport's selection as the first outsider to be named president since the appointment of Robert Wallace in 1928 was a reversal of a long tradition; in the minds of many this marked the new president as a man on probation. Dr Davenport suffered a very public loss of confidence among his faculty when he cancelled the Timms Collections Centre project, and diverted the Timms bequest to building a theatre and drama centre, a move which upset the long-established plans of a score of departments, as well as the Library, which had anticipated recovering the space occupied in Rutherford South by the University Archives. The further announcement of the creation of two new vice-presidential portfolios within the University Administration, at a time of looming cutbacks, proved the last straw, and created a loud uproar among both faculty and students across the campus.[238]

Mr Freeman's somewhat abrupt resignation to answer the call of his first profession left the Library's personnel officer, Mr John Teskey, in the role of Acting Chief Librarian until a successor could be recruited, a process that consumed more than a year. It proved to be a painfully memorable year as many budgetary pressures coalesced. In a lengthy series of memos to Vice-President Peter Meekison and his Associate Vice-Presidents Dianne Kieren and John Tartar, Mr Teskey

7

Ernie Ingles Charts New Courses for the Library, 1989–

gave eloquent voice to the Library's increasing financial dilemma. Following the cancellation of 1200 subscriptions in 1987 for a savings of $250,000, the Library had escaped further cancellations in 1988, but was now facing the need to recover a further $350,000, by making a 12 percent cut in subscriptions, and purchasing approximately 4700 fewer monographs in the coming year. Since duplicate subscriptions had long since been purged in earlier cancellations, this meant the obliteration of as many as 2600 unique journal subscriptions.

The Library depended upon the money from vacant positions in the staffing budget to provide the casual funding to pay the students who reshelved books and maintained long library opening hours. The Library was also expected to support a number of new programs, for which additional funding was not forthcoming, including a $266,000 annual shortfall in support for the East Asian Studies program, despite an annual conditional grant of $58,000 from the government of Alberta. Compounding these problems were the charges levied against the Library by Computing and Network Services (now known as Academic Information and Communication Technologies, or AICT) for computer time, which, in the Library's case, was classified as "administrative computing," and thus subject to billing, as opposed to "academic computing," which was provided free of direct charges. As Mr Teskey recalls, "The real down side of DOBIS was Computing Services' charging mechanism. The Library had no real budget for computing, [but thanks to the OPAC] all of a sudden we had bills for several hundred thousands a year." The annual computing cost of running the on-line catalogue had originally been estimated at $600,000; this sum had never been provided to the Library. Even after the charges were capped at $800,000, the Library confronted a $400,000 deficit in its computing account. He argued that "The Online Catalogue (OPAC) could rightly be compared to a general utility, one which serves the University as a whole and whose use is neither limited nor controlled by the Library. Accessibility to OPAC is essential to the access to information procured by the materials budget." Mr Teskey also raised the possibility of simply shutting it down as unaffordable.

Covering a $400,000 deficit from the staffing budget would require elimination of about 20 positions, which would in turn deplete the vacancy pool that supplied the funding for casual staff. So Mr Teskey proposed an alternative strategy of raising revenues through a combination of increasing fines, applying fines to staff, and charging for inter-library loans, on-line searches, and library cards. In a memo to the GFC Library Committee, he noted that an additional $637,000 would be required to maintain the same level of purchasing in the next year's acquisition budget, a sum that was highly unlikely to be forthcoming; he therefore gave notice of another impending round of cuts and cancellations. As he explained to Mr Peter Meekison, the GFCLC members' "reaction was one of dismay. However, the reaction could have been 'hotter'. Perhaps there is an 'incubation' period. I am sure that you will be contacted by several faculty members over the next few weeks." In a mid-August memo to Dr John Tartar, Mr Teskey announced that library hours would not be reduced for 1989–1990, because the estimated 10 percent, or $50,000 savings, "does not offset the loss of service to the University Community; especially the students." However, in a memo written to Dr Tartar two weeks earlier, he calculated that even by cutting almost $450,000 from the staff vacancy pool and adding $150,000 in revenue sharing from Printing Services' profits from public photocopiers in library locations, the Library would still come up $207,000 short of covering its anticipated deficit. "The question," according to Mr Teskey, "is do I start issuing lay-off notices, or is there any flexibility?"[239]

The Library Committee had been pressuring for some time, without success, for the University Administration to emulate their counterparts at the Universities of Saskatchewan and Toronto, to not merely protect the Library's acquisitions budget from cuts, but also to index it for inflation to halt the steady erosion of purchasing power. It was estimated that in the years elapsed since 1983–1984, at least $1 million had been lost through price inflation, and the share of the acquisitions budget committed to renewing subscriptions had grown from 50 percent to an excessive 75 percent, despite the cancellation of many titles. In the GFC Library Committee's annual report for 1988–1989, outgoing chairman Fred Van De Pitte noted that,

> Throughout the year, a series of questions continued to arise concerning the structure and operation of the Library Committee, as well as the function which the Committee is to serve in a period when it is no longer possible to exercise control over Library finances in the way it had formerly done. The budget of the Library tends to be a hypothetical figure during virtually the entire year. Thus, neither controlling, nor even advising the Library in financial matters is possible in any realistic sense. The Committee is placed rather

in the position of offering its blessing, or moral support from time to time. In addition, there are no longer any discretionary funds to be allotted to individual departments. There are no special project funds to be distributed to energetic departmental representatives striving to build up the strength, or correct the weaknesses of their area[s] of the collection. Thus the Committee has very few substantive decisions to make.

Perhaps this accounts for why the attendance of committee members was so poor during the year. Academic staff and ex officio members averaged five out of the eight meetings for the year. Two out of the last three meetings failed to produce a quorum (50%). A discussion of this issue has been slated for early in the fall.[240]

Although circumstances had certainly reduced the role played by the Library Committee, the incoming chairman, English professor Robert Merrett, was determined not to play a passive role in the face of the growing financial crisis confronting the Library. In November, he proposed a series of 14 questions to be asked of Deans and Directors, "To determine what sort of priority is given to expectations of the Library in the matter of hiring staff, planning research strategies, and devising and amending courses." In a lengthy and detailed letter to President Davenport, Dr Merrett raised questions about the relationship between faculty and librarians, and noted that,

If the Library is to be encouraged to speak more rigorously about the present and future needs of the Collection, it should also be asked to contribute to academic and administrative planning. Inevitably, shortcomings in the library system reflect the quality of the attention paid by faculty and central administration to the Library. Uncertain academic and administrative guidance has prevented the Library from taking important initiatives.

In closing, he raised once again the issue of indexing the acquisitions budget, as well as the discrepancy between the GFC Policy Manual's claim that the Library should account for 8 percent of the University's total budget, and the real figure, which was only 6.5 percent.[241]

Dr Merrett, accompanied by Mr Teskey, met with President Davenport and Vice-President Meekison on 30 November, and then with the Academic Development Committee on 10 January, to discuss the problems confronting the Library. At the latter meeting, Dr Merrett was requested to draw up a list of proposals "that would address the need for the Library, as for other units on campus, to be more efficient in the face of declining resources." Basing his proposals on the Vice-President's assurance that "no fixed, 'hard-dollar' funding increases are to be given to the Library's materials or operating budgets...a concession GFCLC refuses to make and for which I have been criticized," nonetheless, "the proposals oblige me to make an official request for extra and immediate 'soft-dollar' funding since substantial, long-term economies in the Library system are to be realized only if certain short-term investments are made now." Those short-term investments included centralization of Rutherford Libraries' service points in the Galleria, completion of the retro-conversion of all catalogue records, purchase of an integrated, automated, on-line library system to replace DOBIS — measures designed to save time, labour, and free several staff positions — and the expenditure of resources to improve the University's computing infrastructure as well as the Library's inter-library loans operation.

> To GFCLC's current proposals: with great reluctance, the committee accepts the view that budgetary restraints entail a reduction of hours the Library is open and hours circulation service is offered....
>
> GFCLC wishes to propose to GFC one measure that will enable the Library to make efficiencies of several sorts, namely the closing of branch libraries. By closing the three branch libraries, the Library could save $60,000.00 a year from the salaries of two library assistants. The other two assistants could be redeployed to central duties. This closure of branch libraries, besides shutting down three service points, would make a large number of volumes generally accessible. GFCLC accepts the principle that standard hours of opening and service throughout the system increase the efficient use of materials. The costs associated with this efficiency comprise funds for removal and storage, the need to create space within Cameron Library, and inconvenience to formerly privileged users.

The proposals also endorsed revenue enhancement by raising fines, applying them to all categories of borrower, and charging for such services as inter-library loans. The economies to be realized by closing the three branch libraries in question, namely Computing Science, Mathematics, and Physical Sciences, were first raised by Mr Teskey in a letter to the President in December. However, later events proved that those "privileged users" would put up a bitter fight to preserve the status quo. In acknowledging Dr Merrett's proposal-laden letter, the Vice-President noted that with a new Chief Librarian appointed and the Library PACCR, there was an ideal opportunity to make the necessary changes. The new Chief Librarian had, indeed, been appointed in December, but before he could move to Edmonton to take up his new duties on a full-time basis in May, the frustrations on the campus of both faculty and students had reached a boiling point.[242]

Protest Rising: The "Save the Library Committee"

At the beginning of February 1990, Political Science professor Max Mote circulated a petition and covering memo announcing that,

> A group of faculty members and librarians has met to discuss what we believe is a crisis situation in the University Library. The result of our deliberations is the enclosed petition. We plan to present this petition to Dr. Davenport at a Save the Library rally on the steps of University Hall at 12:00 noon on 28 February 1990. Please circulate this petition in your Department among faculty, staff and students and inform them of the rally.

Four days later, the "Committee to Save the Library" issued its first press release, in which it decried the cuts to the Library budget, warned that "The University of Alberta is in danger of losing the research quality of its library because the provincial government won't increase funding to the university," and labelled it "'dishonest' for the University to maintain 'a pretence of excellence' without proper budgets for the library."[243] A front-page article in the University staff bulletin, *Folio*, reported that 300 signatures had been collected, while the Committee's second press release, issued that day, boasted of more than 500 signatures. Several librarians who were active members of the Committee gathered signatures from among Library staff members.

A large crowd gathered for the rally on the south steps of the Administration Building (not, as first advertised, at University Hall), where prominent faculty members addressed them. "I don't think that under the circumstances hard work is really enough," declared E.D. (Ted) Blodgett.

> We can work, and work, and work, but if the cuts continue, all our work will be in vain.
>
> I liken the library to the heart and soul of this University. If you cut one valve, if you cut another valve, if you take away chamber after chamber, you

might as well put it on a life support system and let it go, because that is what is happening.

Prof. Juliet McMaster of the English Department began by quoting from Milton's *Areopagitica*:

> *"A good book is the precious life-blood of a master spirit." I'm talking about the books as our blood, and the fact that we are bleeding.*
>
> *President Davenport, I know you don't want to let our fine library deteriorate....But we hope you will make the Library a high priority in your budgeting for this University, and we want to work with you on this, not against you. The Save the Library Committee will not fade away after this rally.*

Mr Teskey added that, "We have to put more resources into preservation of our existing collection. A great portion of it is turning to dust." And finally, taking aim at the provincial government, the President declared to the crowd,

> *We're going to need to get back to grants that are in the rate of inflation and then some.*
>
> *I believe that over the past several years the library has been a priority.... The message today was that...we should be doing more, and that's certainly a message I'll take back to the Vice-Presidents. This rally will certainly have an effect on me.*

True to Prof. McMaster's word, the Save the Library Committee did not fade away after the rally, but remained both active and highly critical for more than another year. The public pressure the Committee brought to bear on the University Administration may not have been the sole reason for the additional $500,000 allocation to the Library for the following year, but it certainly played a role.[244] It was into this highly fraught atmosphere that the new Chief Librarian arrived in May to find his work cut out for him.

The Man from Regina

Ernest ("Ernie") Boyce Ingles was born in Calgary in 1948, and educated at the Universities of Calgary and British Columbia. Before joining the University of Alberta as Chief Librarian and Director of

Ernie Ingles,
Vice-Provost &
Chief Librarian.
Courtesy of
Ernie Ingles.

Libraries in 1990, he headed the University of Calgary's Department of Rare Books and Special Collections (1974–1978), was founding Executive Director of the Canadian Institute for Historical Micro-reproductions in Ottawa (1978–1984), and University Librarian of the University of Regina (1984–1990). It was just as well that he arrived with a full measure of self-confidence; as he recently revealed,

> *the challenges at Regina were what set me up for success in Alberta, because I learned there how you dealt with restraint, budget cutbacks, and unions. Regina was a wonderful training ground. I threw myself into it, and I think I left a pretty fair legacy; I got them on the map from a collections perspective. It was the beginning of my understanding of the power of cooperation. I developed my first consortium at Regina.*[245]

Mr Freeman had managed, for various reasons, to postpone the Library's self-study for the President's Advisory Committee on Campus Reviews (PACCR) for so long that the task fell to his successor. Because the President's discretionary fund, that had provided additional staff positions to a number of departments that were quick off the mark to complete their PACCR reports, had been well nigh depleted, many might have lacked enthusiasm for undertaking one at such a late date. Mr Ingles, on the other hand, perceived an opportunity to develop a proper strategic plan under the guise of the PACCR review process, and thus lay before the University Administration and wider University community a blueprint for significant change.

Addressing the President and Vice-Presidents less than a month after his arrival, Ingles promised that

> The Library will use the PACCR process as an opportunity to prepare not only a "self-study," but also a "Strategic Plan"; intended to identify the immediate and long-range challenges for itself, and by implication for the University community and for the University administration. The identification and integration of challenges is particularly necessary in a unit such as the Library given that it underpins the totality of the University's functions. Moreover, these three groups share a common and fundamentally important goal: that is, the development of an effective information service infrastructure designed to meet the information needs of instruction, learning and research as this institution strives for excellence through this century and into the next.[246]

B.J. Busch and Douglas Poff were pressed into full-time service as editors, as numerous other colleagues were called upon to provide background research and gather data. Together, under Ingles' direction, by October they produced a densely comprehensive 140-page draft document, with an additional 48 pages of statistical tables and graphs. The plan called for an enlargement and stabilization of the Library's funding base; adoption of a new service model that relied increasingly upon access through cooperation with other institutions and electronic resources, and decreasingly upon ownership of resources; replacement of existing automated systems; greater focus upon the physical preservation of collections; more efficient use of existing physical space on the campus; and, finally, provision of off-site storage with document delivery in lieu of the long-promised Rutherford expansion.

Read today, the plan appears unexceptional, even prescient, as a preview of the direction taken by leading academic libraries over succeeding years. However, like many an idea to appear slightly before its time, it met with a sceptical, even hostile, response among many academics, particularly those in the Faculty of Arts. It was also ill-served by its title *Riding the Wave*, which was seized upon by critics as somewhat puerile, or at least lacking in the gravity demanded by a crisis. Its actual intent and thrust was perhaps best expressed by the University of Michigan's Library Director Richard Dougherty:

> *If we can assume that access to online bibliographic, numeric, and full-text databases will soon be available in many college dormitories and faculty offices...then don't we have to assume that the role of the academic library has to change?...One might try to hide from this reality or make defensive moves designed to counteract it. But it won't go away....In the past we have made organizational alterations at the margins — restructuring, reforming, and retraining. But my feeling is that a wave of change is about to reach us that will require more fundamental transformations. We can ride the crest of the wave or be engulfed by it, but we can no longer stand at the water's edge and ignore it.*

Riding the Wave was supplemented by an implementation plan, an ambitious schedule of activities, and a list of 14 strategic priorities to address the Library's needs for indexed funding, upgraded automated systems, retro-conversion of the remaining manual catalogue records, auxiliary storage space, enhanced document delivery, collection preservation, and the building of alliances to access other resources.[247]

In November and December 1990, following the widespread distribution of *Riding the Wave*, the Save the Library Committee distributed a questionnaire to faculty members to measure perceptions of the Library's subject strengths, recent deterioration, and adequacy for graduate-level research, as well as their reactions to the strategic plan. When the 219 responses were tallied in January 1991, 80 percent of respondents not surprisingly expressed the belief that the Library's collections had deteriorated in coverage. Question number 5 was about *Riding the Wave*; 64 of them responded to it. Of these responses, 18 were "generally positive," 28 were "generally negative," and a further 18 were either neutral or mixed. The tenor of responses ranged from the thoughtful and measured to the mildly hysterical; from "exceptionally well-prepared and pleasing document" to "poorly written document unworthy of high scholarship" to "who wrote this comic strip?" A number of the hostile responses focused exclusively upon the perceived threat to the Mathematics Library posed by the plan's goal of consolidating branch libraries. Even the respondents who were "pleased to see the future described in the document," and found it "very forward looking," expressed scepticism about the degree to which it could ever be implemented, particularly in the fiscal climate. That prevalent campus pessimism was reflected in the year-end message of the Faculty Association's President:

> We are under siege at all levels currently....The provincial authorities are giving every indication that they will be even more tightfisted than last year with the grants for postsecondary education. It is clear that they are unwilling to fund a first class research university. A balanced budget is much more important to them than anything that we might contribute to the education and wellbeing of the people of this province, and even more important than anything that we might contribute to the economy. Apparently we are expendable.[248]

In an attempt to allay some of the anxiety generated by *Riding the Wave*, Mr Ingles and Vice-President Lois Stanford met with the Save the Library Committee on 23 January 1991. Prof. Juliet McMaster, the Committee's Chair, wrote afterward:

> Thank you for coming to our meeting on Wednesday. I found it a very useful exchange of views. Of course our interests coincide with yours of having and maintaining an excellent library....many people are supportive of the main direction of the strategic plan, but even more share our committee's grave concern that the technology will be at the expense of the collection, and that we may end up getting more and more access to less and less material. I hope you will take these reservations seriously. The report tends to construct those who are not in favour of the promised technology as Luddite fuddy-duddies. But in the humanities especially...we have reason to believe that books are beginning to be regarded as the acquisition of the past.[249]

In mid-February members of the Committee were granted an interview with Advanced Education Minister John Gogo, where they pleaded the Library's financial case with statistical documents supplied by the Chief Librarian. The Minister afterwards expressed his thanks "for our recent opportunity to meet and for the frank discussion on funding for the University of Alberta Library." While the Committee representatives did not rehearse their reservations about *Riding the Wave* with the Minister, they had listed them in a seven-page document circulated in January. Those concerns centred around fears that book purchasing would be sacrificed to the purchase of new technologies of unproven and unreliable efficacy, to the particular detriment of the humanities; that auxiliary storage and the consolidation of branch libraries would undermine research in all disciplines; and that the leadership of the Library was out of touch with its primary clientele, and thus only serving the interests of administrative expediency. When the PACCR review committee gave its blessing to the Library's plan, the Save the Library Committee responded by issuing "A Charter for the Future," accompanied by a second petition form requesting signatures, in which it called for the University to seek "adequate on-campus library space"; not to sacrifice collections or staffing to computer automation; to restore the acquisitions budget; to investigate the feasibility of centralizing libraries; and to establish closer contact between the Library and its research and student clientele. A further meeting in Dr Stanford's office brought the two sides no closer together.[250]

The Save the Library campaign was by then generating wider attention and comment in publications such as *Quill & Quire*. Early in April, Mr Ingles wrote to the editor of *The Gateway* in response to an article on 4 April, to deny that the Library's priorities were responsible for "a slide in emphasis away from the Humanities and Social Sciences to the Natural Sciences," which was merely a function of differential increases in publishers' pricing, and that there was ever any intention to "consider suspending book purchasing in order to finance automation. Never has such a possibility been considered. This canard should be put to rest." He admitted that "the Library realizes that auxiliary stacks are not ideal, but we are in a crisis situation with regard to space. Additions to campus libraries have been the University's number one building priority since the early 1980s but no government funding has been forthcoming." And finally he noted that the Library's holdings of books and journals had caused its ranking among North American research libraries to rise significantly. In a letter to Deans and department heads, Vice-President Lois Stanford, writing on behalf of the GFC Library Committee in response to the Save the Library Committee's "Charter for the Future," stressed these same points. Rejecting the charge that the Administration had abandoned hope for the long-promised library building expansion, she emphasized that,

> even if it were to be funded next year, it would not be operational for several years. The problem with library space is now — this spring: the Library is acquiring approximately 99,000 volumes per annum, and they have no

where to put them. The proposal for auxiliary off-campus stacks is the means at hand now to ameliorate the problem. The Library's plans for making available to the academic community the materials housed in auxiliary stacks (e.g., transportation of people and materials, fax, study/work areas on site) make the facility considerably more than "storage." It is to be an interactive facility.[251]

In May 1991 Prof. McMaster stepped down as chair of the Save the Library Committee, and was succeeded by her colleague, Prof. Gary Kelly, who showed every willingness to continue the struggle into the following year. Before departing for England on leave, Prof. McMaster wrote to Mr Ingles:

I want to let you know that I regret the differences that have arisen between us. Obviously, you of the Library and we of the Save the Library Committee share a deep concern for the well-being of the Library, and we have all been doing our best for it according to our lights. I do believe that the publicity that our committee has given to the Library as an issue has been good for it, and that the publicity will help in raising funds, whether from Central Administration, the government, or private donation. (I have recently written a plea for donations for Library Editions; and the committee has some ideas about fund-raising which we will be checking through with the Fund Development office in due course.)

I don't buy the argument that if Central Administration is getting a "mixed message" (the Library calling for East Point off campus, and our Committee continuing to call for a real library on campus), they will see it as a good excuse to give the library nothing at all. I think much better of Central Administration than to believe that they would consider any such dodge. The message they are getting both loud and clear from both you and us is that the Library is in severe trouble, and desperately needs help. And we all agree that it needs help now, before we are absolutely out of space, and not ten years down the road. If [storage at] East Point is the only viable means of enabling us to keep the collection growing, then of course we want East Point, and soon. But our committee views this as only a stop-gap; we want people to remember that a real new library on campus is still a necessity.

I am proud of the initiatives taken by members of the Save the Library Committee (and they have received congratulations from many corners of the university). These are dedicated people. Without official standing, or secretarial support, or financial resources, they have nevertheless managed *to make a difference; and I think you'll find that (even besides the $500,000 for the Library last spring), it's a difference for the better. The university community, and the larger community beyond, have paid attention. And I believe the Library will benefit from that attention. I hope you'll regard us as the Library's friends.*[252]

While they might have differed over questions of strategy, there was complete accord among all parties regarding the ultimate goal of an expanded library building devoted to the humanities and social sciences. Meanwhile, the Arts Faculty Library Committee (AFLC) recognized the urgent need for compromise. Writing to the heads of departments, Classics professor Alastair Small reported that,

The Arts Faculty Library Committee has considered the Strategic Plan very carefully in light of the options actually available to the University, and has, on balance, supported the policies advocated in Riding the Wave. *At its meeting last month it passed, with one dissentient vote, a motion supporting the policy of developing remote stacks at East Point. It did so since this appeared to be the best available solution to a problem of shelving which has become urgent, and since the aim of the Library continues to be to construct a new building on campus as soon as the Provincial Government can be persuaded to finance one.*

Prof. Small went on to advise members of the Faculty of Arts to refrain from signing the second petition of the Save the Library Committee (SLC) until they had become more fully acquainted with the issues. He nonetheless ended by paying tribute to the good work of the Committee: "Although the AFLC differs from the Save the Library Committee on some matters, it recognizes that the SLC is having a very valuable impact on the University's policies for the Library."[253]

Students Protest Proposed Cuts to Hours

While faculty concerns and active protests focused upon maintaining the quality of the Library's collections and pressing for further library construction, students were primarily concerned with the libraries as study space and their hours of access. This concern had even prompted the Student Union to provide the Library with the additional funding required to extend late-night hours of opening during exam periods. While the students and their leaders had quietly supported the efforts of the Save the Library Committee, the implementation of reduced library hours for the fall term, 1990, elicited their outspoken anger and outrage. "Overall," *The Gateway* reported,

> the Health Sciences, Cameron and Rutherford Libraries will be open for 21 fewer hours every week compared to last year. Other libraries were not as hard hit by the cuts as Rutherford and Cameron, but all have been forced to close their doors at least a little bit earlier. The Law Library, for example, will be open for thirteen fewer hours per week than last year, and the Education Library will lose three hours.

The Chief Librarian explained that "The money just isn't there." "In the past," the report continued,

> the money used to pay for extended hours came from three prime sources: photocopying revenue, fines revenue, and from the money saved when staff members resigned and were not immediately replaced.
>
> Ingles explained Monday afternoon that these sources of revenue have dried up or disappeared altogether over the years. Revenue from photocopying is no longer directed to the libraries and "the revenue projections that were made on the basis of increased fines never materialized," said Ingles. He said he realizes that some students may be adversely affected by the reduced hours but argued that priority has to be given to the acquisition of books and periodicals. "We feel a library has certain primary functions and development of the collection is certainly one of these."[254]

As student anger over the cuts to weekend hours grew, the Student Union Council entered the controversy to denounce the decision and lack of consultation with students: "The only opportunity for student input came in June," *The Gateway* reported, "when the library administration sent a letter to the su and the G[raduate] S[tudent] A[ssociation] asking for their opinions on 'improvements to the library.' The letter did not mention the planned reduction to the library's operating hours." The su Executive responded by announcing a protest "study-in" to be held in the Rutherford Library from 10 P.M. till midnight on 18 September. After a "heated debate" the Graduate Student Association voted 24 to 10 to support the Student Union's protest "after it was made clear that the su was not asking the University to sacrifice the quality of its book collection." Paul Skelhorne, *Gateway's* editor-in-chief, asked rhetorically,

So who is to blame for this mess?...Who else? The provincial government, even though it sounds like an old and tired melody. They consistently refuse to acknowledge the importance of education to the province. Oh, they acknowledge it vocally, without a doubt. The rhetoric spewed in the legislature about the importance of higher education could rot the ears off a titanium-alloy monolith. When it comes to the pocket-book, however, they remain remarkably close-mouthed.

So it is that we end up in the predicament we now face, with a book collection to be proud of, but an administration that feels the need to cut back our access to it. The University might as well burn down the library, for all the support they seem to be giving it.

The following month the medical students gathered more than 300 signatures on a petition to restore the hours in the Scott Health Sciences Library. The letters to the editor columns of *The Gateway* were filled with students' protests over the cuts to hours, including one writer who compared it to Saddam Hussein's recent invasion of Kuwait. At length, the University Administration proposed a compromise, and offered to fund extended hours during mid-term exams, a two-week period, at a cost of $4620, a sum su President Suresh Mustapha deemed too small an economy to have justified the cuts in the first place. Having won this limited victory in challenging the University Administration, Mustapha did not rule out future protest actions, and declared it an object lesson that "Students are going to have to realize that we have to protest in order to be taken seriously."[255]

Pursuing its campaign for the full restoration of Library hours, the Student Union undertook a user survey which revealed that half of the 496 students who responded indicated a desire "to continue studying beyond the library's ten o'clock closing time." The Library and University Administration had taken the position that there was insufficient demand for late night hours as attested by reader head-counts. But while the libraries may not have been crowded with late-night patrons, there was no question that they were crowded during the day time. As more and more book shelving was erected to accommodate the ever growing collection, study spaces continued to be lost. Consequently over-crowding in the Libraries was a concern not merely to students and Library staff, but also to the University's Fire Marshal, whose job it was to

monitor and maintain evacuation routes. The immediate answer
to that problem lay in the option so dreaded by the Save the Library
Committee, among others, the creation of off-site, auxiliary storage.

Conjoined Solutions: BARD and DRA

Despite the reduction in the rate of the Library's accessions, the
space problem could no longer be deferred; the Save the Library
Committee's campaign had ensured that the Library's dilemma
was very widely known. Mr Jamie Fleming of the University's
Investment and Property Management Office had identified a
building for potential redevelopment as a storage facility. The site
of the former IKEA store was located on 50th Street in Edmonton.
The former shopping centre, hard hit by the recession and IKEA's
move to the West Edmonton Mall, was being promoted as the
"Eastpoint Technology Park" by its new owner, the Hong Kong Bank
of Canada Ltd, which viewed the University Library as a preferred
potential tenant. The 46,460-square-foot facility was vacant, suitable for remodelling, and offered at a favourable rent. Once
renovated, the more than 300,000 volumes then stored in the basement of Cameron Library would find an immediate home, to be
followed by annual deposits of at least 50,000 volumes thereafter.

Following the GFC Library Committee's endorsement in principle of an off-site facility in March 1991, the Library appointed an
"advisory task force" to study all options; its members reported in
favour of a high-density, climate-controlled storage facility, to be
modelled to some extent upon the depository run by the Harvard
University Archives in Massachusetts, which this author visited that
fall, and described in a detailed report. Successful operation of such a
facility, in which books were sorted by size, and tracked and retrieved
by bar-code, required a system of inventory control that could not
be managed by the Library's 25-year-old, home-grown circulation
system. A replacement was in order, and that could best be supplied
by replacing the DOBIS system — which Mr Ingles characterized
to *The Gateway* as "old, it's cranky, and it's inefficient...not where we
should be in terms of technology" — with a new automated library
system, with fully integrated on-line catalogue, circulation, acquisitions, and serials management modules. This would also serve to
liberate the Library's cataloguing operation from dependence "upon
a commercial database utility [Utlas] whose precarious financial situation places its continued existence in question!" The cost of both

the new computer system and of creating the new storage facility was estimated at a total of $4.6 million; the two were presented as an interdependent package. In February the Library had suggested that the purchase of a new automated system could be funded by shutting down the OPAC, and recouping the $800,000 in annual computer service fees that it required. "This institution managed to do research and students managed to get degrees using the COM [fiche] catalogue up until a very few years ago," Mr Ingles told *The Gateway*. Less than two weeks later, *The Gateway* afforded the Chief Librarian another opportunity to publicize the need to replace DOBIS, and in the process repatriate its electronic catalogue records from Utlas to a University of Alberta-based system, when it reported that the University Administration had vetoed any notion of closing down the OPAC.[256]

At its meeting on 22 October 1991, the Board Building Committee recommended leasing the Eastpoint Centre; on 1 November the Board of Governors, upon recommendation of its Finance Committee, approved leasing the property "on the understanding that the rental and facility operating costs would be funded by Alberta Advanced Education and that the program operating costs would be provided from within the Library's existing operating budget." In other words, no funding would be provided for additional staff. Having accepted this necessary compromise to achieve a solution to the space crisis, events proceeded on the assumption that all hurdles had been cleared. A tender was issued for the new integrated, automated system, and the contract was won by Data Research Associates (DRA) of St Louis, Missouri. The new DRA system, with its integrated modules, represented a major advance over its predecessor in several respects. As James Heilik explained,

> The first on-line catalogue system, IBM's DOBIS/LIBIS, was based on mainframe technology in which a central computer controls everything. Its replacement, DRA, was based on a technology where work is shared between the machines which manage the library records and the devices the users use. This brought us to personal computers and networks. By the time the DRA project was done, the Library had one of the largest local area networks on campus with some 500 computers scattered over ten buildings. The project coincided with the establishment of the NEOS consortium of libraries who cooperated as our partners in acquiring and sharing in the new system. Part of my role was to ensure the new systems would work for the nascent consortium.[257]

The installation and configuration of the new automated system, and the downloading of the Library's electronic catalogue records, was a major operation that consumed months before the system was ready for its public debut in September 1993.

Concurrently, the final retro-conversion of the remaining manual catalogue records was undertaken with major funding for temporary staffing provided by a grant from Immigration and Employment Canada. Retro-conversion had been progressing slowly since the mid-1970s, when, in 1989, an exceptionally favourable contract was negotiated with the Utlas cataloguing utility to convert the manual records to digital, electronic form at a cost of 35 cents per title, a rate that prompted Utlas Account Manager Karen Taylor to exclaim to John Teskey, "You have managed to squeeze blood from a stone!" This would finally provide access through the OPAC to *all* of the Library's holdings, including those of the Bibliothèque Saint-Jean. The cost of the project was reduced still further by deploying the work force in shifts, thus cutting equipment rental costs by speeding up the processing. Ms Kathy Carter, who served as the Recon Project Coordinator, remembers "the intensity of the final years of our recon project. I supervised the 10 temporary and 2 permanent staff who reconned the last half-million monographs in 1991–92. We had 3 shifts going from 8:00 AM to 11:00 PM, including weekends. Some of those temporary staff were great workers. One day, one of them worked her shift until 11:00 PM, then went straight to the hospital to deliver a baby later that same night!"[258]

Inspired, perhaps, by such examples of dedication, and lulled by assurances of capital funding from Alberta Advanced Education, all was proceeding smoothly, when the province's 1992–1993 budget was delivered from the printers. Repeated searches through its pages revealed no trace of the promised $5 million in additional capital funding. It was no mistake. Eleventh-hour trimming of minor targets by Alberta Treasury officials had deleted the promised funds. An official letter from the Minister to Board of Governors' chair Stanley Milner later confirmed the denial of funding, but held out some faint hope for its restoration in the 1993–1994 budget process. Events at this stage, however, were so far advanced, that when the provincial government proved unwilling to provide the necessary support, the University Administration acknowledged and addressed the pressing need by dipping into its capital reserve funds:

Nevertheless, the Library System has no acceptable alternative but to proceed with the Eastpoint project. This is the only alternative within financial reach which will enable the Library to maintain its role as a research library....A side benefit, but an important feature of this initiative, with the accompanied reorganization of Library space on campus made possible by moving millions of volumes to Eastpoint, is that about 1500 additional study spaces will be provided within the Library buildings on campus.

Moreover, it was still hoped that the government would provide the building's operating costs.[259]

On 27 July 1992, architect Kees Prins of the firm of Maltby & Prins was officially named prime design consultant for what was still known as the "Eastpoint Project," and serious planning for the facility began. While most people were relieved to see the project underway, and to anticipate an imminent solution to the storage problem, not everyone was pleased. Dr Alastair Small, who had counselled the Arts Faculty Library Committee to endorse the project, confessed to this author his unhappiness with the loss of browsability caused by sorting books by size, and not keeping them in shelf-list order for retrieval. Not that books stored in drawer-like, box-board trays on shelves as much as 20 feet off the ground would have proven amenable to browsers in any event. When confronted with a series of floor plans and shelving arrangements that ranged in capacity from a scant half-million to almost 4 million volumes, and in recognition of the more than 300,000 volumes already in dense storage in Cameron Library's basement, Dr Small surrendered to pragmatism, and admitted that his concern was not for volumes of Greek and Roman history, which could easily be found with the aid of the OPAC. Rather, it was for easy access to catalogues of classical art and archaeological field studies that he relied upon to identify artefacts recovered on his summer field excavations in Italy. The issue of browsability and serendipitous discovery by researchers is, indeed, the single greatest drawback to high density storage of this kind. But it was to some degree ameliorated by soliciting recommendations from each faculty and department regarding the material in their respective disciplines that required consultation in a traditional, browsable setting, regardless of their infrequent use. However, not everyone was so easily persuaded.

When *The Gateway* announced the project in its first issue of the new fall term, the story appeared under a leader that read "Prof Upset

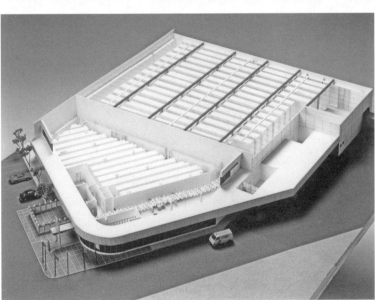

Above: President Paul Davenport (left) and Minister Jack Ady officially opening the BARD, *February 1994. Courtesy of UofA Creative Services.*

Left: Model of the Book & Record Depository (BARD). *Courtesy of Maltby and Prins Architects.*

Over Plan to Store Books," followed in smaller type by "But 500 to 700 New Study Spaces Will be Created on Campus." After a joke about how "IKEA is Swedish for library storage space," reporter Christopher Spencer quoted Mr Ingles' explanation that "the library ran out of space. We have had to cannibalise as much of our study space as we can for storage stacks." The rest of the article was devoted to the vehement objections of Dr Gary Kelly, who still headed the remnant of the Save the Library Committee, and who remained irreconcilable.

> This is the worst act of vandalism against the University ever....
> It is pretty clear that the students and staff do not want this, and they, not the government or the university administration, should be Mr. Ingles primary concern....

It is clear that the University is denigrating its library, which has made it one of the top three universities in Canada.

The University does not want to protest too much against chronic government underfunding, and thus there have to be cutbacks. The Library is one of those places where cutbacks are taking place.

Though his language may have been intemperate, his sentiments were shared by many who viewed the new Book and Record Depository, or BARD as it was soon to be known, as a cheap consolation prize for an unfulfilled promise of a building on campus.[260]

The Library's advisory task force on auxiliary storage worked with the Development Office to produce a Detailed Space Program for the new facility, and delivered its own final report later that fall. Tenders were issued for the building renovations, shelving, and retrieval systems, and for custom-designed book storage trays and archival boxes made of acid-free, double-faced, corrugated Kraft board. Major construction of BARD began in July 1993, and continued through the fall and early winter, including installation of 127,208 linear feet (24 miles or 38.8 kms) of book shelving, 27,170 linear feet (5 miles or 8.2 kms) of archives shelving, an electronically guided stock-picker retrieval system, and state-of-the-art climate control and security systems. The project was completed on schedule, and $200,000 under its $2.9 million budget. The task of moving to BARD tens of thousands of seldom-used volumes from Cameron Library, and moving the University Archives and its thousands of boxes of records from old Rutherford Library, was accomplished during the first half of February 1994. At last, on 15 February, the new facility was officially opened by President Paul Davenport and Advanced Education Minister, the Hon Mr Jack Ady. The event was celebrated with a day-long open house, during which transportation was provided to give all interested Library staff members their first glimpse, as well as tours, of BARD. The new facility supplied books to campus on a daily and overnight basis, became a major delivery and transit hub for resource sharing through inter-library loan, and provided the Library with the capacity needed to accommodate its ever-growing collections. Removal of less frequently consulted titles from campus libraries soon led to the recovery of more than 1000 study spaces. The BARD project was honoured with two awards: the 1993 Quality and Productivity Award of the Canadian Association of University Business Officers — the first of several CAUBO awards received by the Library — and the 1994 Innovative Achievement Award of the Canadian Library Association and Canadian Association of College and University Libraries. By 2005, however, it was clear that BARD was within a few years of reaching its full capacity, and planning for a new, purpose-built successor was begun with architectural consultants. Final approval and funding of plans for a new BARD are currently pending.[261]

Struggling to Do More With Less

The fiscal stringency that Mr Ingles confronted when he arrived in May 1990 only worsened as the decade wore on. In 1991, a further round of serials cancellations, the third such exercise since 1987, resulted in the loss of another 2085 subscriptions, for a total saving of $518,000. Negotiation with the Alberta Heritage Foundation for Medical Research of a final, three-year phase-out of support for library resources in the health sciences promised to bring additional pressure to bear on the acquisitions budget by 1995. The compilation and distribution of a cumulative listing of the 8360 subscriptions cancelled between 1987 and 1991, in the form of a printed document more than 4 centimetres thick, made abundantly clear the degree of loss the Library and its clientele had suffered.[262]

The year 1992 proved to be pivotal. On the positive side of the ledger, it marked the long-anticipated completion of the digital retro-conversion of all of the Library's catalogue records, the approvals needed to proceed with the BARD and DRA system projects, and a new ruling by the Academic Development Committee that it would not entertain future proposals for new or enlarged programs without an accompanying formal Impact Statement in which the Library detailed potential cost increases for staffing and collections. While these statements would not always result in budget augmentations, they at least allowed the Library to document the full costs of new programs. On the other side of the page, the Library, as well as the University, ended the 1990–1991 year in a deficit position, despite having implemented many economies. Following the release of the provincial government's budget figures for 1991–1992, the University was forced to impose yet another "stringency tax" and consider seriously restructuring the institution and its programs in order to live within its reduced income. In a 10-page letter addressed to all Library staff in March 1991, Mr Ingles announced that the Library would be required to cut its budget for 1991–1992 by $344,000, a figure that would grow to nearly $1 million, when added to commitments for casual staffing and the administrative computing fees charged for operating the on-line catalogue. He outlined the principles that would guide the budgeting process, namely avoidance of layoffs, if possible; reviewing and refocusing of both staff and services; and support for restructuring initiatives. The strategies adopted included reorganization or restructuring of Library units, surrender of vacant positions, and creation of a central vacancy pool to reallocate staff positions where most needed. To that end, he announced the Bibliographic Verification Unit would be closed by month's end, its four staff members to be reassigned elsewhere, and three vacant librarians' positions would not be filled. As for future directions, Mr Ingles observed that the Library's administrators would have to consider consolidation of service points, expanded use of book approval plans, curtailing circulation of periodicals, and even possibly closing the on-line catalogue, and reverting to one on microfiche.[263]

Although development of the Book and Record Depository brought hope of imminent relief from the chronic shortage of space for both study and collections, and acquisition of the DRA automated system would soon free the Library from the onerous charges for central computing time, the budget outlook for 1992–1993 brought no cause for joy. Indeed, the Student Union once again organized a late-night "study in" to protest the budget cuts by occupying the Rutherford Library's Periodicals and Microforms Reading Room on 20 February. "The Library closes at ten and we're going to stay until they move us," a student organizer told *The Gateway*. "'It's a question of doing something to get students' blood boiling....This is not going to be a milk-and-cookies type event,' he said, referring to last year's protest at Rutherford North in which chief librarian Ernie Ingles offered coffee and doughnuts to the 450 protesters." The truculent mood that under-funding and annual tuition hikes were creating among the student body was very much on display when, on Friday, 13 March, 3000 students and other protesters marched across the High Level Bridge to the Legislature, where Advanced Education Minister John Gogo was heckled, shouted down, and pelted with an egg. This demonstration was smaller than one the previous year, when 5000 marched to the Legislature in -25° weather, but the crowd members' noisy anger made up for their smaller numbers.[264]

The students' anger was shared in the Library, where a budget reduction of 2.4 percent was set to cut a further $380,625 from the coming year's budget. In a letter to Vice-President Lois Stanford, Mr Ingles wrote that,

> the Library feels strongly that it has demonstrated a willingness to assist the University, at every recent call, in terms of reducing operating expenditures. Indeed, we continue to take significant rebuke from the University community for our strategic planning efforts, and resulting initiatives, which are predicated on a long-term reduction in real support from provincial funding sources.
>
> But, we feel strongly that the University must demonstrate its commitment (not only to the Library, but to the faculty) for library-based research by supporting, in some reasonable measure, the collections on campus. There is no doubt that the deterioration to date has gone well beyond what might be considered reasonable even within our present financial environment.

Four days later, *The Gateway* interviewed Mr Ingles, and announced to its readers that,

> Libraries at the University of Alberta are feeling the bite of inflation and the GST, and as a result, book acquisition and staff positions have been slashed, according to director of libraries Ernie Ingles....The cost of budgetary restrictions can also be seen in the faces of library staff, according to Ingles. He said the ten percent staff cut Libraries has [sic] faced in the last few years adds up to create much stress. "We're in a decline, partially in staff and also on the book side. The user population has not decreased and we have a lot of services which must continue. The staff are overstressed having to do a lot more with much less."[265]

In the minds of many faculty, staff, and students, the University's financial situation appeared to be hitting bottom. But there was still worse to come. In December 1992, Alberta's ruling Conservatives elected a new leader, former Calgary mayor Ralph Klein, and went on the following year to win a provincial election that they were widely expected to lose. Under Premier Klein's leadership, the government made balanced budgets and retirement of the province's outstanding debt its paramount objectives. It demonstrated that it meant business by cutting 2500 of the province's 32,000 civil service positions, and reducing its own cabinet from 26 ministers to 17. Its plan to reduce its expenditure on the province's universities by 11 percent ushered in what the University's official historian, Rod Macleod, characterized as perhaps the worst financial crisis in the institution's history. The University's operating budget was cut sharply over a three-year period, with support units such as the Library bearing a heavier tax — a total of 22 percent — than that imposed on the teaching faculties and departments. Mercifully, the Library's book budget, already hammered by skyrocketing costs of books and, especially, of journals, was sheltered from these cuts.[266]

Pressured by the provincial government, the University was forced to roll back staff salaries by 5 percent (10 percent in the case of the president and vice-presidents). The support staff accepted a similar cut, half of it taken as unpaid leave days. To cope with the onset of three years of deep cuts, the Library Administration chose to freeze its vacancy pool, and authorize staff replacements only with a tourniquet-like restraint. It also began to look more seriously at deep restructuring initiatives. Against the advice of some of his senior staff, Mr Ingles had made a commitment to the Library's employees that he would tender his own resignation before he would order any layoffs. The unprecedented, albeit small number of layoffs he had been forced to make in 1991 had been a bitter experience he never wished to repeat. To those who counselled caution, he replied that he could not expect the staff to cooperate in making the structural changes required of the organization, if they believed they were merely going to help organize themselves out of some of their jobs. Therefore, his commitment to a policy of "no layoffs" stood, and, after their anticipated initial scepticism, they soon witnessed layoffs occurring everywhere else across the University, but none in the Library.

Drastic times, it is often said, call for drastic measures. And sometimes for courageous ones. With the endorsement of the GFC Library Committee and the encouragement of Vice-President Stanford, Mr Ingles was at last resolved to grasp the stinging nettle of branch library consolidation. This issue had festered just below the surface for years, arising whenever discussion turned to implementing budget cuts. At the end of January 1991, Prof. Werner Israel, one of the most distinguished scientists on the campus, circulated a survey "to canvas the opinions of those who will be directly affected" by the amalgamation of the branch science libraries. To no one's great surprise, the respondents were overwhelmingly opposed to the idea. Indeed, all but 8 of the 178 respondents implied that the need to walk an average of 150 metres to the Cameron Library without so much as stepping outside, and being deprived of 24-hour, key-holder access, would seriously impede their research, if not also their teaching. Prof. Israel passed a summary of the survey to Mr Ingles with an expression of hope that "the results of this survey will be of help in the difficult task that confronts you." The Library's recent success in implementing a related initiative, curtailing the circulation of periodicals, a policy known as "anchoring serials," may have buoyed up Mr Ingles' confidence excessively. Allowing periodicals to circulate not only created considerable work, requiring additional circulation staff to check them in and out, but also meant that many issues were unavailable for other readers to consult for the duration of their loan periods. Predictably, faculty and students had objected, and were unimpressed to learn that very few other academic libraries allowed their periodicals to circulate. However, a compromise was arrived at, that allowed limited loans to be made after 3:00 P.M. on days prior to weekends and holidays. Not a complete win for the Library, but better than a draw.[267]

In the face of large annual budget cuts, even before the advent of Ralph Klein's government, the issue of branch library amalgamation could no longer be avoided. It was unveiled in the form of a formal Discussion Paper at a GFC Library Committee meeting in the fall of 1992. Word of a proposal to close the Computer Science, Mathematics, and Physical Sciences reading rooms, and amalgamate their collections within Cameron Library, was bound to spread like wildfire through several departments, even before they had an opportunity to see a copy of the discussion paper explaining it in detail. First to post his objections to Vice-President Stanford was Professor Ron Bercov, head of the Mathematics Department, whose members had gained temporary possession of the Library's math collection three decades earlier, and refused ever since to consider returning it:

> The Mathematics Department, and undoubtedly others, should have an opportunity to oppose such a proposal at all stages of the decision making process....[and] should have a full opportunity to respond, not only to the discussion paper, but to any recommendations for change which the Library may make. We would of course hope that as a result of responses to the discussion paper there will be no major changes recommended.

Prof. Bercov and his colleagues followed up at the end of January by sending Vice-President Stanford a 14-page brief rejecting the

Library's case for amalgamation, accompanied by a petition signed by 69 faculty, 16 post-doctoral fellows, and 76 graduate students in the Departments of Mathematics and of Statistics and Applied Probabilities.[268]

In a letter to the Editor of *The Gateway*, Prof. Israel, a veteran member of the Save the Library Committee, questioned the Library's claims that the closures would yield significant savings, and ended by declaring that, "The financial constraints upon the Library system are recognized and deplored. At the same time, one can only wonder at the priorities of a Library administration that allows its services to users to progressively deteriorate as it sinks $4.8 million into ware-housing and cataloguing!" President Davenport and Vice-President Stanford's mailboxes were soon filling with letters protesting the closures from a host of chemists, mathematicians, physicists, and statisticians, who offered a plethora of well-worn arguments in defence of their branch libraries. In addition to their local letter-writing campaign, their friends and colleagues at other universities as far afield as Memorial of Newfoundland and Nova Scotia's Dalhousie University also sent letters. The GFC Library Committee accumulated a file of protest letters several centimetres thick.[269]

On 4 February 1993 *The Gateway* published a report on the simmering controversy, and noted that another protest petition had been gathered, this one bearing the signatures of 290 graduate students and 66 post-doctoral fellows in the departments that felt threatened. When apprised of this,

> Chief Librarian Ernie Ingles said he could easily get an equal or greater number of petition signatures supporting the amalgamation.
>
> "It's just an expression of people's opinion and that's no problem," he said. Ingles said the library kept the amalgamation option as a last resort but budgetary pressures made cuts necessary.
>
> "You can't maintain the same amount of service when you have lost 30 per cent of your staff. It's just that simple."

Celebrated chemist Norm Dovichi, who provided a lone voice in support,

> said his colleagues are not focusing on the correct issue which is increasing Cameron library hours. He added that library centralisation would be more convenient.

"If you know what you are looking for, it's no more difficult to find material in Cameron than it is in Physical Sciences," he said.

Gary Kelly, chair of the Save the Library committee, said amalgamation would start a domino effect ending at Rutherford, reducing its collections as books are displaced into the Eastpoint Stacks facility, off campus.[270]

A week later, secure in the knowledge that reason was on his side, Mr Ingles met with 120 or more representatives of the science departments affected by the amalgamation proposal. It quickly became clear that they had circled their wagons, made up their minds, and were quite unprepared to listen seriously to what he had to say. Prof. Israel spoke at great length, and delivered a masterpiece of condescension, laced with sarcasm, the four-page text of which has been preserved. His concluding remarks were both prescient and not a little ironic.

I believe the day is almost upon us where we shall hardly need the Library any more at all for access to current information. Many of us now in physics (and very soon most of us in all the sciences) use our personal computers every day to access in one second, at no cost, more information (and information more immediately up-to-date) than all the Document Delivery Services could ever provide at $20 a shot.

Those expensive journals, which for the moment we still have to worry about cost-sharing, were a 20th century aberration that is already fading into history.

What we really need is direct and continuous access to the knowledge base not yet available in electronic form — the stuff that is stored in monographs and journals of the last 20 and 30 years. We have this now. We are aiming to keep it.

A coup de grâce of sorts was delivered three days later by Dean of Science Richard Peter, who wrote Vice-President Stanford to express his own opposition, and added: "The issue of closure of science branch libraries has gotten greatly overheated. To defuse the situation, I request that you will quickly resolve the situation by cancelling any further moves towards closure of the branch libraries. This will enable members of the Faculty of Science who are so greatly involved in the issue to turn their focus to the important functions of teaching and research." At that point, the Chief Librarian scarcely needed the Dean's counsel. Having wisely decided that this issue was not the hill to die on, he recommended at the next meeting of the GFC Library

Committee that the proposal be withdrawn, saying, "I'm just going to have to find my savings somewhere else." One positive outcome of this dispute was the commitment by the heads of the Chemistry and Physics Departments to provide the Library with funding to extend the Physical Sciences Library's hours to equal those of the Cameron Science and Technology Library, and thus provide equal access for all students. As for Prof. Israel's vision of a library-less future for the sciences, it has in large measure come to pass, as those "aberrant" paper journals are now available to scientists and students in electronic form. But providing scientists with access to them is still the responsibility of the University Library, at an annual cost to it of several million dollars. If the tussle over science branch libraries left the Chief Librarian feeling bruised and chastened, he was soon winning accolades for the success of the Library's subsequent initiatives.[271]

At the beginning of 1995, the arrival of the University's eleventh president, Dr Roderick Fraser, an alumnus and native Albertan, brought a renewed sense of enthusiasm and purpose to the University after more than a year during which, in Prof. Macleod's words, it had a "governing structure in something approaching chaos." As part of President Fraser's "faculty renewal" program begun that year, generous severance packages were offered to academic staff who were at least 50 years of age, to encourage early retirements. Nearly a dozen of the librarians who were eligible took advantage of this opportunity. Although their severances had to be amortized by the Library over three years, this did offer some budgetary relief, at the expense of depriving the Library of their skills and experience.[272]

As the Library's rate of acquisitions rose exponentially during the 1960s, the staff had to be significantly increased to deal with the flood of books. When acquisitions entered a period of decline after 1971, despite the attrition of positions, the number of technical services staff did not decline in direct proportion. The introduction of automation made for labour saving efficiencies, if not also lower costs. For example, Bibliographic Services Coordinator Kathy Carter recalls that the simple expedient of closing the card catalogue, and dispensing with catalogue card production, with its endless checking, editing, and filing, was calculated at the time to have eliminated work that had occupied a score or more full-time employees, or their equivalent. Automation also reduced the amount of original cataloguing required, since catalogue records stored in large, bibliographic databases could be located and copied on-line at smaller cost. "When I first came here," Mr Ingles recently recalled, "we were, to be quite blunt, more than adequately staffed. I just didn't think all the staff were deployed particularly well. We had, if memory serves me, well over 400 staff. Of course, we lost a lot of those positions in the 1990s, and have never recovered them. Staffing has always been a struggle." The challenge, as Ingles viewed it, was to find a way to preserve as many of those positions as possible through the era of escalating budget cuts, while obtaining the greatest benefit from their labour. The answer, he realized, lay in outsourcing the bulk of the Library's more routine cataloguing work to an outside agency, and redeploying many of the technical services personnel to the public service units that were becoming increasingly understaffed.

> People were truly amazed that we were able to do this. We were lucky for a variety of reasons. We had some good people who were prepared to look at some interesting and different approaches to things. I don't think it could have been put together at many other institutions, both because of our people, but also because we've been extraordinarily well-served by our collective agreements. This is ameliorated by the fact that so many people here are open to trying new things, even if not without some grumbling.[273]

Not the least amazed was Vice-President Lois Stanford, who wrote, "Thank you for the draft discussion paper on the Library's outsourcing project for cataloguing and processing. Being interested in the details of how libraries are run, I found it fascinating reading, and I also realized from it what an enormously complex task you are undertaking." In 1995 a contract was awarded to Information Systems Management (ISM) of Winnipeg, to perform the bulk of the Library's routine monograph cataloguing at a significant unit cost saving to the Library. Newly purchased monographs are shipped directly to Winnipeg by the vendors, and delivered "shelf-ready" to the Library along with electronic catalogue records. The Library continues to catalogue serials, rare books, and titles in East Asian languages, as well as duplicate copies, in-house. This outsourcing initiative was truly innovative, for it allowed the Library to reassign 40 technical services staff members to public service duties, and avoid any staff layoffs.[274]

"I also wanted to enhance the University of Alberta Library's reputation," Ingles admits today, "and we got a lot of attention with the outsourcing." It also brought the Library another Quality and Productivity Award in 1995, the second in a whole series of CAUBO awards received by the Library in recent years. "Putting it in Winnipeg wasn't actually our choice," he explained.

> We simply chose to find a vendor, a company interested in getting into this area of outsourced technical services, and become their main client. The University of Manitoba signed on later, but we're still the primary client. They just happened to be in Winnipeg. Later they were sold to IBM, who sold them in turn to OCLC. But we were the ones who actually created it as a service, and we might have franchised it. Soon publishers and book vendors began to provide shelf-ready processing as part of the acquisitions-purchasing process as a service on behalf of their customers. We actually changed the way the industry works, setting the ball in motion. So now you can buy your cataloguing where you buy your books, and you can change vendors at will.

While the early retirements played their part, the Library saved much of its 22 percent in operating budget reductions through the outsourcing. "People said to me, 'How could you have saved any money when you didn't lay anybody off?' The real savings," Ingles explained,

> lies in the "opportunity costs," which can be quantified. In a large academic institution with a collegial environment, many of the staff do things other than what they were specifically hired to do. We were losing up to 40 percent of the productivity of our cataloguers by having them serve on a variety of committees, performing some public services, and so forth. I'm not saying these extra activities weren't worthy or important, but that they didn't neces-sarily need the input of cataloguers, who, as a result, weren't nearly as productive than if they'd worked in a shop totally dedicated to cataloguing things.[275]

Because not even the largest library can be wholly self-sufficient, the Library has focused considerable energy and effort upon building library partnerships and consortia to facilitate the sharing of access to books and other information resources. "For much of its history," Mr Ingles recalls,

> this Library had a long tradition of focusing inward. I can recall very few interactions with the University of Calgary Library from my time there in the

1970s; the two institutions had pretty much gone separate ways. Until Peter Freeman took command, the Library neither pursued, nor received the national, let alone international, recognition it might have deserved, and it was often seen by other institutions as rather isolationist. That had begun to change thanks to Peter's efforts here, Alan MacDonald's at Calgary, and when I was at Regina. We worked together to invigorate COPPUL [Council of Prairie and Pacific University Libraries], and had some modest successes, with things like our inter-library loan initiatives.[276]

In 1994 the Library spearheaded formation of the NEOS consortium, an alliance of academic and government libraries created to participate in the University's newly acquired DRA automated system, create a union catalogue of their regional holdings, and thus provide cost-efficient access to facilitate the sharing of library resources. Over the years it has grown to include 18 member institutions with 49 branches across the northern half of the province, that exchange services. The NEOS consortium's geographic expansion quickly made the name NEOS — which stood for "Networking Edmonton's On-line Services" — obsolete, but the acronym stuck. The University of Alberta Library also played a leading role in obtaining provincial government funding in 2001 to create The Alberta Library (TAL), a consortium of 43 public, university, college, technical institute, and special libraries, united to promote universal, barrier-free access to information for all Albertans. Under the umbrella sponsorship of The Alberta Library, the University of Alberta and the University of Calgary spearheaded the successful campaign to establish the Lois Hole Campus Alberta Digital Library (LHCADL) in 2005, which embraces 35 post-secondary educational institutions, including the libraries of six First Nations colleges. Funded by a grant from the provincial government, this initiative, named for a much beloved Lieutenant Governor of Alberta, is designed to provide province-wide, affordable access to licensed, on-line, electronic, information resources. The Lois Hole Digital Library project was awarded the CLA/CACUL Innovative Achievement Award for 2008. To enable the full participation of the First Nations college libraries, Ms Sharon Marshall and Ms Anne Carr-Wiggin of the University Library worked closely with the First Nations college librarians to automate and retro-convert their catalogue records, and create the First Nations Information Connection website, with additional funding raised by Ms Mary-Jo Romaniuk.

Other consortial projects in which the Library played a key role include Alberta's Health Knowledge Network (HKN), established to provide clinical practitioners and researchers across the province with timely, on-line access to information resources, thus continuing and updating a service provided by the Library to the medical profession since 1928, and the Canadian Research Knowledge Network (CRKN), a non-profit corporation funded by 64 universities and matching grants from provincial governments, that provides licensed access to electronic journals and information databases. "Some people inside the University looked upon cooperation with suspicious eyes," Ingles recalls,

> because in every case we were partnering with institutions smaller than our own. I made a case at the time, for which I had no proof at the beginning, but which has been proven right, that the benefits to the University would be much more than political. Yet in every case, people asked "Why is he doing this? Times are tough. It's costing us money and taking time away from whatever we should be doing instead." But I felt it was the right thing to do as part of that mainstream notion that libraries exist to serve the wider community. I felt we would develop a reputation for being cooperative, friendly, and right-thinking, which would hold us in good stead in the future.[277]

As a result of that growing reputation, the Alberta government gained a new appreciation for the stature of the University and the larger role it is able to play in the emergence of the wider information culture and the so-called knowledge economy.

> When the provincial government was developing the idea of "Campus Alberta," they looked to the University of Alberta Library. It may be something of a mixed blessing for NEOS, that today, in 2009, it's considered so matter-of-fact that no one really thinks about what it is or where it came from. Even now people in the government are often genuinely surprised when they find that their entire government library services are being underpinned by the University of Alberta Library because all of those libraries are part of NEOS, and that most of the colleges north of Olds are also part of NEOS. So it has served us very well; I honestly don't think that The Alberta Library or the Lois Hole Digital Library would have come into existence without the work we did in creating NEOS. It's produced benefits for all Albertans, earned us kudos, and put us on the map, so to speak. It moved us further away from

small "p" provincialism, and made us seen as a place where people know what they're doing. People building consortial networks came from places like Minnesota and Ohio to see how we did NEOS, and they're still coming.[278]

Relais and OneCard

Once the Library had achieved the major technological leap with the adoption of the new DRA system, other computer-based initiatives were made possible. NEOS was the prime example that reached beyond the campus. A second was the development of the Relais system, which was based on technologies to facilitate inter-library lending by enabling the retrieval and digital conversion of paper texts, and their delivery over the internet. "It seems commonplace now," Ingles observed, "but it was challenging when we developed it in a partnership with Network Support Inc (NSI), and it won the North American Workflow Gold Excellence Award of the Workflow and Reengineering International Association (WARIA). Much credit is due to Doug Poff, our former head of ITS on the systems side, and to Tina James and Alexis Gibb on the I-LL side."[279]

Other new services were developed specifically for the campus community, such as self-service checkout machines for circulating books. The current generation of this equipment, a vast improvement over the earliest versions tested, have reduced the staff-mediated checkout of books, and made line-ups of people clutching piles of books a far-less-frequent occurrence. The replacement of traditional library cards with the unified, multi-service OneCard has been described earlier. James Heilik, who was responsible for organizing and implementing the OneCard initiative, now admits that,

> *The OneCard is a strange thing for a library to operate; a vehicle with which students can operate photocopiers, buy food, gain entry to restricted facilities, operate laundry machines, use vending machines, buy books, lock and unlock doors, and do a host of other things including borrowing books from the Library. We placed the operation in the Cameron Library, and the first applications were student identification, library card, and photocopying. In looking at the list of things one can do with a OneCard, it is clear that it requires intense co-operation among many departments and that there is still great potential for growth.*

If some of that potential has yet to be realized, it is not for lack of enthusiasm on the part of students, who appreciated the convenience they afforded, whereas, before the OneCard was introduced, as Mr Ingles observed in *The Gateway*, "It's possible today for someone to [have to] wander around campus with six or seven cards in their pockets."[280]

Associate Vice-President (Learning Services)

In 1995, Mr Ingles assumed additional administrative responsibilities as Associate Vice-President (Learning Services) — later styled Vice-Provost — and Chief Librarian. These included Computing and Network Services, the University Bookstores, Museums and Collections Services, and the University Press. "It wasn't something that I sought," he explains,

> but I was encouraged to take on those things. Those were hard times, and the Administration was looking for ways to reconfigure the administrative structure without recruiting expensive new people, but instead by exploiting available human resources, expanding people's portfolios. That's essentially how it happened, and I still had enough residual ego to see it as a good career move, and to feel that I was moving upstream.

Although the added assignments took him away from the Library — literally, by moving his office to University Hall — and left less time and attention to devote to Library business, he feels that it yielded numerous benefits for the Library, through closer working relationships with publication-oriented operations such as the Bookstores and the Press. "In retrospect, and I've thought on numerous occasions of what life might have been like had I stayed at the Library and done my own thing, with my head down, the reality is that the Library is now better served for my having been over there."[281]

Soon, however, the burden of work, and the sometimes conflicting demands and agendas of the Library's six Associate Directors, prompted Ingles to recruit a trusted surrogate to whom he could delegate the daily administration of the Library. Ms Karen Adams, the Executive Director of the Canadian Library Association, and former Saskatchewan Provincial Librarian, was appointed Director of Library Services and Information Resources at the end of 1997, and arrived early in the new year. As a skilled administrator and amiable colleague, she proved to be an ideal choice. "Karen provided a steadying hand," Ingles recalls,

she has an extraordinary ability to smooth the waters and get people's oars
pulling in unison. Her contribution during that period was important, while
I was an absentee landlord, so to speak; she did an excellent job of keeping
things moving, and developing services and projects in her own right. At the
same time, I have to give much credit and praise to Ms Mary-Jo Romaniuk,
who has so ably managed the finances of the Learning Services portfolio for
the past decade. Karen Adams and the other senior Library managers kept
the wheels on, but without Ms Romaniuk's fine work, there might not have
been any tyres on the wheels.[282]

One of the major projects in which Ms Adams played a key role
was the development of the Canadian National Site Licensing
Project (CNSLP, later renamed the Canadian Research Knowledge
Network, CRKN), launched in Halifax in September 2001. A consortium of 64 Canadian academic libraries, the project secured tens
of millions of dollars in provincial and institutional grants, and
successfully negotiated licensed access to a wealth of electronic journals and databases. It succeeded where the joint serials renewal
project attempted in the late 1980s did not; in the process it also
provided a model for the Lois Hole project. CNSLP also won top
honours in the CAUBO Quality and Productivity Awards for 2001.
Much to her colleagues selfish regret, Ms Adams left in June 2008
to become the University Librarian at the University of Manitoba.

New Facilities for a New Century
Reflecting upon the Library's seemingly endless need for more space,
Mr Ingles says that it represents the biggest single disappointment of
his nearly 20 year career at the University of Alberta.

> *When I came I was promised as an inducement — one of the carrots held*
> *out at my interview to tempt me to take the job — that I would be able to*
> *build a big, brand-new library. It was to be a major complex connecting the*
> *Cameron and Rutherford Libraries, and gobble up all the space in between.*
> *It was the highest item on the planning agenda. Well, that ended pretty*
> *quickly, and we've fought for space ever since, with a few positive results*
> *along the way. We were the first university library in Canada, and one of the*
> *first in North America to build a major depository like the BARD. We did it*
> *on the cheap, but it was innovative. Pound for pound, the BARD was a good*
> *investment, but it wasn't what I'd signed on for.*[283]

Ernie Ingles officially opening the Cameron Library renovation as Mayor Stephen Mandel looks on, March 2009. Courtesy of UofA Creative Services.

While the long-promised Rutherford West Library remained a ghost of unfulfilled hopes, the Library system was able to undertake a number of development projects even in the lean-budget years of the 1990s. A series of renovations in the Cameron building led to the creation of the Professors Emeriti Room on the third floor; renovations to offices (and more asbestos removal) on the 5th floor; development of the Knowledge Common, Technology Training Centre, and study hall on the lower level; creation of the Inter-library Loans suite on the second floor; complete replacement of the entrance foyer, curtain-wall façades, and windows on the east and west sides of the building; and, most recently, complete renovation of the main floor, a project opened in September 2008, and officially dedicated six months later. As part of this most recent renovation, Ms Mary-Jo Romaniuk proposed a new partnership with the Edmonton Public Library (EPL), which agreed to open a lending branch in Cameron Library to provide University students and staff with more convenient access to EPL's stock of books, CDs, and DVDs. Capital funding for renovations often depends upon making a case for long-term savings through enhanced efficiency or reduction in labour and staffing costs. Thus, a major series of renovations were undertaken in the two Rutherford Libraries, designed to reduce the number of public service points that required staffing, as well as to accommodate relocation of the Music Library. Over the past decade, major renovations were also undertaken in the Scott Health Sciences Library, the Weir Law Library, and the Coutts Education Library, designed in each case to increase efficiency of operation and maximize the number of computer workstations for library users.[284]

Also, after years of enduring impossibly crowded conditions in their library, staff and students of the Campus Saint-Jean, the University's French-language, affiliate college, received a splendid new library as a result of a generous $6 million dollar grant provided by the federal government. The spacious new Bibliothèque Saint-Jean, the centrepiece of the entire project, was completed and officially opened its doors in January 1997. As this book is being published, the latest addition to the Library system is under construction at the University's Augustana Campus in Camrose, where a splendid new library building is scheduled to open for the fall term 2009.[285]

Collection Development

In the years following Mr Ingles' arrival, financial stringency prompted several academic departments to close their independently run, departmental libraries, and transfer their collections to the University Library. These 'orphaned' collections adopted by the Library include those devoted to circumpolar studies, data, film studies, geography, geology, maps, music, and political science. Budget cutting by the provincial government also yielded some 'orphan' collections, most notably the Department of Transportation and Utilities' collection and the entire contents of the Government of Alberta Libraries' Central Periodicals Depository. Mr Ingles never hesitated to adopt collections in need of a home, for as he explains, "as an institution, we have a fiduciary responsibility to preserve collections entrusted to us, both the ones we've inherited as stewards, and those which build on them. We're not collecting for 10 years, or 50 years, or 100 years, we're collecting for 500 years, and perhaps even longer." Ingles' goal has been to establish and maintain the Library as a library of record, and a destination for scholars. "What makes a top 10 university?" he asks rhetorically.

> They have destination libraries; libraries people seek out. People go to Cambridge, Oxford, Harvard, Yale, and Texas because there are libraries there with collections of importance to scholarship. We may not share the same subject strengths with those libraries, but the OCLC database reveals

that our collection has more unique titles than all but a handful of other
North American research libraries. That's our drawing card.[286]

Granted a wide mandate to augment the Library's collections
with still greater retrospective strength in printed books, the author
has sought out, identified, and acquired significant collections,
both large and small, either by purchase, or, more often, through
donation. These efforts have been amply rewarded by the annual
acquisition of tens of thousands of additional volumes, quanti-
ties that often taxed the capacity of the staff in the Gifts Unit and
Bibliographic Services to absorb. Colleagues throughout the Library
have contributed to the effort, whether by identifying potential donations and encouraging donors among their personal contacts or by
pitching in occasionally to help pack or unpack major donations.
Since his arrival as Director of Development (Learning Services)
in 2003, Mr Josh Bilyk has also provided invaluable support in the
ever-demanding responsibilities for stewardship that major donations entail. In 2008, to help mark the University's centenary, the
Library negotiated the purchase and repatriation to Canada of the Sir
Samuel Benfield Steele Collection, an immensely significant archive
related to the early history and development of Western Canada.
It was purchased entirely with funds raised through federal, provincial, and corporate grants, as well as several large contributions
from private donors. The Steele Collection, which includes over
100 diaries and thousands of letters, is now being inventoried and
undergoing conservation treatment. It has attracted wide attention
among scholars and researchers who are eager to study its contents.

The University Library's collections have benefited from the
generosity of donors from the outset. Premier Rutherford took
great interest in the library of his beloved University, to which he
made some of the earliest donations it received. Offers to donate
books were generally welcomed, but major gifts-in-kind were relatively few, and would have been subject to the constraints of the
Library's limited space and processing capacities. Financial limitations also constrained the pursuit of large collections to purchase
until the major expansion of budgets and collections in the 1960s.
Mr Ingles' reaffirmation of the University Library's mandate to
collect, and to collect aggressively, established the tone for the subsequent development of the Library's gifts-in-kind program. In the
first decade of the new century, appraised and receipted gifts-in-

kind have totalled $15,290,000, for an annual average of $1.7 million, contributed each year by nearly 400 donors. By contrast, in 1981– 1982, receipted donations-in-kind numbered only 66, for a total of $40,550.[287] Raising public awareness of the value of the Library's Special Collections for research and scholarship has also been a major focus of activity in recent years. Here the work of Special Collections and Rare Books Librarians Jeannine Green and Robert Desmarais, and Map Librarian David Jones, have made enormous contributions by providing visitors with tours of their collections, introducing classes of students to their valuable, antiquarian resources, and mounting regular exhibitions, that are frequently accompanied by beautifully designed, illustrated catalogues that have gained wide attention and admiration, as well as consistently winning awards.

For all the enthusiasm for building the Library's collections of printed books, the University of Alberta Library has not shunned the digital side of collection development. It has forged ahead with major digital initiatives, from the Peel's Prairie Provinces website, which highlights the Library's particular specialty in Prairie materials through the provision of thousands of keyword searchable full-texts, to a major project to digitize 20 million pages of Canadiana in cooperation with Canadiana.org (formerly the Canadian Institute for Historical Microreproductions, CIHM). Still another partnership has been undertaken with the University of Toronto Library to share digital copies of books from that vast collection. "One of my audacious goals," Ingles reveals,

is that some day every printed title in our collection will have a digital surro-gate available on-line. It won't happen in my lifetime, but someday the great university research libraries will have their deep, rich research collections of printed material, carefully preserved, but with digital surrogates available through the internet to serve most workaday research needs. You won't ever satisfy every type of scholarship with digital copies, but having said that, we must nonetheless satisfy young and future generations of scholars with digital alternatives. When I retire, I will walk right out the door and into the sunset believing, as a former special collections librarian, that collections are what research libraries are all about. We perform services around those collections, and services are important. We need to help people find the collection resources, but none of those services would be relevant if there were no resources to find. Collections are the most important thing.[288]

Above: President Samarasekera's Charter Day Dinner, Rutherford Library South, main reading room, May 2008. Courtesy of UofA Creative Services.

Right: Pierre Ouvrard at the launch of the exhibition and book Pierre Ouvrard: Master Bookbinder/ Maître relieur *with Merrill Distad (left) and rare book dealer Alfred Van Peteghem (right), June 2000. Courtesy of UofA Creative Services.*

Looking Back

Reflecting upon his two decades as University Librarian, Ernie Ingles believes that, "over those 20 years I think the Library has been treated reasonably well by the institution. And, I think that the University itself has done as well as, or better than, many others in terms of the investment it has made in its Library, though God knows we've had our ups and downs." In recent years, the solid support of Dr Carl Amrhein, our Vice-President (Academic) and Provost, has been especially valuable." While our Library is not unique in having suffered chronic shortages of space, staff, and dollars,

The Augustana Library nearing completion, April 2009.
Photo by Chantal Beesley, Augustana Campus.

the calibre of the people we have at the University Library, and the calibre of those we've attracted over the years, has been superb. Kathleen DeLong has managed our human resources and staff training and development program with a sure hand, and ensured that we've been able to hire the cream of the crop, and while I wish we had more of them, where we lost out in numbers, we gained in competency, dedication, and shoulders-to-the-wheel. Almost 10 percent of our librarians possess, or are completing PhDs. Our librarians conduct research and publish because they choose to, not because they have to; they're true academics who are regularly invited to speak and present papers at national and international conferences. They are a Library staff who 'get it,' and who have pushed the institution forward instead of pulling it backward.

After coming through an era of such incredible change in both the profession and the University, I think we've come out of it better than we entered it. As proof of that, 20 years ago, our Library wasn't even ranked among the top 30 of the more than 100 North America institutions in the Association of Research Libraries, except in size of collections, where we were ranked as the 29th largest. By 2006, ours was the 17th largest collection among ARL libraries, and still more impressively, Alberta has risen steadily in the ARL's Membership Criteria Index, a sophisticated algorithm that analyses multiple criteria, to rank 13th overall in 2006. That's being in pretty rarified company when one's library is only surpassed by a dozen much older and more famous institutions.

People elsewhere in Canada, and more generally in North America, are talking about the University of Alberta and its Library; these people know who we are, but didn't 20 years ago. Our fame is far greater than anyone on staff may think. We've reached the point where we're not only recognized as the province's preeminent library, but as one of the top two or three in Canada. We've also achieved a measure of recognition in North America. I'm hoping that in the last few years of my tenure, that we may make further progress in developing a more visible international profile. When that day arrives, that might well be my, and, indeed, our proudest achievement as an academic library.

For today, however, we certainly take pride in the collections, the facilities, and the traditions that our predecessors have provided us, as well as in the gratitude expressed by those we serve, and in whom we also seek to instil pride in their University and its Library.[289]

Library pride

Libraries are good things, and at the U of A we're lucky to have a fully stocked series of such establishments throughout campus. In fact, last year's Maclean's university rankings showed us that the U of A has the second largest holdings in Canada and the most books per student in the nation.

That's a record we should all be proud of, and as well, we should be proud of our librarians for admirably tackling the not-so-small feat of keeping the records of our society in a searchable order.

All the libraries I have known: I salute you.

—JHENIFER PABILLANO,
News Editor, *The Gateway*, 8 October 2002[290]

Although its mission and centrality to teaching and research remain fundamentally unchanged, the University of Alberta Library of today bears scant resemblance to its earliest incarnations. During its first century, it weathered frequent moves and much adversity, and witnessed many changes within the University and the world at large, as it gradually evolved into one of North America's largest academic research libraries. But throughout those 100 years, the commitment and dedication of its staff to service, innovation, and, occasionally, improvisation have remained constant.

Endnotes

Abbreviations

Report BofG = Report of the Board of Governors of
the University of Alberta

UAA = University of Alberta Archives

1   "An Act to Establish and Incorporate a
University for the Province of Alberta,"
Alberta Statutes, 1906, Cap 42, 382–389;
Corbett, *River Lot 5*; Babcock, *Alexander
Cameron Rutherford*, 35–36.

2   A.P. Low, Deputy Head and Director,
Geological Survey of Canada, to Rutherford,
2 November 1906 (UAA 69-164-2/3/6-8).
The McGill extension programs laid the
foundation for the later establishment of the
University of British Columbia.

3   Gordon, "University Beginnings," 490–491.

4   Senate minutes, 30 March 1908 (UAA
70-98-1); Corbett, *Henry Marshall Tory*, 97;
Tory to Rutherford, Ottawa, 14 April 1908,
Tory to Rutherford, Young's Hotel, Boston,
23 May 1908 (UAA 69-164-2/3/6-8). The
following year, W.A.R. Kerr (MA, Toronto;
PhD, Harvard) was appointed to the chair
of Modern Languages at a salary of $2,600.
He later served the University as Dean of
Arts and Sciences and as president (Senate
minutes, 10 June 1909 [UAA 70-91-1]).

5   Edmund Kemper Broadus, "Dr. Tory — An
'Appreciation'," *The Gateway* (8 December
1927): 3.

6   Alexander, *The University of Alberta*, 9; cf. "A
Retrospect," *The Gateway* (1 April 1912): 11.
Miss Archibald's appointment as university
librarian, at an annual salary of $900, was
not formally confirmed by the Senate until
10 June 1909, at which meeting it also
authorized future construction of a main
building, separate men's and women's
residential buildings, and a library building
(Senate minutes, 10 June 1909 [UAA 70-91-1]).

7   Senate minutes, 6 July 1908 (UAA 70-91-1).
Two years later, the Finance Committee
reported a clear profit earned by the
University Bookstore of $263.74 (Senate
minutes, 15 July 1910 [ibid.]).

8   M.J. Griffin to Rutherford, 23 June 1909;
J.-L. Gouin to Rutherford, 8 February 1910;
Rutherford to J.P. Robertson, 7 May 1910;
Robertson to Rutherford, 14 May 1910;
Rutherford to Lord Strathcona, 3 December
1909; Strathcona to Rutherford, 1 March
1910 (UAA 69-164-2/3/6). See also Babcock,
Alexander Cameron Rutherford, 45, 134. The
Government of Canada also supplied copies
of the Debates of the Senate and House of
Commons.

9   Corbett, *Henry Marshall Tory*, 103. Prior
to World War I, prices of academic titles
averaged as little as $2 and rarely cost more
than $5 a volume.

10   Senate minutes, 7 September 1909 (UAA 70-
91-1); Tory Papers (UAA 68-9-204); Johns, *A*

History, 28–29, 230. Gould (1855–1919) was "considered the leading Canadian librarian of his day and one of the foremost in North America" (*Dictionary of Canadian Biography,* XIV: 428b).

11   "The Home of the University of Alberta," *The Gateway* (1 October 1911): 15; Lister, *My Forty-Five Years,* 10–12.

12   Gordon, "University Beginnings," 491.

13   *University of Alberta, 1908–1933,* 19; Gordon, "University Beginnings," 491–492. Commenting on the expanding curriculum, a student wrote, "Our library also has grown in proportion to the departments of study organized, and now contains some fifteen thousand volumes" (*The Gateway* [1 April 1915]: 15). See also "Dept. [of] Extension has Big Library: Over 4,000 Books of History, Travel and Fiction Open to Students," *The Gateway* (17 October 1922): 1. The total figure cited includes the Extension Department Library.

14   Schoeck, *I Was There,* 146; Gordon, "University Beginnings," 493. See also "The Opening of the Main Teaching Building," *The Gateway* (1 November 1915): 3.

15   In an interview with President Robert Newton in 1945, Librarian Donald Cameron referred to the Cutter system as having been "adopted from McGill" (Newton, Memo: "Conf[erence] with Mr D.E. Cameron, 5.2.45" (UAA 68-1-3/4/5/4-1). Charles Ammi Cutter (1837–1903), one of the founders of modern librarianship, pioneered such innovations as card catalogues, systematic rules for cataloguing (*Rules for a Dictionary Catalogue,* 1st ed. 1876, 4th ed. 1904), and an expandable classification scheme adaptable to library collections of any size. His death before he could complete and publish the final, most detailed level of his system, and the absence of later revisions, ensured its eventual obsolescence. However, "Cutter numbers," his alpha-numeric system of abbreviating authors' names, remain in use in most libraries that employ either Library

of Congress (LC) or Dewey Classifications. Although the Cutter System was later largely supplanted in academic libraries by the Library of Congress Classification, LC drew heavily upon Cutter's system. The curriculum of the Summer School for Librarians founded by C.H. Gould at McGill in 1904, which later evolved into Canada's first post-graduate program in librarianship, included Cutter's classification, described as "one of the most complete and logical of all classifications now in use...[and] modified to suit Canadian libraries" (*McGill University Summer School for Librarians 1914,* prospectus [UAA 68-9-204]).

16   *Vancouver Sunday Province* and *Bulletin of the Maritime Library Association,* quoted in Marble, *The Archibald Family,* 321–322. Bruce Peel, in the first edition of his history of the Library, cited marriage as the probable reason for Miss Archibald's resignation (Peel, *History* 1965, 5). In the second edition, Mr Peel deleted this claim, perhaps for lack of clear evidence (Peel, *History* 1979, 1). In fact, Miss Archibald never married.

17   "Our New Librarian," *The Gateway* (1 October 1912): 35; W.A.R. Kerr, "An Appreciation of F.G. Bowers," *The Trail* 1 (1920): 9-10. Cecil Race, described as "a prince among men, modest, retiring, capable, of outstanding character, and impressive ability," was recruited from the staff of Alberta College by President Tory, who often said "the best day's work Alberta College ever did was to give the University of Alberta the services of Cecil E. Race" (Riddell, *Methodism,* 275).

18   Bowers to Tory, 27 March 1913 and 15 January 1914; F.G. Bowers, "Librarian's Report, 27 March 1913" (UAA 68-9-204).

19   Bowers to Acting President W.A.R. Kerr, 18 February 1919 (UAA 68-9-205).

20   A. Calhoun to J.M. MacEachran, 28 March 1913; A.E. Ottewell to Bowers, 3 April 1913; K. Calhoun to C. Race, 17 April 1913; C. Race to K. Calhoun, 26 April 1913, making it clear that the decision on hiring rested with President Tory; and K. Calhoun to Tory, 15 November

1924 (UAA 69-9-204). Ironically, Alexander Calhoun (1879–1979) lacked any formal library training, and had only been appointed to head the Calgary Public Library two years earlier, in 1911 (Lohnes and Nicholson, *Alexander Calhoun*, 6). While in Edmonton in 1924 to paint the official portrait of founding Chancellor C.A. Stuart, Group of Seven artist Frederick Varley made a charcoal sketch "Head of Kathleen Calhoun," now in the University Print Room (Acces. 1971.5.37).

21 Gordon, "University Beginnings," 490.

22 K. Calhoun to Bowers, 6 May 1919; W.A.R. Kerr (Acting President) to K. Calhoun, 13 May 1919; Tory to K. Calhoun, 18 August and 3 September 1919; K. Calhoun to Tory, 26 August 1919; G. Lomer to Tory, 26 November 1920; G. Locke to Tory, 21 December 1920 (UAA 69-9-204). See also Library Committee minutes and correspondence, 22 December 1920 (UAA 90-148-1).

23 Gordon, "University Beginnings," 489.

24 Tory to E.F. Slocock, 1 October 1920 (UAA 69-9-205); see also Samuel, "An Early History," (Winter 1953): 143–147.

25 Bursar D.S. Mackenzie to Kerr, 29 December 1917; Tory to W.H. Alexander inviting him to serve on the Library Committee, 14 November 1917 (UAA 69-9-205).

26 Library Committee minutes and correspondence, 22 December 1920 and 3 May 1921 (UAA 90-148-1/1); Kerr, "Appreciation of F.G. Bowers," 9; Macleod, *All True Things*, chapters 1 and 3; Corbett, *Henry Marshall Tory*, 109, 131; Peel, *History* 1979, 2.

27 Library Committee minutes, 3 May 1921 (UAA 90-148-1); Tory to Capt. David Corbett, 29 May 1922 [*sic?*], quoted in Johns, *A History*, 67, *cf.* 75–76, 87; Macdonald, *History*, 32–33. Prof. Cecil Burgess, speaking as a member of the Mayfair Golf Club, established near the University in 1922, recalled that, "D.E. Cameron, the librarian, was the best golfer of us all" (Ruth Bowen, "Interviews and draft stories, 1969" [UAA 79-112-8], quoted in Schoeck, *I Was There*, 170).

28 *The Gateway* (21 March 1919): 4–5, (20 March 1923): 2, and (16 October 1934): 1.

29 Corbett, *Henry Marshall Tory*, 133–134. Macleod notes that Tory's version was overly dramatic; the award was publicized in advance, and the so-called cheque was merely a bank transfer (Macleod, *All True Things*, chapter 4, esp. 71–72).

30 "Fill Library–Fool the Supps.: Librarian Advertises His Wares," *The Gateway* (17 October 1922): 1.

31 D.E. Cameron, "Librarian Urges You to Use Books: 26,000 Volumes at Your Service–Card Catalogue Simplifies Reference," *The Gateway* (9 October 1923): 1, 4.

32 Cameron, Librarian's Annual Report for 1924, quoted in Johns, *A History*, 91–92; *cf.* "Fill Library–Fool the Supps." At the end of the decade, Library hours were more limited: the main reading room was open 8:30 a.m. to 5:00 p.m. (till 1:00 p.m. on Saturdays), and again from 8:00 p.m. to 10:00 p.m. on Mondays, Wednesdays, and Fridays ("Library Notice," *The Gateway* [24 October 1929]: 6).

33 Cameron, Librarian's Annual Report, in *Report of the Board of Governors of the University of Alberta, 1928–29*, 40–41 (hereinafter cited as *Report BofG*).

34 Cameron to R.C. Wallace, 24 November 1928 (UAA 68-1-3/2/5/5-1).

35 Jean Lehmann, "Memories of the Arts Library at the University of Alberta in the Twenties," *Library Editions* (Summer 1990): 7. As an ordained minister, Cameron often performed campus weddings, including that of Ms Millar to Jack Lehmann, later a professor of botany at the University of Toronto.

36 Ibid., 8. During Mr Cameron's convalescence, President Wallace provided the Library with temporary, casual support staff (Wallace to Cameron, 31 March 1930 [UAA 68-1-3/2/5/5-1]).

37 Blackburn, "Reminiscences," 5. Blackburn, the undergraduate advised by Cameron, took his first library degree at the University of Toronto, served as its Chief Librarian from

1954 until his retirement in 1982. He wrote that, "Cameron could not have imagined a day when Alberta would have its own library school or when a building bearing his name would be headquarters of a multi-million volume library" (ibid.).

38 Cameron, Librarian's Annual Report, in *Report BofG*, 1931–32, 32.

39 Peel, *History* 1979, 3, 6.

40 Robert Newton, "I Passed this Way, 1889–1964+," 201–202 (UAA 71-87); *cf.* Johns, *A History*, 105, where after recounting this incident, Johns noted that, "Dr. Tory's word was law...." Appropriately, the Cameron Library was built on the site claimed by Mr Cameron in 1928. Plant Pathology's West Lab was demolished in 1966 to make way for the new Student Union Building (SUB).

41 C.S. Burgess, Memoranda, "UofA Library Plan," 3 December 1928 (UAA 68-1-3/2/5/5-1). Cecil Scott Burgess (1870–1971) left McGill to supervise building construction at the University of Alberta, and remained as resident architect and professor of architecture in the Faculty of Applied Science. Following his retirement in 1940, architecture was permanently dropped from the curriculum.

42 Alexander, *The University of Alberta*, 29; R.C. Wallace, President's Annual Report, in *Report BofG*, 1928–29, 55.

43 Wallace, President's Annual Report, in *Report BofG*, 1929–30, 59; ibid., in *Report BofG*, 1930–31, 52.

44 Cameron to Wallace, 12 February 1930 (UAA 68-1-3/2/5/5-1); Cameron, Librarian's Annual Report, in *Report BofG*, 1931–32, 32; "Nucleus of New Group U. of M. Buildings to be Constructed," *The Gateway* (3 October 1931): 7.

45 "Proposed Library Association for the Province of Alberta, and Proposed Conference on Library Service," 1 March 1930 (UAA 68-1-7); "Alberta Library Delegates Hold Successful Conference Here," *The Gateway* (19 December 1930): 2, 9, 10; Cameron to Wallace, 1 March,

30 October, and 12 December 1930 (UAA 68-1-3/2/5/5-1).

46 "Some Library Suggestions," *The Gateway* (19 December 1930): 4.

47 Johns, *A History*, 123–124; see also correspondence with Carnegie Corporation (UAA 68-1-3/2/5/5-1), including a five-page reply of 3 February 1932 to the Carnegie Corp.'s "Request for Information" in connection with the application for a library grant, that provides an informative summary of the University and Library's staffing, budget, and library policies.

48 Wallace, President's Annual Report, in *Report BofG*, 1933-34, 30. Instead of the desired library building, the $50,000 Carnegie grant was used for faculty and student research, travel, and publication grants, as well as "for apparatus and books needed for research" (ibid.; see also Johns, *A History*, 124).

49 L.L.A. [Larry Alexander], "Brief History of the University, 1929–1950," *The Gateway* (5 December 1929): 5; "Faculty Makes Daring Admission," *The Gateway* (13 February 1931): 1. Sixteen years later, another student editor reprinted Larry Alexander's humorous chronology without comment (*The Gateway* [26 October 1945]: 6).

50 B.D., "U.B.C. and U. of A.– A Contrast," *The Gateway* (17 February 1933): 5. Total seating capacity of the University of Alberta Library's several branches as reported to the Carnegie Corporation in 1932 was 225 (UAA 68-1-3/2/5/5-1).

51 "Thoughts of a Reader," *The Gateway* (16 October 1934): 2.

52 Murray Bolton, "University Library Has Six Branches: Sixty Thousand Volumes Listed: Periodicals and Scientific Journals on Shelves," *The Gateway* (17 December 1936): 9. Efforts to improve the frequently criticized ventilation in the Arts Building Library, though largely unavailing, included the trial installation of a Kelvinator Corozone ozone converter in the autumn of 1930: "The Corozone is a simple electrical device

that converts ordinary oxygen into ozone. Ozone is a revitalized zestful form of oxygen surcharged with abundant energy....the instant it collides with tobacco smoke or the thousand odours that daily plague us it oxidizes them–literally burns them up. The ozonized air becomes pure, and charged with the breath of life" ("Corozone Placed in Library: Long-felt Need Finally Satisfied–Treat to Watch Students Inhaling Ozone," *The Gateway* [30 October 1930]: 1). Results of this experiment are unrecorded, but a year later a *Gateway* editorial expressed amazement at students' apparent zeal for studying, and noted that "The library, once the abode of the élite, the refuge of the exclusive, is now crowded by the vulgar throng" (M., "This Studying," *The Gateway* [27 November 1931]: 5).

53 Schoeck, *I Was There*, 271; "The Common Rooms," *The Gateway* (1 December 1936): 2.

54 "University Library Performs Increasingly Large Function," *The Gateway* (16 November 1937): 3; "No Room in Library Since Registration," *The Gateway* (5 October 1937): 1.

55 "Three Decades of Progress," *The Gateway* (16 December 1937): 4.

56 Alex Cairns, "Reporters Track Down Castles in the Air: Approach Dr. Wallace on Student Union Building Question: Library Needed," *The Gateway* (18 October 1935): 2; *cf.* "The President...said that what was wanted at Alberta was a smaller edition of [Toronto's] 'Hart House,' and he stated that unquestionably the University would some day have such a building" ("Students' Union Building Finds Favour: President Favours Idea of Students' Union Building: Suggests that Students Start Fund and Later Secure Outside Assistance," *The Gateway* [8 February 1935]: 1). In 1920–1921, escalating costs of the new medical building led to postponement of plans drawn up by C.S. Burgess for both a student union building and a gymnasium with swimming pool ("History of the Gymnasium Project," *The Gateway* [3 October

1930]: 1). A Student Union building, now known as University Hall, was finally completed in 1950.

57 "Thoughts of a Reader," *The Gateway* (16 October 1934): 2; "'We Protest'," *The Gateway* (11 February 1936): 2; R.F. Brey to the editor, *The Gateway* (14 February 1936): 3; D.E. Cameron, Librarian's Annual Report, in *Report BofG, 1934–35*, 23; D.E. Cameron, Librarian's Annual Report, in *Report BofG, 1938–39*, 30. As a further space-saving measure, steel shelving was purchased to replace wooden units, until war-time restrictions halted its manufacture (D.E. Cameron, Librarian's Annual Report, in *Report BofG, 1937–38*, 33, and *1941–42*, 33).

58 "Faculty Jottings: German Library," *The Gateway* (16 November 1928): 6; Cameron to Wallace, 24 December 1929 (UAA 68-1-3/2/5/5-1); D.E. Cameron, Librarian's Annual Report, in *Report BofG, 1932–33*, 40. Later, Gourlay became Librarian of the Edmonton Public Library.

59 "Varsity Library in Possession Rare Books: 55,000 Volumes and 500 Periodicals Form Tremendous Bulk for Local Library," *The Gateway* (6 December 1935): 1. "Rare Books" in the title is rather misleading, as the first paragraph of text made clear. More than three decades would pass before a library school was founded at the University.

60 Bolton, "University Library has Six Branches"; "Varsity Library in Possession Rare Books."

61 "University Library Performs Increasingly Large Function." That small Paracelsus volume is now in the Health Sciences Library.

62 "Library Fund Gets Donation," *The Gateway* (27 October 1939): 1; D.E. Cameron, "Byways For Bookworms," *The Gateway* (5 October 1937): 2 (reprinted from *The Canadian Student*).

63 Blackburn, "Reminiscences," 4; Blackburn, "University of Alberta," 10.

64 Cameron, Librarian's Annual Report, in *Report BofG, 1931–32*, 31. Cost estimates for the renovation totalled a mere $745, exclusive of shelving (Cameron to Wallace, "Note on Sketch Plan for Library Storage,"

12 January 1933 [UAA 68-1-7]; Peel, *History* 1979, 8). Other library expansion schemes considered included building additions to the Med building and to the Power Plant, but these were dismissed as not cost effective (Cameron, [Memorandum] "Extension of Medical Building," 15 December 1933 [UAA 68-1-3/2/5/5-1]).

65 Cecil Burgess, "University of Alberta, Building for Library and Literary Classes. Scheme 20.2.31," 18 January 1934, and "...20.2.31. Memorandum of Accommodation Provided," 18 March 1934 [UAA 68-1-7]; D.E. Cameron, Librarian's Annual Report, in *Report BofG*, 1933–34, 24; D.E. Cameron, Librarian's Annual Report, in *Report BofG*, 1936–37, 21; D.E. Cameron, Librarian's Annual Report, in *Report BofG*, 1939–40, 32.

66 The fullest summary of the war's impact is to be found in Thomas, *The University of Alberta in the War of 1939–45*. See also Macleod, *All True Things*, chapter 8, and Johns, *History*, chapter 13.

67 D.E. Cameron to President Newton, 1 September 1942 and Newton to Cameron, 25 September 1942 (UAA 68-1-3/4/5/4-1). Cameron's request for a leave from the same day as the date of his letter suggests that such requests were largely pro forma. Only in later years did Margaret (Peggy) O'Connor Farnell reveal that her "confidential" employment was with British Intelligence's western hemisphere branch run by Sir William ("Man Called Intrepid") Stephenson; much later still she recorded her experiences in a self-published memoir, *Mummy Was a Spy* (Edmonton, 1996).

68 D.E. Cameron to President Newton, 3 March 1943, and Newton to Cameron, 5 March 1943 (UAA 68-1-3/4/5/4-1).

69 D.E. Cameron, Librarian's Annual Report, in *Report BofG*, 1939–40, 32; D.E. Cameron, Librarian's Annual Report, in *Report BofG*, 1940–41, 30.

70 D.E. Cameron, Librarian's Annual Report, in *Report BofG*, 1941–42, 33. Prior to December

1941, while the United States remained neutral, imported publications from Europe could be redirected and delivered to addresses there.

71 D.E. Cameron, Librarian's Annual Report, in *Report BofG*, 1942–43, 36. The following year, Cameron reported having made little progress on this worthy project, "owing to lack of space" (D.E. Cameron, Librarian's Annual Report, in *Report BofG*, 1943–44, 44).

72 D.E. Cameron, Librarian's Annual Report, in *Report BofG*, 1944–45, 39–40. Alvan Sherlock Mathers was a founding partner of the firm of Mathers & Haldenby, who, with their sons Douglas Haldenby and Andrew Mathers, later designed Canada's National Library and the then ultramodern Robarts Library complex at the University of Toronto.

73 Johns, *A History*, 211.

74 Newton to Manning, quoted in Johns, *A History*, 223, *cf.* 190, 211, 224; Newton, President's Annual Report, in *Report BofG*, 1944–45, 12. At the same time, the President acknowledged the retirement, following 32 years of service, of Miss Jessie Montgomery, the Department of Extension's first librarian. That same month the *Edmonton Journal* (17 May 1945) announced the appointment of Miss Flora Mcleod as Extension Department Librarian; see also *The New Trail* 3, no. 3 (July 1945): 170.

75 Newton, Memo: "Conf[erence] with Mr. D.E. Cameron, 5.2.45" (UAA 68-1-3/4/5/4-1). Miss Clever was then on leave to complete a bachelor of education degree.

76 Marjorie Sherlock, Librarian's Annual Report, in *Report BofG*, 1945–46, 49; "Former Librarian: Mr. D.E. Cameron," *The Gateway* (18 October 1946): 1.

77 "Donald Cameron, Former Librarian, Dies on Saturday," *The Gateway* (22 October 1946): 1. Henry Marshall Tory's death at Ottawa, on 6 February 1947, followed Cameron's by only three and one-half months.

78 Calhoun to Newton, 13 January 1945 (UAA 68-1-3/4/5/4-2). Miss Sherlock had, for a brief

period, been employed by Calhoun at the Calgary Public Library.

79 Newton to Calhoun, 6 February 1945; Calhoun to Newton, 8 February 1945 (ibid.).

80 Letters of application, search committee candidate assessment notes, and other related correspondence (ibid.). Mr Thomas Barcus, University Librarian at Saskatchewan, withdrew his application upon accepting a position at the Library of Congress in Washington, DC. David Appelt left his cataloguer's post at the University of Alberta to succeed Barcus at Saskatchewan, where he served as that university's chief librarian for nearly three decades. Miss Flora McLeod was, indeed, appointed Extension Librarian.

81 Assessment notes and minutes of the search committee, 14 April 1945 (ibid.). Bruce Peel believed that Cameron had groomed David Appelt to succeed him (see Jobb, "Biography of a Librarian," 19). However, the search committee's minutes reveal that Cameron deemed Marjorie Sherlock and University of Western Ontario's James Talman the best qualified candidates. Some of the comments recorded on the assessment notes would give today's human resources officers apoplexy, e.g., "Dismissed for drinking," "Does not practice religion in any established form [but] not anti-religious," and "Physically handicapped – slightly lame."

82 "Librarian has Varied Career," *The Gateway* (12 October 1945): 5. See also Freifield, "Marjorie Sherlock Grayson-Smith" and Peel, "Miss Sherlock," 5–6, 8; Wendy McDonald, "Had Successful Librarian's Career: Mrs. H. Grayson-Smith," *The Gateway* (28 October 1955): 11.

83 Newton, President's Annual Report, in *Report BofG*, 1945–46, 11–12. Somewhat lower enrolment figures were cited by Samuel in "An Early History," (Spring 1954): 186–187.

84 Marjorie Sherlock, Librarian's Annual Report, in *Report BofG*, 1945–46, 49. Miss Sherlock's annual reports generally contained considerably more detailed statistics than those of her predecessor.

85 Marjorie Sherlock, Librarian's Annual Report, in *Report BofG*, 1946–47, 46–47. The need for this change was obvious as early as 1928, when Donald Cameron was driven to ask the Board of Governors for a grievance hearing arising from his dissatisfaction over his rank and salary, compared with what he had originally been promised upon appointment (Cameron to President Wallace, 26 November and 7 December 1928 [UAA 68-1-3/2/5/5-1]).

86 Sherlock, "The Role," 62–63. Miss Sherlock's other great achievements were the conversion of the Library's catalogue from the Cutter to the Library of Congress classification, and the creation of the Rutherford (now Rutherford South) Library.

87 Sherlock to Newton, 14 March 1946 (UAA 68-1-3/4/5/4-1).

Library Salary Schedule Effective 1 April 1946

Librarian	$3500–4500	Miss Sherlock	$3600
Assistant Librarian	2700–3300	(Yet to be appointed)	
Reference Librarian	2000–2600	Miss Hamilton	2000
Chief Cataloguer	2000–2600	Miss Farquharson	2000
Circulation Librarian	2000–2600	(Yet to be appointed)	
Senior Assistant Librarian	1800–2000	(Yet to be appointed)	
Junior Assistant Librarian	1400–1700	Miss Freifield (Circulation)	1600
		Miss Giffen (Med Library)	1600
		Miss Nancekivell (Orders)	1500
		Miss Leversedge (Cat/Circ)	1400
Non-prof. graduates	1200– 1400	Mrs Lillian Gue (Assistant & typist)	1200

Annual increments were initially set at $200.

88 Quoted in Jobb, "Biography of a Librarian," 24–26. Post-war inflation soon stimulated

the movement to unionize among university support staff, so the academic recognition and improved salary scales for the University of Alberta's librarians was most timely in helping Alberta resist that trend (see Macleod, *All True Things*, 151–153). By 1951 the salary schedule for librarians, by then classed in ranks labelled from I to V, had risen by nearly 60 percent in only five years.

89   The first North American university to do so was Columbia in 1911; Illinois did so in 1946, the same year as Alberta. Still far from being universal, by the 1990s only 79 percent of North American universities had done so, and the precise definition and privileges conferred thereby varied widely (see Sanders, "Faculty Status").

90   Peel, "Miss Sherlock," 6; see also Freifield, "Marjorie Sherlock Grayson-Smith." Prof. Glyde received no remuneration for the mural, but obtained $650 to pay for three summer student assistants, paint, and other supplies (Board of Governors minutes, 21 March 1950, 59 [UAA 71-164-12]).

91   Quoted in Jobb, "Biography of a Librarian," 31–32; I.F. Morrison to Newton, 16 February 1946 (UAA 68-1-3/4/5/4-1).

92   Dean R.D. Sinclair to Newton, 30 April 1948; Newton, "Branch Libraries," memo to self, 29 April 1948, initialled by WHJ[ohns], May 5/48 (UAA 68-1-3/4/5/4-1).

93   Newton to Sherlock, 21 February and 14 April 1949; Sherlock to Newton, 11 March 1949; minutes of meeting to discuss use of Library 3rd floor, 4-page typescript, 11 March 1949 (UAA 68-1-3/4/5/4-1). The walls of the third floor gallery space were covered with wood sheathing and burlap, for the sake of hanging pictures, at an additional cost of $1500 (Board of Governors minutes, 21 March 1950, 59 [UAA 71-164-12]). The University of Alberta Archives was not formally established until 1968.

94   Salaries and benefits for new staff positions were projected at $25,000, additional binding of books and journals at $2,000, and building

maintenance and janitorial service at $33,000 (MS Presidential memo, "The additional cost of maintaining the Library in its new quarters," 9-12-50 [UAA 68-1-3/5/5/6-1]).

95   Newton to Sherlock, 20 June 1950, quoting Board of Governors' minutes of 16 June 1950; Sherlock to Newton, 23 June 1950 (UAA ibid.).

96   Sherlock to Stewart, 22 November 1950 (UAA ibid.). The branch libraries in question were Agriculture, Chemistry, Law, Medicine and Dentistry, Mining, Nursing, and the Research Council. The deposit collections were primarily located in Botany, Engineering, Genetics, Geology, Pharmacy, Plant Pathology, and Soils Science, while "various smaller collections [existed] all over Campus, signed out by faculty members."

97   Minutes of the Library Committee, 20 December 1950 (UAA ibid.). Those "views" amounted to special pleadings on behalf of various departments eager to retain their local collections that filled five pages of typed minutes. Scheduling the meeting less than a week before Christmas at 4:30 p.m. served to limit the proceedings to a mere 90 minutes.

98   Stewart to Deans, Directors, and Heads of Departments, 2 April 1951; O.J. Walker to Stewart, 11 September 1951 (UAA ibid.).

99   *The Gateway*, quoted in Schoeck, *I Was There*, 327; Peel, *History* 1979, 11; Johns, *A History*, 229–230 and note. The cornerstone was found resting behind St Stephen's College ("Library Ceremony Conducted Thursday: Stolen Cornerstone Recovered in Time," *The Gateway* [26 November 1948]: 1; *cf.* "To Lay New Library Corner Stone Thurs.: Lieut.-Gov., Premier to Officiate at Ceremony," *The Gateway* [19 November 1948]: 1, and "Students May Attend Library Ceremony Thurs.," *The Gateway* [23 November 1948]: 1).

100 Transcription in UAA First Facts Reference File: "Rutherford Library"; "New Rutherford Library Said Best on Continent," *The Gateway* (25 September 1951): 5. *Cf.* "A Preview," *The Gateway* (17 October 1950): 3.

101 "Special Materials Contribute to Beauty: Oak Featured in Woodwork," *The Gateway* (23 November 1956): 7. The lovely bronze balustrades with acanthus leaf motif, which some thought "an over-ornate design," were substituted for the wrought-iron ones originally specified in the plans because of the general, post-war shortage of iron and steel (W.J. Johns, minutes of Rutherford Library Advisory Committee, 6 January 1950 and MS memo on the balustrades by President Newton, 9 January 1950 [UAA 68-1-3/5/5/6-1]).

102 Sherlock, "The Role," 63–64. Law students were upset to find that smoking in the new library was confined to a designated "smoking room" and to the music room ("All About Rutherford," *The Gateway* [23 November 1951]: 2 and "Music Room Pleasant Spot to Relax, Smoke," *The Gateway* [30 October 1951]: 3).

103 Jobb, "Biography of a Librarian," 18, 30.

104 Sherlock, MS memo [1950], Library Committee minutes and correspondence (UAA 90-148-2).

105 Peel, *History* 1979, 14; Library Committee minutes, 26 April 1951, esp. 4–5, Stewart to Dr H. Rawlinson [Medicine] 27 April 1951 inviting him to serve on the expanded Committee, and Rawlinson to Stewart, 1 May 1951, accepting the invitation, and expressing complete confidence in Miss Sherlock (UAA 68-1-3/5/5/6-1).

106 Library Sub-Committee minutes, 12 July 1951 (UAA ibid.). The other members of the initial Sub-Committee were G.W. Govier (Engineering), H. Rawlinson (Medicine), and O.J. Walker (Chemistry).

107 Sherlock to Stewart, 24 September 1951; Stewart to Sherlock, 26 September 1951 (UAA ibid.).

108 "Resolution of the Library Sub-Committee and Memorandum re Reclassification of University Library," Sherlock to Stewart, 22 and 31 March, 3 April 1952 (UAA 68-1-3/5/5/6-2).

109 Jobb, "Biography of a Librarian," 32–33; Stewart to Sherlock, 7 April 1952 and Sherlock to Stewart, 9 April 1952 (UAA ibid.). In his letter, President Stewart added a cautionary note that the extra personnel "will not be considered library staff," and "cannot expect to be transferred to the permanent Library staff." McGill University Library retained the Cutter system well into the 1960s, an era of massive collection building, and exemplified Miss Sherlock's dire predictions of the escalating cost of delaying LC conversion.

110 "Reclassify 100,000 books at University's New Library," *Edmonton Journal* (24 July 1953): 1, 4; "Book Reclassification Causes Little Hardship," *The Gateway* (15 October 1953): 4; Sherlock, "Report of the Chief Librarian to the President, 1953–54" [typescript version], 29 April 1954 (UAA 68-1-3/5/1/2-24); Peel, *History* 1979, 14; Jobb, "Biography of a Librarian," 33. An additional $9,000 was required to complete the initial reclassification project.

111 Sherlock, "Survey of the Budgetary Needs of the Library for Books, Periodicals, and Binding, April, 1953"; Sherlock to Stewart, 31 January, 12 February, and 31 March 1953; Stewart to Sherlock, 10 February 1953; Stewart to Sherlock, 22 April 1953 (UAA 68-1-3/5/5/6-2). Student Library Fees were then covering 40 percent of the cost of periodical subscriptions.

112 Sherlock to Newton, 11 February 1947; Sherlock to John Macdonald, Dean of Arts and Sciences and Acting President, 14 July 1948 (UAA 68-1-3/4/5/4-1). Two days later, President Newton replied that the Executive Committee of the Board of Governors approved the purchase of Rowan's books for $1,038, to be paid from the Library's reserve funds.

113 Library Sub-Committee, "Apportioning Book Funds Based on Evidence of Book Need and Cost of Materials," 4 (UAA 68-1-3/5/1/4-24).

114 W.A.R. Kerr to R.B. Bennett, 23 April 1938; *cf.* Kerr to Bennett 10 and 19 February 1938; Bennett to Kerr, 14 February and 15 March

1938; Cameron to Kerr, 21 February 1939; Rutherford to Kerr, 8 March 1938; Stanley McCuaig to Kerr, 29 March 1938; Kerr to McCuaig, 12 April 1938 (UAA 68-1-3/3/5/6-1); "Old West in Rare Book Room," *The Gateway* (25 February 1955): 6.

115 Newton to Sherlock, 23 June 1947; Walter Johns, "Memorandum on Rutherford Collection of Books," reporting a meeting with Cecil Rutherford and D.F. Hunter, University Purchasing Agent, n.d. [January 1950]; Hunter to Newton, "Rutherford Collection," [January 1950]; Johns to Newton, 25 January 1950 (UAA 68-1-3/4/5/4-1). The appraiser was Toronto bookseller Dora Hood, who was recommended by Prof. W. Stewart Wallace, Librarian of the University of Toronto (Dora Hood to Sherlock, 28 July 1949; Johns to Hunter 25 March 1950; Sherlock to Johns, 28 April 1950; Inventory of the Rutherford books; Johns to Sherlock, 29 April 1950 [UAA 68-1-3/5/5/6-1]).

116 Jobb, "Biography of a Librarian, 34–35.

117 Peel, "Miss Sherlock," 8; quoted in Jobb, "Biography of a Librarian," 90–91; Peel, *History* 1979, 14; see also McDonald, "Had Successful Librarian's Career," *The Gateway* (28 October 1955): 11.

118 "Rutherford Library Offers Many Facilities," *The Gateway* (24 February 1956): 9; Ted Young, "New Device Reproduces Printed Material Quickly," *The Gateway* (14 January 1955): 4.

119 "Esther Halstein, "Rutherford Library Vital: 160,000 Volumes for Students," *The Gateway* (23 November 1956): 6; Peel *History* 1979, 15; see also McCalla, *Development of Graduate Studies*, 31-32. Mr Peel summarized these trends in Jobb, "Biography of a Librarian," chapter 3, "The Great Leap Forward: 1957 to 1967," 37–41, passim.

120 Library Sub-Committee minutes, 29 November 1956, 1; see also 1, 8, and 22 November, and 7 and 13 December 1956 (UAA 90-148-7).

121 Library Committee minutes, 24 October 1958 (UAA 90-148-2). A motion that adequate staffing be provided in the expanded library was also passed (Library Sub-Committee minutes, 14 October 1959 [UAA 90-148-8]; "Library Doubles Book Content in Ten Years," *The Gateway* (4 December 1959): 3; Bill Samis, "30,000 New Books, 5,500 New Acres, 1,000 New Students, and One New Building," *The Gateway* (3 February 1961): 1.

122 Library Sub-Committee minutes, 8 March 1960 (UAA 90-148-8); Reg Jordan, "Supermarket Style Library Proposed," *The Gateway* (21 October 1960): 1.

123 Jordan, "Supermarket Style Library"; Library Committee minutes, 10 August 1960 and 6 December 1961, emphasis added (UAA 90-148-2). The North Labs building was designated "temporary" when it opened in 1919.

124 Library Sub-Committee minutes, 8 March, 2 June, and 9 September 1960 (UAA 90-148-8); Library Committee minutes, 5 April 1961 (UAA 90-148-2); Jobb, "Biography of a Librarian," 53–54. The chemists continued to complain that too many journals had been retained in the central library (Library Committee minutes, 6 December 1961 [UAA 90-148-2]). The "Phys-Sci" Reading Room was finally closed more than 40 years later, when internet access to science journals had usurped its role.

125 Samis, "30,000 New Books"; "Library Smoking Room Will Give Way to Books," *The Gateway* (1 December 1961): 1, *cf.* issues for 27 January, 3 and 23 February, 17 March, and 24 November 1961. Seven years earlier, smoking, especially by law students, and cigarette litter in the lobby of the Rutherford Library, led to a smoking ban enforced with fines. As a compromise with the law students, "who need to discuss cases," the "no talking" rule was lifted in the smoking room, and smoking permitted in the music room (Library Sub-Committee minutes, 25 November and 15 December 1954, Sherlock to Sub-Committee, 10 December 1954 [UAA 68-1-3/5/1/4-24]; "Rotunda Smoking Favored," *The Gateway* [7

January 1955]: 1; "Many Students Find Serious Faults in Library–Gateway Investigates," *The Gateway* [23 November 1951]: 1; "All About Rutherford," *The Gateway* [23 November 1951]: 2). With the exception of the old Law Reading Room, Rutherford was the first library on campus to offer any accommodation for smokers; *cf.* E. Lekshun, "No Smoking," *The Gateway* (20 March 1926): 5.

126 Peel to Members of Teaching Departments, "Schedule of moves to the new Cameron Library," 18 November 1963 (UAA 69-123-694.1); Peel *History* 1979, 16, 18–19; *The Gateway* (24 September, 18 October, 19 and 22 November, and 13 December 1963); "Library Built for Additions," *Edmonton Journal* (25 November 1963): 35. In the end, Cameron Library cost more than $3 million.

127 Ian Pitfield, "SUB Plans to Run Gauntlet," *The Gateway* (11 October 1963): 1; Valerie Mae Becker, "Cameron Library Idle, Transfer Complete Soon," *The Gateway* (18 October 1963): 8; "Geraniums and Architecture," *The Gateway* (8 October 1963): 4; Lawrence Samuel, "Survey Finds Majority Dislike New Library," *The Gateway* (22 November 1963): 9; David Estrin, "Plan for Aesthetic Architecture Does Exist–Must Consider Costs," *The Gateway* (15 November 1963): 3. Students soon began referring to Cameron as the "Bronze Pagoda."

128 D.M. Ross to Johns, 22 April 1964; Johns to Ross, 24 April 1964; Peel to Ross, 28 April 1964; Ross to Peel, 30 April 1964 (UAA 69-123-696). Prof. Ross backed down graciously, but nonetheless asked that Library usage figures be supplied to the General Faculties Council. The open-plan Cameron building was deemed more suitable than the Rutherford building for housing the graduate research library because it placed readers in closer proximity to the collections (Peel, *Program for Library Service on the Edmonton Campus of the University of Alberta [With Special Reference to the New Research Library]*, June 1961, 1).

129 Bruce Peel, "Book Fines," *The Gateway* (10 January 1965): 5. *Cf. The Gateway* for Larry Krywaniuk, "Many Feel Book Fines 'Bad Idea'," (24 January 1964): 1; "Library Fines Start in October" (29 September 1964): 2; "High Library Fine to Penalize Students Hoarding Overdue Books" (6 October 1964): 2; see also Peel, *Report of the University Librarian*, 1965–1966 and 1966–1967. Library fines, a form of "voluntary tax," continued to yield annual revenues of six figures, and to stir controversy ("Library Fine Reduction Urged," *The Gateway* [15 February 1973]: 1).

130 Library Committee minutes, 6 December 1961 (UAA 90-148-1/1-2). The first incumbents were Mr Sidney Harland, later Chief Librarian of the University of Regina, responsible for Public Services, and Mr Donald Baird, later Chief Librarian at Simon Fraser University, responsible for Technical Services.

131 Peel to Armstrong, 2 August 1963, forwarding E.E. Williams, Harvard University, to Peel, 29 July 1963, and three telegrams from prospective candidates (UAA 69-123-696); Library Committee minutes, 24 May 1966 and Appendix A: "Selection Librarian" job description (UAA 90-148-3); Johns to Peel, 20 January and 31 March 1965 (UAA 69-123-696); Peel, *History* 1979, 28. The post of Coordinator was filled until her retirement in 1980 by Ms Norma Freifield.

132 Ralph Melnychuk, "Lack of Space Hurts Library: Needed Additions to Cameron Delayed at least Two Years," *The Gateway* (26 January 1966): 1; "U of A Enrolment Rapidly Outrunning Library Facilities," *The Gateway* (2 December 1966): 3; Library Committee minutes, 8 August 1967, 28 February, and 13 March 1968 (UAA 90-148-4); Academic Development Committee minutes, 20 March 1968 (UAA 80-91-1). Dr Gunning was disdainful of the need for an adequate central library facility after his department obtained a separate library in 1961.

133 Peel, "North Garneau Library: Programme for the Construction of a Library Building Complex to be the Central Library and House the Humanities and Social Sciences

Collection: A Research Library East of
112th Street, Revised Draft, September 20,
1967." The final version, dated 2 June 1968,
envisaged a four-phase project to create
613,460 square feet of net space (UAA
99-2 Box 13); see also "Cameron Expansion
Imminent," *The Gateway* (26 January 1968):
11 and Glenn Cheriton, "Cameron Cheaper
than Figured," *The Gateway* (11 October 1968):
16. The south façade of the Cameron building
still retains its 'temporary' cladding.

134   Library Committee minutes, 15 March,
5 April, and 6 September 1966 (UAA 90-
148-3); Peel to B.E. Riedel and J.R.B. Jones,
12 September 1966 (UAA 69-123-696). Mr
Peel noted that 175,000 volumes would
require 17,500 square feet of conventional
bookstack accommodation, while 7500
square feet would be needed to accommodate
60 additional library staff. The Extension
Library then occupied 7500 square feet in the
Rutherford Library.

135   Peel to Johns, 5 May 1966 (UAA 69-123-694.1).

Budgets for Fiscal Year 1966–1967

Library	Salaries	Acquisitions	Binding	Supplies	Instit. budget	% for library
Alberta	$1.025M	$971,000	$116,000	$76,000	$35M	6.3
BC	1.382M	1,250,000	55,509	61,219	28.876M	9.8
Toronto	2.299M	965,000	100,000	219,158	N/A	N/A
McGill	1.006M	508,325	47,250	52,065	28.348M	5.7

136   McCalla, *Development of Graduate Studies*,
1–3, passim; Macleod, *All True Things*, 180.
Dr Gunning began campaigning to keep
the Library open a minimum of 16 hours a
day, seven days a week. He also revived the
decade-old demand for a separate chemistry
library (Library Committee minutes, 28
October 1958 [UAA 90-148-2]).

137   Library Committee minutes, 29 October
1959, 27 November 1962, and 27 February
1964 (UAA 90-148-2).

138   These developments are summarized in
Macleod, *All True Things*, 190–194.

139   Library Committee minutes, 27 February
1964 (UAA 90-148-2); Peel to Johns, 3
February 1964, Johns to Peel, 6 February

1964, Parr to Johns, 27 February 1964, Johns
to Parr, 3 March 1964 (UAA 69-123-697).
Donald Baird's appointment as University
Librarian at Simon Fraser University was also
announced at the February 1964 meeting.

140   Peel to Johns, 16 March 1964; Johns to Peel, 18
March 1964; Armstrong to Johns, 30 March
1964; Johns to Armstrong, 1 April 1964; [Peel],
"Reorganization of Library Committees,
University of Alberta," 14 April 1964; Johns to
Peel, 24 April 1964 (UAA ibid.).

141   [Ex GFC minutes], "REPORT OF THE
COMMITTEE ON RECONSTITUTION OF
THE LIBRARY COMMITTEE," September
1964, [MS.Note: "GFC passed Nov 25/64"],
emphasis added; Bowker to Johns, 2
December 1964 (UAA ibid.).

142   McCalla to Peel, 13 May 1964; Kreisel to Johns,
21 May 1964, copies to Peel and Hanson;
Johns to Kreisel, 2 June 1964 (UAA 69-123-
694.1).

143   McCalla "Confidential" to Johns, 27 May
1964; Hanson "Confidential" to Johns, 29 May
1964, emphasis added (UAA 1-123-694.1).
Ironically, Dean McCalla registered his
irritation when colleagues raised objections
based on practices in other universities,
and, moreover, had nothing to say about the
role of the Library and its collections in his
relentlessly statistical work, *Development of
Graduate Studies*, 42.

144   Johns "Confidential" to McCalla, 12 June 1964;
Johns to Hanson, 12 June 1964 (UAA 69-123-
694.1).

145   Hanson to Johns, 29 July 1964, emphasis
added (UAA ibid.).

146   Ibid.

147   *To all Members of Staff and Student
Representatives: Announcement of Review of
Policies by the New Library Committee*, March
1965; *Library Requirements in the Decade
Ahead: A Report by the Library Committee*,
November 1965 (UAA 81-54-69); Jobb,
"Biography of a Librarian," 65–66. The "poet
with imagination" was Elias Mandel; the
"economist" was Eric Hanson.

148 Jobb," Biography of a Librarian," 69; Peel to Johns, 26 April 1965 (UAA 69-123-1013).

149 Johns to Hanson, 19 April 1965; *cf.* Hanson to Johns 5 April 1965 (UAA 69-123-694.1). Eric Hanson reported that some of the Board's reluctance stemmed from Calgary's decision not to participate (Library Committee minutes, 23 June 1965 [UAA 90-148-3]).

150 The other members of the team were Dr Robert Downs (University of Illinois), Father Paul-Émile Filion (Laurentian University), and Professor Peter Russell (University of Toronto). Funding was provided by the Canada Council and the American Council on Library Resources (C.G. Andrew, Executive Director AUCC, to Johns, 25 January 1966, Johns to Andrew, 28 January 1966, Peel to Johns, 10 February 1966 [UAA 69-123-696]; "Press Release / Communiqué: Study of Canadian Academic Libraries," 25 July 1966 [UAA 69-123-694.1]; see also Peel to Johns, 12 August 1966, 9 January 1967, 11 January [but dated December] 1967, as well as Johns to Peel, 18 August 1966, 10 January, and 7 February 1967 [UAA 71-101-205.1]).

151 "University Professional Librarians Group, Brief to Library Consultants" [Resolution of 20 December 1965 meeting of Librarians to discuss the November 1965 report of the University of Alberta Library Committee] (UAA 69-123-694.2); Library Committee minutes, 7 December 1965 (UAA 90-148-3); Jobb,"Biography of a Librarian," 67–68. The revised University Act, which took effect in April 1966, provided for a restructured General Faculties Council, which itself recommended the inclusion of the University Librarian *ex officio* and two other librarians elected by their peers (Johns, *History,* 443). A decade later, rank-and-file librarians were still seeking seats on GFC ("Librarians Ask for Representation," *The Gateway* [15 November 1973]: 3). Mr Peel appears to have been excluded when the Library Committee met to brief the consultants (Library Committee minutes, 9 January 1966 [UAA 90-148-3]).

152 Stephen McCarthy and Richard Logsdon, "Survey of the University of Alberta Libraries, [March] 1966," Preliminary chapter, 8, and Main report, 6–7, 9 (UAA 69-83-1). This initial draft copy bears Bruce Peel's handwritten annotations, including this note on the cover: "Draft report by the consultants received about March. This report was considered unacceptable by the Library Committee and consequently a change in tone etc. will be noticed in the final draft. Bruce Peel." For the revised final draft of the report see UAA 81-54-69.

153 Johns, "Memorandum on 'Survey of the University of Alberta Libraries'," 13 July 1966, Hanson to Johns, 14 July 1966, Johns to Hanson, 15 July 1966, McCarthy to Johns, 26 July 1966 (UAA 69-123-694.2); Library Committee minutes, 15, 22, and 29 March, 5 April, and 5 July 1966 (UAA 90-148-3); Peel, *Report of the University Librarian to the President, 1965–66,* 6; ibid., *1966–67,* 6–8; Peel to Johns, 9 March 1967 (UAA 71-101-205.1). Mr Geoffrey Turner was promoted to the position of Associate University Librarian; Mr Rod Banks, whose background was accounting, was transferred from the University's Data Processing Centre to serve as the Library business officer (Library Committee minutes, 27 January 1967 [UAA 90-148-3]; Jobb, "Biography of a Librarian," 46). The Library Committee approved an estimate of $85,000 to cover the purchase of all American scholarly books in 1967–1968 (Library Committee minutes [UAA 90-148-3]). Following the bankruptcy of the Richard Abel Company in the early 1970s, John Coutts Library Services, a Canadian firm, acquired the American contract.

154 Peel, "The Library Committee at the University of Alberta: Considerations and Recommendations of the Librarian," 3 October 1966, Library Committee, 1966–72 (UAA 89-10-1); Library Committee minutes, 6 December 1966, emphasis added, 21 February 1967, and Appendix A, "University Library

Committee Terms of Reference" (UAA 90-148-3).

155 Peel to Johns, 11 December [sic, January] 1967 (UAA 71-101-205.1); Library Committee minutes, 11 October 1966 (UAA 90-148-3).

156 McCarthy-Logsdon Report, preliminary chapter, 8–10. The *entire* University operating budget for the Edmonton campus in 1966–1967 was only just over $27 million, and that of the newly independent Calgary campus (then still under the same Board of Governors) stood at $9.77 million (Johns, *History*, 450).

157 Peel, "Speculation on Developments to A.D. 2000 Affecting the Growth of the University of Alberta Library Book Collection," 20 September 1967 (UAA 77-25-88); Peel to Johns, 10 February 1967, Johns to Peel, 13 February 1967, Johns to McCalla, 15 February 1967 (UAA 71-101-205.1).

158 Johns to Peel, 27 July 1967; Peel to Johns, 26 July 1967 (UAA 71-101-205.1).

159 Assoc. Dean Eric Hanson had already left the Library Committee, after chairing his last meeting on 11 July. His successor, long-serving Library Committee member Prof. Henry Kreisel, chaired the next meeting on 25 July.

160 Johns "Personal and confidential" to Peel, 3 October 1967; Peel "Personal and confidential" to Johns, 6 October 1967 (UAA 71-101-205.1). Bruce Peel composed no memoirs *per se*, but did tell his biographer that during those frustrating years, when he was often tempted to resign, his friend and colleague Geoffrey Turner provided unfailing support, advice, and counsel: "So, I owed a great deal to Geoff" (Jobb, "Biography of a Librarian," 69).

161 Library Committee minutes, 28 June and 5 July 1966 (UAA 90-148-3); Hanson to Johns, 16 August, Johns to Hanson, 18 August 1966, A.D. Cairns, Registrar, on behalf of GFC/Executive, to Hanson, 22 September, Hanson to Cairns, 6 October 1966 (UAA 69-123-697).

162 Library Committee minutes, 15 and 30 August 1966 and "Appendix A: Policy Statement on Library Decentralization"; 1 and 15 November 1966; 13 March, 24 April, and 26 June 1968; 8 May, 15 July, 10 September, and 20 October 1969; 1 June, 16 November, and 14 December 1970 (UAA 90-148-4).

163 This section is heavily indebted to University of Calgary Librarian Barbara Brydges, and her forthcoming article, "Older than it Looks: Origins of the University of Calgary Library." See also Macleod, *All True Things*, 181. President Johns was equivocal about projecting enrolment numbers: "I must confess I did not recall having agreed that an enrolment of 6000 in 1972 seemed a reasonable figure for U.A.C. on which planning might be based, but in a moment of weakness, I might have conceded this point" (Johns to C.E. Challice, 15 December 1959; *cf.* Library Committee University of Alberta at Calgary minutes, 10 December 1959 [UAA 68-1-2006]).

164 Malcolm Taylor to Johns, 10 April 1960; Johns to Taylor, 14 April 1960 (UAA 68-1-2006).

165 Peel to B.W. Brooker, 25 November 1959; Brooker to Peel, 30 November 1959; University of Alberta at Calgary, Library Committee minutes, 10 December 1959 (UAA 68-1-2006).

166 UAC Library Committee, "Report to the Faculty of Arts & Sciences," 21 January 1960, Taylor to Johns, 11 and 18 October 1963, Johns to E.W. Hinman, 18 October 1963 (UAA 68-1-2006 and UAA 69-123-1002); Brydges, passim; "Grant Given for Books," *The Gateway* (22 February 1963): 2.

167 Brydges, passim; "History of the Doucette Library," http://education.ucalgary.ca/doucette/History; Library Sub-Committee minutes, 7 December 1956 (UAA 90-148-7); Macleod, *All True Things*, 176–177, 192–193; "The Feasibility of Establishing a Medical School in the University of Alberta at Calgary, Private Report" (UAA 69-123-1044).

168 Peel to Johns, 21 March 1966; [BoG Agenda item], "Professional Librarians Salary Scale 1966-67," 3 December 1965 and Johns to Peel, 10 December 1965, announcing BoG approval of library salary scales for 1966–1967, thus: Grade 1: $5800–$6800; Grade 2: $6800–$7800; Grade 3: $7200-8200; Grade 4: $7800-$9800 (UAA 69-123-696).

169 Brundin, *From the Codex to the Computer*, 1–4; Jobb, "Biography of a Librarian," 58–59. Other members of the Coburn Committee were David Appelt (USaskatchewan), David Foley (UManitoba), and Bruce Peel. President Johns initially favoured supporting UBC's library program, but soon concurred that the local solution was preferable (Johns to Samuel Rothstein, Director, UBC Library School, 17 March 1964 [UAA 69-123-694.1]). Johns later expressed frustration over the difficulty of finding a director for the new Library School (Johns to Peel, 10 August 1966 [UAA 71-101-205.1]). Johns made it clear to the Library Committee that the Director would be a member of GFC and would report directly to him (Library Committee minutes, 11 October 1966 [UAA 90-148-3]).

170 Peel, *History* 1979, 23; Library Committee minutes, 3 January 1967 (UAA 90-148-3). In 1969 the Library produced a handsomely illustrated, 20-page *Staff Handbook*, complete with a glossary of library terminology, to aid in the seemingly endless task of providing orientation and training for new staff.

171 T. Kelly to R. Buck, 9 February; Peel to Kelly, 5 March and 26 April; Kelly to Peel, 8 April 1968 (UAA 71-101-205.1). President Johns then wrote to Mr Peel, "I have observed this exchange of views with great interest and I think you've made a very good case for the Library" (Johns to Peel, 2 May 1968 [UAA ibid.]).

172 Peel, *History* 1979, 20; Peel, *Speculation on Developments*, 20 September 1967; Ralph Brinsmead, "Costly Periodical Service, University Library Feature," *The Gateway*

(21 January 1954): 4; Jobb, "Biography of a Librarian," 43–44, 47.

173 Peel, *History* 1979, 20; Jobb, "Biography of a Librarian," 44–47. Library collections statistics can be confusing. Volumes (as opposed to titles) ordered, volumes received, and volumes catalogued in any given year usually need to be expressed as three different numbers. The figures given in this study include monographs and serials, but, unless otherwise stated, exclude government documents and microforms.

174 Quoted in Jobb, "Biography of a Librarian," 94–95; Peel, *History* 1979, 28. Reicher went on to head the library at Université de Montréal. Mr Olin Murray served as collections coordinator until his retirement in 1986, when the author was hired to succeed him.

175 Library Committee minutes, 27 February 1964 (UAA 90-149-2); Peel to Johns, 28 April 1964 (UAA 69-123-694.1). President Johns was moved to query the utility of spending $55,000 on the Salzburg Archiepiscopal library, although that sum represented only $16 a volume on average for 2768 titles in approximately 3500 volumes, with virtually no duplication of extant Library holdings (G. Hermansen to Johns, 7 and 10 December 1965; Johns to Hermansen, 8 December 1965 [UAA 69-123-697]); "The Salzburg Collection," *Library Editions* (Winter 1992): 5–7. For the Bunyan collection, see Peel to Library Sub-Committee, 27 April 1964, G.G. Turner to Johns, 20 November 1964, and Press Release, 23 November 1964 (UAA 69-123-694.1); "The Progress of a Rare Book Collection," *Library Editions* (Winter 1990): 2–6.

176 Library Committee minutes, 10 October 1967, 17 January, 14 February, 26 June, and 13 November 1968 (UAA 90-148-4); Lucinda Chodan, "Library Now Two Million Strong," *The Gateway* (10 October 1979): 17. Peel erred in recalling the final price of the Woods Collection as only $70,000. Had Gutteridge lost the bidding war, he was authorized to negotiate with California to purchase titles

that duplicated their holdings, apparently unaware of California's policy of routing duplicates around their multi-campus system.

177 Library Committee minutes, 2 and 16 March 1972 (UAA 90-140-5); Peel to department heads and library representatives announcing spending restrictions, 2 October 1973 (UAA 79-152-84); Peel, *Report of the University Librarian to the President, 1971–1972, 1972–1973,* and *1973–1974.* The recently established PhysEd branch was already on sufferance because of low use (Library Committee minutes, 18 November 1971 [UAA 90-148-5]; "Library Economizes on Books," *The Gateway* [7 March 1972]: 6).

178 Library Committee minutes, 17 and 27 September, 18 October, 22 November, 11 and 13 December 1973, 4 April 1974 (UAA 90-148-6); Peel to Vice-President W.P. Allen, 21 January 1974 (UAA 90-148-6); "Inflation Hits U Libraries," *The Gateway* (9 October 1973): 3; "Library Crisis Averted," *The Gateway* (8 January 1974): 1; Greg Neiman, "U libraries Face New Financial Problems," *The Gateway* (1 October 1974): 1; Peel, *Report of the University Librarian to the President,* 1974–1975.

179 Library Committee minutes, 16 March 1972 (UAA 90-148-5); Library Committee minutes, 28 September 1972, 4 April, 1, 2, and 6 May 1974 (UAA 90-148-6); Peel to All Academic Staff regarding new loan policy, 8 June 1972, John Forster to All Academic Staff rescinding 1 September implementation of loan policy, 17 July 1972 (UAA 75-12-181); Peel, *Report,* 1972–1973. In 1969 the Library Committee formed a sub-committee to explore adoption of an allocation formula, without results (Library Committee minutes, 25 March 1969 [UAA 90-148-4]).

180 Library Committee minutes, 30 October 1968 and 6 April 1970, "Library Committee Report to the General Faculties Council, 1967–68," 14 October 1968 (UAA 90-148-4); Peel, *Report of the University Librarian,* 1968–1969, 10, and 1970–1971, 13–14.

181 Peel, *Report of the University Librarian,* 1973–1974; Jobb, "Biography of a Librarian," 79–82; Peel, *History* 1979, 25; Library Committee minutes, 8 and 23 May 1972 (UAA 90-140-5). In 1973, when the Humanities and Social Sciences research collections were moved from Cameron Library to the Rutherford complex, a Coordinator of the Rutherford Libraries replaced the position of Assistant University Librarian for Public Services, and assumed responsibility for circulation, reference, microforms, government publications, rare books and special collections, the undergraduate library, and Inter-Library Loan (these last two located in Cameron Library). In 1974, the 14-year-old Periodicals Division was phased out and its functions transferred elsewhere. In 1971, several 'housekeeping' units were amalgamated into the Division of Administrative Services, and the word "Division" replaced "Department" in the organization chart.

182 Peel to Library staff, 2 June 1976, quoted in "Management Survey of the Library of the University of Alberta [1977]," 1 (UAA 81-54-73). In a cover letter accompanying a questionnaire sent to all faculty, Mr Peel named "financial uncertainty" as the principal motive for the self-study (Peel to Faculty, 7 July 1976 [UAA 79-152-84]).

183 Mr Peel's efforts to be accepted as a member of Deans' Council initially won him only the right to be invited when budget planning was under discussion (Peel to President Wyman, 18 March 1971 and 24 February 1972, Wyman to Peel, 28 February 1972 [UAA 75-12-181]).

184 Peel, *Report of the University Librarian,* 1976–1977, 6–7; "Management Survey," 11–43 (UAA 81-54-73).

185 Peel, *Report of the University Librarian,* 1976–1977, 6–7; Philip G.C. Ketchum (lawyer representing Ms S.E.H. Rooney) to the Canadian Association of University Teachers and Association of Academic Staff, University of Alberta, 15 January 1976, AAS:UA Executive

Committee minutes, 27 January 1976 (UAA 73-162-99); Management Survey, 44–47. Further documents related to the S.E.H. Rooney appeal case are in UAA 73-162-100; Peel to J.B. Dea of Field, Owen (representing the University of Alberta), 7 January 1975, James Plambeck (AAS:UA) to President Gunning, 4 November 1975, Gunning to Plambeck, 17 November 1975 (UAA 79-152-84).

186 Peel, *Report of the University Librarian*, 1977–1978, 5–6; Horowitz to Advisory Committee on Library Surveys, 1 February 1978, Horowitz to Staff of the Library, "Re Vice-President (Academic)'s Advisory Committee on Library Surveys," 31 July 1978 (UAA 83-12-114). Over the course of three meetings the Library Committee unanimously rejected the decentralizing recommendations (Library Committee minutes, 18 and 20 October, 1 November 1977, and "General Reactions of the GFC Library Committee to the Report of the Library Management Survey Team" [UAA 81-54-53]).

187 Peel to Roderick MacCosham, 30 July 1980 (UAA 83-12-113); "Half Million Towards Libraries from MacCosham Estate," *The Gateway* (11 February 1975): 1, 6.

188 Peel, *Report*, 1975–1976, 5; Library Committee Annual Report, 1977–1978, 3. "Editorial" [re Blaeu *Atlas*], *The Gateway* (13 January 1977): 4; "Library Hours Hassle," *The Gateway* (21 September 1976): 1–2; "Library Hours Still Unknown," *The Gateway* (7 October 1976): 3; Randy Read, "Library Hours Will Increase," *The Gateway* (26 October 1976): 1. The Library does now, however, possess two complete sets of Blaeu's atlas in facsimile editions.

189 D. McIntosh, "Editorial," *The Gateway* (9 March 1978): 4.

190 Wayne Kondro, "Library Quality will be 2nd Rate," *The Gateway* (14 March 1978): 8. See also D. McIntosh, "Editorial" [re budget cuts], *The Gateway* (9 March 1978): 4; Macleod, *All True Things*, 237–238; Mike Ekelund, "It Really Began in '77," *The Gateway* (9 March 1982): 8.

191 Adam Singer, "Library Situation 'Critical': Cutbacks in Staff, Acquisitions," *The Gateway* (19 September 1978): 3; A.E. Hohol, Minister of Advanced Education and Manpower to John Schlosser, Chairman, Board of Governors, 26 October 1978 (UAA 83-12-113); "College Libraries get $9 Million," *The Gateway* (3 November 1978): 1; Adam Singer, "Library in Holding Pattern: Extra Funding Urgently Needed," *The Gateway* (24 November 1978): 1; see also Randy Read, "In 3 Years the Real Crunch, Til Then Fewer Books, Staff," *The Gateway* (16 March 1979): 6. Both Murray and GFC motion quoted in Peel, *Report*, 1979–1980, 5.

192 Jobb, "Biography of a Librarian," 70–71.

193 Ibid., 72–73; Peel, *Report*, 1966–1967, [8].

194 Heilik, personal communication, 9 March 2009; Library Committee minutes, 18 April and 19 May 1967 (UAA 90-148-4). The Epic terminals for 'reading' the punched Hollerith cards replaced the obsolete IBM 1030 terminals, for which replacement parts could no longer be obtained (Peel, *Report*, 1979–1980, 12); Lynne Shalom, "Library Service terrible!" *The Gateway* (18 October 1979): 4; Norma Freifield, "Defence of Library," *The Gateway* (25 October 1979): 5; Bruce Peel, "Slow Library Explained," *The Gateway* (22 November 1979): 4; Julie Green, "Library Delays Still a Problem," *The Gateway* (19 February 1980): 3; Mike Walker, "Changes Delay Cards," *The Gateway* (9 September 1980): 9.

195 "New Circulation System for Library," *The Gateway* (10 October 1969): 3; Peel, *History* 1979, 23.

196 Heilik, personal communication.

197 Ibid., see also Library Committee minutes, 15 and 27 April 1970 (UAA 90-148-4); Peel, *Report*, 1977–1978, 1978–1979, 1979–1980, 1980–1981; "Library to Modernize Cataloguing," *The Gateway* (12 October 1978): 2; Mike Walker, "Automated Books: Computers Take Over Library," *The Gateway* (23 September 1980): 9; Pat Just, "Fiching for

Tomes: Library Computerizes," *The Gateway* (17 March 1981): 1. As a sheer cost-saving measure, the University of Toronto Library closed its card catalogue at the end of June, 1976 (Blackburn, *Evolution of the Heart*, 292).

198 Peel, *Report*, 1980–1981, 15–16; Jobb, "Biography of a Librarian," 70, 74–75.

199 Peel, *Report*, 1976–1977, 5.

200 Peel, *Report*, 1979–1980, 21–22, and 1975–1976, 19–20; *Library Staff Information Bulletin No. 48* (28 December 1965): 1; "Tattle-tape Makes Library Books Safe," *The Gateway* (9 September 1975): 3; David Patterson, "Turnstiles a Hazard," *The Gateway* (29 September 1981): 5.

201 *University of Alberta News Release*, 2 October 1979; Chodan, "Library Now Two Million Strong."

202 Peel to R.E. Phillips (VP Planning and Resources), 4 January 1980 and "Revised Detailed Program Rutherford Storage Faculty," January 1980 (UAA 83-12-113); *University of Alberta Library Space Proposal*, [n.d.], 1–4 (UAA 83-35-72).

203 Peel to R.E. Phillips, Chairman, Facilities Planning Committee, 26 March 1981, and three-page "History of Library Planning and Construction" (UAA 83-35-72); Peel to Horowitz, 9 August 1982 (UAA 84-136-63).

204 Peel to Gunning, 27 June; Gunning to Peel, 9 July 1979 (UAA 83-12-113). See also Adam Singer, "Library in Holding Pattern: Extra Funding Urgently Needed," *The Gateway* (24 November 1978): 1; *University of Alberta News Release*, 27 October 1980 (UAA 83-12-113).

205 Peel to Horowitz, 12 January, Horowitz to Peel, 3 February, Peel to Horowitz, 15 May 1981; Peel to Library Representatives, 6 July 1981 (UAA 83-12-113). The University of Alberta's share of the third and final instalment of the AHSTF grant was $920,000 (James Horsman, Minister of Advanced Education to John Schlosser, 9 July; G.D. Prideaux to Horowitz, 7 December; Horowitz to Prideaux, 30 December; E.D. Blodgett to Horowitz, 29 December; Horowitz to Blodgett, 30 December 1981 [UAA ibid.]).

206 Peel to Horowitz, 3 December, Horowitz to J.D. Horsman, 4 December 1981 (UAA ibid.); Horsman to Peel, 10 December 1981 (UAA 83-35-72); Peel to Horsman, 31 December 1981 (UAA 83-12-113); Horsman to Horowitz, 11 March 1982, emphasis added (UAA 84-136-63); Greg Harris, "Province Cuts Libraries Back: Fund Cancelled," *The Gateway* (9 December 1981): 3; Greg Harris, "Library Funds Up in the Air," *The Gateway* (12 January 1982): 1.

207 "Libraries Strangled by Fieldhouse," *The Gateway* (19 January 1982): 6; "The Finer Points of Library Strangulation," and Greg Harris, "Modern Libraries Must Keep Resources Up to Date," *The Gateway* (9 March 1982): 9.

208 Peel, *Report*, 1980–1981, 3.

209 B.W. Wilkinson to Gunning, 1 March; Peel to Gunning, 21 April 1977 (UAA 79-152-84). Peel also enclosed copies of congratulatory letters from Harvard, CUNY, and the University of Minnesota Library School that were sent in response to his annual reports, and added, "In 21 years this is the only negative reaction I've had to my report."

210 Peel to Horowitz, 26 August 1982 (UAA 84-136-63); see also Jens Andersen, "Librarian Retires," *The Gateway* (10 November 1981): 14.

211 Library Committee minutes, 14 October and 6 November 1981 (UAA 87-96-24). Neither the one local, nor the three internal applicants made the short-list for an interview (C.D. Evans to J.G. Kaplan, 1 March 1982; Kaplan to Evans, 8 March 1982 [UAA 84-136-63]). Quoted from a personal interview with Peter Freeman, 3 March 2009. First-person quotes from that interview hereinafter are cited as "Freeman, interview."

212 Peel, *Report*, 1970–1971, 29–30; Freeman, interview. Half of the Law Librarian's salary was charged to the budget of the Dean of Law.

213 Freeman, interview; Freeman to Horowitz, 21 January 1982 (UAA 84-136-63); Library Committee minutes, 22 September 1982 (UAA 87-96-28); Cathy McLaughlin, "U

of A Supreme Librarian," *The Gateway* (16 November 1982): 3; "Library to Begin Self-Study of its Collections," *Folio* (17 March 1983): 3. The CAP study led to the deferment of another scheduled self-study, since the Library staff could only undertake one at a time, and the CAP study was deemed to take precedence. Thus, the Library became the last university unit to submit a report to the President's Advisory Committee on Campus Reviews (PACCR). For PACCR, see Macleod, *All True Things*, 248–249.

214 Freeman, interview; B. Abu-Laban, Assoc. VP (Research) to G. Baldwin, Dean of Arts, 28 February 1983 (UAA 87-64 Box 10). Ms Busch and Ms Rooney were granted administrative stipends, yielding a net saving of the balance of the Associate's salary (Freeman, Triennial Report, 1982–1985, B-9 [UAA 91-102-22]).

215 Freeman, interview; L.C. Leitch to Freeman, 23 January 1984, Freeman to B. Abu-Laban, 13 March 1985, Freeman to Leitch, 12 March 1985, "Proposal to the Alberta Heritage Foundation for Medical Research for the Funding of Library Resources," 2 January 1985 (UAA 87-64 Box 10); Brent Fennell, "Periodicals Face Cuts," *The Gateway* (19 October 1987): 3; Annual Report of the GFC Library Committee, 1984–1985 (UAA 90-104-4).

216 Freeman, interview; Zane Harker, "Library Hurts Too," *The Gateway* (3 March 1983): 3; Sheila Read, "Helpful Librarians Overdue," *The Gateway* (1 February 1983): 4; Denise Workun, "Where's the Money, Myer?," *The Gateway* (3 April 1984): 4; Gilbert Bouchard, "Libraries Crunched," *The Gateway* (6 March 1984): 4. The Library's Rod Banks, who was probably Bouchard's original source of information, wrote on 20 March to correct one small detail. In 1980–1981, the University of Alberta was in "Group 7" in terms of acquisitions, and had fallen 22 places to 26 out of 101 ARL libraries reporting (Banks, "Library Agrees," *The Gateway* [20 March 1984]: 4).

217 Peter Block, "Council Gives to Library: Building Policy Referendum Called," *The Gateway* (6 December 1984): 1–2; Peter Block, "Bucks for Books?," *The Gateway* 6 December 1984): 4. As a good journalist, Block covered the Council meeting objectively, and reserved his criticism for his editorial column in the same issue.

218 Library Committee minutes, 16 October 1968 (UAA 90-148-4); "Library's Future in Doubt," *The Gateway* (27 November 1973): 3; Macleod, *All True Things*, chapter 15; Freeman, interview; Annual Report of the GFC Library Committee, 1986–1987; Library Committee minutes, 9 December 1987, 13 January 1988, 10 February, 19 May, and 16 June 1989 (UAA 90-104-3). Participating libraries in the Joint-serials renewal project were found to have a collective total of 14,626 subscriptions to 2113 different journals published by the eight publishers in question, at a total cost of $9,517,313.68 ("U of A Leads Fight for Lower Journal Prices," *Library Editions* [Winter 1990]: 1–2).

219 H. Hargreaves to R.G. Baldwin, 22 January 1973 (UAA 81-54-68).

220 Library Committee minutes, 25 January and 20 February 1980 (UAA 87-96-23), 14 January and 15 April 1981 (UAA 87-96-24), 8 December 1982 (UAA 87-96-28); F.P. Van De Pitte to the GFC/LC, 6 February 1984 (UAA 87-118-29). Mr Rod Banks had provided a list of concerns to be addressed in plans for that facility (R. Banks to T. Miner, Director, Design & Construction, 30 March 1982; APRA, *University of Alberta Library Facility Planning Study*, May 1984 [UAA 87-118-29]).

221 Library Committee minutes, 13 June, 11 July, 26 September, 10 October, and 7 November 1984 (UAA 87-96-32); J.G. Kaplan to L.C. Leitch, 2 October 1984 (UAA 87-118-29); T.C. Miner to Freeman, 10 December 1984; Freeman to Miner, 14 December 1984 (UAA 87-118-29).

222 L.C. Leitch to Freeman, 4 January 1985, "Library Space Planning for the Humanities

and Social Sciences, February 11, 1985," 7, and Library Committee Annual Report, 1984–1985 (UAA 90-104-4); Freeman to Horowitz, 9 September 1986, Horowitz to Freeman, 10 September 1986 (UAA 90-41-17).

223 Freeman, interview; Freeman to Library Committee members, 28 July 1986 (UAA 87-118-29). Whether or not there was any substance to Mr Freeman's notion, the Timms Collections Centre project was itself cancelled in November 1989, when its staffing costs appeared unaffordable (Sarah Ahmad, "Timms Centre Underway," *The Gateway* [17 October 1989]: 3; Dawn Lerohl, "Timms Cancelled," *The Gateway* [9 November 1989]: 1; Diane Wild, "Collection Centre Closure Causes Concern," *The Gateway* [16 November 1989]: 3).

224 B. Abu-Laban to Freeman and G. Morcos, Dean, FS-J, 16 June 1983 (UAA 87-64 Box 10); "Draft Proposal on the Integration of the Faculté Saint-Jean Library with the University of Alberta Main Library, June 24, 1983," Freeman to Morcos, 7 September 1983, and B. Abu-Laban to Freeman and Morcos, enclosing signed integration agreement, 15 September 1983 (UAA 87-118-30). The Library assumed responsibility for half the salary of the BS-J Librarian, Ms Juliet Henley, who was appointed in October; the President's contingency fund covered the first year's integration costs of $44,595.

225 Jens Andersen, "Asbestos Program Refueled," *The Gateway* (9 November 1982): 3; Freeman to R.E. Phillips, 21 and 22 October, 8 November 1982, 27 June and 25 August 1983, B. Abu-Laban to J.G. Kaplan, 1 November 1982, G. Walker, NASA Manager to all Members, 17 and 25 November 1982 (UAA 87-118-28); Brent Jang, "Workers Find Floors Shaky at Cameron," *The Gateway* (3 November 1983): 1; Freeman, interview. Phase 1 of the project was scheduled for completion by the end of 1983, and Phase 2 by September, 1984.

226 Library Committee minutes, 13 April 1983 (UAA 87-96-29), 12 October 1983 (UAA

87-96-30), 4 April 1984 (UAA 87-96-31), 7 November 1984 (UAA 87-96-32); Library Committee Annual Report, 1984–1985 (UAA 90-104-4); Freeman to D. Norwood, 9 June 1983 (UAA 87-118-29). The announcement that the medical collection would be moving to the new hospital complex instantly created anxiety among the biological sciences faculty (W.R. Kaufman to Chairman, GFC/LC, 9 May 1979 [UAA 81-54-55]). A consulting survey of the Music Resources Centre was prepared by Mr Michael Keller, then of Cornell University. Consolidation of library resources for music had been an issue for at least a decade ("A Brief Regarding Library Service in Music at the University of Alberta" [UAA 81-54-57]; see also UAA 81-54-56).

227 [Press release], "Library Introduces an Expanded Computerized Catalogue," 15 September 1986, Freeman, invitation to Faculty and Staff, 15 September 1986 (UAA 90-41-17); Heilik, personal communication.

228 Heilik, personal communication; Library Committee minutes, 9 and 15 April 1980 (UAA 87-96-23), 9 and 23 February 1983 (UAA 87-96-29); Freeman, Triennial Report, 1982–1985, B6–B7, Triennial Report, 1985–1988, 5–7 (UAA 91-102-22); Tom Wilson, "On-line Catalogue," *The Gateway* (12 January 1984): 7; Alex Shetsen, "Library Modernization Goes On," *The Gateway* (30 September 1986): 7.

229 Freeman, interview; Shirley Norris, personal communication, 22 March 2009.

230 Heilik, personal communication; Freeman, Triennial Report, 1985–1988, 6; Schoeck, *I Was There*, 571–572; Greg Lockert, "Bar Code Speeds Checkout," *The Gateway* (14 January 1988): 1.

231 Norris, personal communication. When this author first reported for work at the Library and requested a typewriter, Mr Freeman replied with feigned indignation, "And here I've spent *years* taking typewriters *away* from librarians."

232 "University of Alberta Library Collection Analysis Project Final Report, December,

1985" and CAP Task Force on Collection Policies, "A Proposed Collection Development Policy for University of Alberta Libraries, June 1985" (UAA 87-118-32).

233 "The Javitch Collection," *Library Editions* (Summer 1988): 4–5; "'A Spirit of Joy in Printing': The Curwen Press Collection," *Library Editions* (Winter 1989): 7–8; Green, *A Spirit of Joy*; Denise Leroy, The Curwen Press: A Checklist of Material Held in the Bruce Peel Special Collections Library, University of Alberta (finding aid in Peel Library); "The Folkways Collection," *Library Editions* (Summer 1989): 2–3.

234 Peel to R.G. Baldwin, 22 February 1980, H.J. Jones to Peel, 11 March 1980 (UAA 81-54-55); Mike Sadava, "U of A Buys Collection of Rare Books," *Edmonton Journal* (20 December 1985): B1; Freeman to President Horowitz, 17 September 1985 (UAA 87-64 Box 10); Dick Johnstone, Minister, Advanced Education to B. Evans, 27 March 1986 (UAA 90-41-17).

235 Freeman, Triennial Report, 1985–1988, 8; Freeman, interview.

236 Freeman, interview; "The Libraries of Alberta Universities, Proposal for Cooperative Network Development," revised draft, 1 November 1983 (UAA 87-118-32).

237 Freeman, interview; Freeman to Myer Horowitz, re resignation, 23 October 1988 (UAA 90-41-17).

238 Macleod, *All True Things*, 271–277; Charles Hobart and Gerwin Marahrens, "Professors Attack Davenport," *The Gateway* (27 February 1990): 5–7; Gil McGowan and Teresa Pires, "One Year Later: Is the Honeymoon Over?," *The Gateway* (25 September 1990): 14–15. Dr Lois Stanford, who was appointed to the new post of Vice-President (Student and Academic Services) was given responsibility for the Library and the Chief Librarian, who formerly reported to the Vice-President (Academic) (Davenport to GFC Executive Committee, 17 September 1990 [UAA 94-132-40]).

239 John Teskey, personal communication; Teskey to D. Kieren, 24 February 1989, Teskey to J. Tartar, 6 and 31 March, 18 and 29 August 1989, Teskey to GFCLC, 14 April 1989, Teskey to P. Meekison, 20 April 1989 (UAA 94-54-8). Academic staff were exempt from fines, save for overdue reserve books and periodicals, for which infractions an annual average of 200 had their borrowing privileges suspended. In the event, there were no layoffs, and the Library ran a large deficit in 1989–1990.

240 Library Committee Annual Report, 1988–1989, 4-5 (UAA ibid.).

241 Merrett to Members of GFCLC, "Draft Topics for a Letter to Deans and Directors," 24 November 1989, Merrett to Davenport, 24 November 1989 (UAA ibid.). Throughout his term chairing the GFCLC, Dr Merrett continued to press for greater influence upon, and transparency in, the Library's budgeting process; see Gil McGowan, "Library Committee Wants Wider Budget Consultations," *The Gateway* (8 November 1990): 2.

242 Academic Development Committee, "An Outline of the Issues, Re: Discussion of the University Library," 18 December 1989; Merrett to Meekison, 25 January 1990; Teskey to Davenport, 6 December 1989; Meekison to Merrett, 30 January 1990 (UAA 94-54-8).

243 Dr Max Mote to Library Representatives and other concerned parties, 1 February 1990 (UAA 90-41-17); Committee to Save the Library, Press Release #1, 5 February 1990 (UAA 96-24-6).

244 Committee to Save the Library, Press Release #2, 15 February 1990 (UAA ibid.); "Committee to Save the Library Starts by Circulating Petition," *Folio* (15 February 1990): 1; Brian Champion, Hope Olson, and Alan Rutkowski, unpublished letter to the editor of *The Gateway*, 14 February 1990, Brian Champion, Media Liaison, to CKER Radio, 16 February 1990 (UAA 96-24-6); G. Paul Skelhorne, "Committee Rallies to Save Library," *The Gateway* (27 February 1990): 1; Paul Kiermam, "Fight for Books: Higher Priority Urged for Library," *The Gateway* (1 March 1990):

1. The petition itself is preserved in the University Archives (UAA 90-96-2). In addition to the $500,000 augmentation to the Library's acquisitions budget, President Davenport revealed most welcome news that the Administration was paying off the Library's 1989–1990 operating deficit of $613,143, "on the firm understanding with the Vice-Presidents that your unit is currently planning to run a balanced budget in 1990/91, and should an unexpected deficit occur, that deficit would be fully flexed forward in 1991/92" (Davenport to Ingles, 21 July 1990 [UAA 93-63-34]).

245 Quoted from a personal interview with Ernie Ingles, 16 February 2009. First-person quotes from that interview hereinafter are cited as "Ingles, interview." Upon the arrival of Mr Ingles in May 1990, John Teskey assumed the role of Associate Director, while retaining responsibility for the Library's human resources portfolio. Before the end of the year, Ms B.J. Busch and Ms Sieglinde Rooney were also made Associate Directors. Early in 1991, Mr Teskey left to become University Librarian at the University of New Brunswick; Ms Rooney inherited the management of human resources.

246 Ingles to President, Vice-Presidents, and Assoc. Vice-Presidents, 22 May 1990 (UAA 94-132-40).

247 *Riding the Wave: University Library Draft Strategic Plan, 1990–1995*, October 1990 (UAA ibid.); R.M. Dougherty, "Editorial: Riding the Wave of Change," *Journal of Academic Librarianship* (November 1990): 275; *University of Alberta Library Strategic Priorities: Operationalizing the Plan* (UAA 94-132-40).

248 Save the Library Committee, [Questionnaire] "Your Views on the State of the Library," November 1990; [Summary of] "Views on the Library," January 1991; "President's Column," *AAS-UA Newsletter* (December 1990): 1 (UAA 93-63-40).

249 McMaster to Stanford, 25 January 1991; McMaster to Ingles, 3 December 1990 and 28 January 1991; Ingles to McMaster, 14 January 1991 (UAA ibid.).

250 McMaster to Stanford, 8 February 1991, Ingles to Stanford, 14 February 1991, Gogo to Rutkowski, 8 March 1991, [Save the Library Committee], "The Save the Library Committee and the Library Crisis at the University Library, January 1991," and "A Charter for the Future: The Response of the Save the Library Committee to the Library Crisis at the University of Alberta [n.d.]" (UAA 96-24-6); Stanford to McMaster, 14 March 1991 (UAA 93-63-40).

251 "Movement to 'Save' U of A's Library," *Quill & Quire* (April 1991): 16; Christopher Spencer, "Staff Organizes to Protest Library Decline," *The Gateway* (4 April 1991): 1–2; Ingles to Skelhorne, 8 April 1991, Stanford to Deans and Chairs, 16 April 1991 (UAA 93-63-40).

252 McMaster to Ingles, 2 May 1991, Kelly to Skelhorne, 19 April 1991 (UAA 96-24-6); Kelly to Stanford, 10 April 1992 (UAA 94-132-40); Juliet McMaster, "Please Keep the Life-Blood Circulating," *Library Editions* (Summer 1991): 1. The "ideas about fund-raising" probably included a proposal for a benefit concert made to the agent who represented Alberta pop singer k.d. lang (A. Rutkowski to Larry Wanagas, Bumstead Productions, 12 April 1991 [UAA 96-24-6]).

253 A. Small to Arts Faculty Chairmen, [8 April 1991] (UAA 93-63-40).

254 Fiona Cameron, "Cameron Late Night Study Hours a Success," *The Gateway* (16 January 1990): 3; Gil McGowan, "University Slashes Library Hours," *The Gateway* (11 September): 1. Mr Ingles might have added that the Library's acquisitions budget was soon to be slapped with the new federal Goods and Services Tax (GST), only part of which would be recoverable (Heidi Modro, "GST Cuts Library Purchasing Power," *The Gateway* [6 December 1990]: 3).

255 Gil McGowan, "Students Excluded from Library Decision," *The Gateway* (13 September 1990): 1; Gil McGowan, "SU Plans Library

Protest," *The Gateway* (18 September 1990): 1;
Gil McGowan, "GSA Votes to Support Library
Protest," *The Gateway* (18 September 1990):
3; G.P. Skelhorne, "Library Decision Short-
sighted," *The Gateway* (18 September 1990): 4;
"Letters," *The Gateway* (20 and 27 September,
4 and 16 October 1990); Gil McGowan,
"Longer Library Hours Pledged," *The Gateway*
(11 October 1990): 1; "Agreement Reached
on Library Hours," *Folio* (11 October 1990): 1.
Multiplied over a 13-week term, however, the
cost of those extended hours would have been
$33,000, equivalent to a year's salary for one
staff position.

256 Teskey to D.G. Bellow, Assoc. V-P (Facilities),
"Proposed Book Storage Facility – 50th Street
and Sherwood Park Freeway," 17 January 1990
(UAA 94-54-8); Ingles to Bellow, "University
Library Capital Requirements," 1 May 1991
(UAA 93-63-39); Gil McGowan, "Library
Considers Closing Computer Catalogue
System," *The Gateway* (28 February 1991): 3;
Gil McGowan, "DOBIS Saved from Closure,
but, Ingles Warns That System May Fail
Soon," *The Gateway* (9 March 1991): 2. The
head of University Computing Services was
not amused by the threatened loss of revenue
from maintaining DOBIS.

257 Heilik, personal communication; Benjamin
Chan, "Libraries to Receive New Database,
Borrowing Policies Remain to Be Set," *The
Gateway* (4 March 1993): 13; "Library Asks for
Volunteers to Aid Implementation of New
Automated System," *Folio* (26 February 1993):
1; "Library Opens The GATE, DOBIS's Days
Dwindling," *Folio* (3 September 1993): 1.

258 K. Taylor to Teskey, November 1989, K.
Carter to Cataloguing Staff, 26 July 1990 and
5 September 1991 (Technical Services Office
files); Kathy Carter, personal communication.

259 Office of the Vice-President (Finance &
Administration), "Eastpoint Auxiliary Stack
Facility, Appointment of Prime Consultant,
[n.d.]" (UAA 94-132-40); Gogo to Milner, 11
May 1992 (UAA 93-63-39); [D.G. Bellow],
"Eastpoint Auxiliary Stack Facility," 14 April

1992 (UAA 94-132-40); Library Committee
Annual Report, 1991–1992 (UAA 93-155-50).

260 Christopher Spencer, "Prof Upset Over Plan
to Store Books," *The Gateway* (3 September
1992): 2.

261 "Eastpoint Library: Detailed Space
Programme," October 1992; "Eastpoint
Auxiliary Storage Facility: Advisory Task Force
Report," 12 November 1992; News Release: U
of A finds $3 million solution to $70 million
library problem," 16 February 1994 (UAA
93-63-39). The $70 million figure was an
impromptu doubling of the original, $35
million cost estimate for the Rutherford West
project proposal, to account for inflation. See
also Neal Ozano, "Welcome to the BARD,"
The Gateway (9 March 1995): 4; Gordon Kent,
"Where Old Books Go to Rest," *Edmonton
Journal* (20 April 1997).

262 "University of Alberta Journal Cancellations,
1987–1991," January 1992 (UAA 93-63-35). A
total of $2,010,386 in expenditure was saved
as a result of these cancellations (Library
Committee Annual Report, 1991–1992 [UAA
93-155-50]).

263 W.J. McDonald, V-P (Academic) to ADC
members, "Library Impact Statements," 17
September 1992 (UAA 94-132-40); Ingles to
Stanford, "Library Impact Statements," 22
March 1993 (UAA 93-63-34); Ingles to All
Library Staff, 19 March 1991 (UAA 94-54-
8). A total of 26 positions were sacrificed,
18 of them vacancies, including 3 librarian
positions designated for cataloguing,
preservation, and computer systems. These
brought the cumulative staff losses over a
decade to "97 positions to budget tax and
transfer, approximating 25% of the staff
complement" (Library Committee Annual
Report, 1991–1992 [UAA 93-155-50]).

264 Karen Unland, "Protest Planned," *The Gateway*
(20 February 1992): 1; Warren Ferguson,
"Thousands Protest," and "Egg on Gogo's Face
No Yolk," *The Gateway* (17 March 1992): 3.

265 Ingles, Confidential to Stanford, "Budget
Reduction," 8 March 1992 (UAA 93-63-34);

Warren Ferguson, "A University Without Books?," *The Gateway* (12 March 1992): 3.

266 Macleod, *All True Things*, 289–290, *et passim.*

267 W. Israel to Research Personnel in Chemistry, Mathematics, Statistics, Computing Science, and Physics, 30 January 1991, Israel to Ingles, 6 February 1991 (UAA 93-63-37); Ingles to Deans Council, "Changes in Library Service," 25 August 1992 (UAA 93-63-34); Vice-President Stanford, correspondence re anchoring serials (UAA 93-63-37); "Decision Not to Circulate Journals Will Save Libraries $193,600 Over Two Years," *Folio* (12 June 1992): 1.

268 Library Committee minutes, 19 October 1992 (UAA 93-155-47); Library Committee minutes, 11 January 1993 (UAA 93-155-48); *Discussion Paper on the Amalgamation of Science Branch Libraries with the Cameron Science and Technology Library*, Autumn 1992, Bercov to Stanford, 19 October 1992, Bercov to Stanford, 28 January 1993 (UAA 93-63-37); "Response of the Mathematics Department to the Library's Discussion Paper on the Amalgamation of the Science Branch Libraries with the Cameron Science and Technology Libraries," and "Petition" (UAA 94-102-89).

269 W. Israel to editor of *The Gateway*, dated 20 January 1993 (UAA 93-63-37); "Science Professors Oppose Plan to Amalgamate Branch Libraries," *Folio* (22 January 1993): 1. Other correspondence files devoted to these protest letters include UAA 93-63-38 and UAA 93-155-49.

270 Peter Moore, "Just Say No to Library Merger," *The Gateway* (4 February 1993): 1, 3.

271 W. Israel, "Meeting of Math, Computing, Chemistry and Physics Depts with Chief Librarian Mr. E. Ingles 12 Jan. 1993," R.E. Peter to Stanford, 15 February 1993 (UAA 93-63-37); Ingles quoted in Peter Moore, "Separate Science Libraries Preserved, Amalgamation Avoided At Least for Now," *The Gateway* (9 March 1993): 5.

272 Macleod, *All True Things*, 289.

273 Ingles, interview.

274 Stanford to Ingles, 13 June 1994, Ingles to President's Executive Committee re outsourcing discussion draft, 1 June 1994 (UAA 95-80-196); Ingles to R. Fraser, 5 December 1994 (UAA 96-112-90).

275 Ingles, interview.

276 Ibid.

277 Ibid.

278 Ibid.

279 Ibid.

280 J. Heilik to Deans, Chairs, Department and Unit Heads, "Campus OneCard: request for information," 27 July 1995 (UAA 90-41-17); Heilik, personal communication; Chris Jackel, "Smart Cards Planned for Sept 95, One-step System Could Make Life Easier for Students," *The Gateway* (22 September 1994): 5; Darren Zenko, "Universally Carded," *The Gateway* (11 April 1995): 3; Dagmar Skrpec, "The One and Only, Student IDs are Now Library Cards, Copy Cards, and Calling Cards," *The Gateway* (5 September 1996): 10; Ingles, interview. The functions OneCard serves continue to grow, for example as a transit pass between the North Campus and downtown.

281 Ingles, interview.

282 Ibid.

283 Ibid.

284 Ingles to Meekison, "Reading Room – Professors Emeriti," 15 August 1991, W. Berg, Chair, Dept of Music, to Ingles, 11 March 1991 (UAA 93-63-37); Stephen Notley, "Facelift for Cameron," *The Gateway* (8 September 1994): 9; Lynn Lau, "Rutherford Renos in Record Time," *The Gateway* (30 September 1993): 5; Celina Connolly, "Two for One, Library Renovations Combine Collections," *The Gateway* (17 September 1996): 5.

285 Michael Robb, "Federal Funding Directed to Faculté Saint-Jean Library," *Folio* (19 November 1993): 1; Sandra Halme, "Faculté Saint-Jean Renovations Improve Learning Environment," *Folio* (24 January 1997): 1; Tim Shoults, "Nouveau Saint-Jean, Deputy PM Officially Opens U of A's Renovated French Campus," *The Gateway* (21 January 1997): 5.

286 Ingles, interview.

287 "Gifts to the Library Always Welcome," *Folio* 1,
     no. 21 (1965): 3; Teskey to Tartar, "Statistics on
     Library Gifts and their valuation," 19 January
     1990 (UAA 94-54-8).

288 Ingles, interview.

289 Ibid.; Caitlin Crawshaw, "U of A Library
     Ranked Second in Canada Despite Cutbacks,"
     The Gateway (11 September 2003): 1, 4. The
     University of Alberta Library ranked 13th
     in ARL's 2006 Membership Criteria Index,
     immediately behind Harvard, Yale, Columbia,
     UC/Berkeley, Toronto, Michigan, UCLA,
     Cornell, Illinois, Wisconsin, Texas, and
     Indiana.

290 Jhenifer Pabillano, "Library Pride," *The
     Gateway* (8 October 2002): 5.

Bibliography

Alexander, William Hardy. *The University of Alberta: A Retrospect, 1908–1929.* Edmonton: University Printing Press, 1929.

———, et al. *These Twenty-Five Years: A Symposium.* Toronto: Macmillan, 1933.

Babcock, Douglas R. *Alexander Cameron Rutherford: A Gentleman of Strathcona.* 2nd ed. Calgary: Friends of Rutherford House and University of Calgary Press, 1989.

Blackburn, Robert H. "Reminiscences," *Library Editions* (Winter 1989).

———. *Evolution of the Heart: A History of the University of Toronto Library up to 1981.* Toronto: University of Toronto Library, 1989.

———. "University of Alberta, 1936–1941: I Was There." UAA 2009-20: 4–5.

Brundin, Robert E. *From the Codex to the Computer: Twenty-Five Years of the School of Library and Information Studies.* Edmonton: School of Library and Information Studies, 1995.

Campbell, Duncan D. *Those Tumultuous Years: The Goals of the President of the University of Alberta during the Decade of the 1960s.* Edmonton: University of Alberta Library, 1977.

Corbett, Bryan. *River Lot 5: A Home for the University.* Edmonton: University of Alberta Library, 2007.

———. *Charter Day, May 9, 1906–2006.* Edmonton: University of Alberta Library, 2006.

Corbett, E.A. *Henry Marshall Tory: Beloved Canadian.* Toronto: Ryerson Press, 1954.

Freifield, Norma E. "Marjorie Sherlock Grayson-Smith." Unpublished MS. UAA biography files.

Gordon, R.C. "University Beginnings in Alberta." *Queen's Quarterly* LVIII:4 (1951): 487–496.

Green, Jeannine. *A Spirit of Joy: Notes from an Exhibition of Books, Periodicals, and Ephemera Printed at the Curwen Press During Its Heyday, 1916–1956.* Edmonton: University of Alberta, 1990.

Ingles, Ernie B., and N. Merrill Distad. "Bruce Braden Peel (1916–1998): Prairie Bibliographer and Librarian." In *Peel's Bibliography of the Canadian Prairies to 1953.* Revised and enlarged ed. Toronto: University of Toronto Press, 2003. Pp. xxi–xxviii.

Jobb, Patricia A. "Biography of a Librarian: Bruce Braden Peel." MLS thesis. Edmonton: School of Library and Information Studies, 1987.

Johns, Walter Hugh. *A History of the University of Alberta: 1908–1969.* Edmonton: University of Alberta Press, 1981.

Kerr, W.A.R. "An Appreciation of F.G. Bowers." *The Trail* 1 (1920): 9–10.

Lehmann, Jean. "Memories of the Arts Library at the University of Alberta in the Twenties." *Library Editions* (Summer 1990): 6–8.

Levasseur-Ouimet, France. *D'hier à demain: connaître l'histoire de Saint-Jean, c'est savoir qui nous sommes.* Edmonton: La Faculté, 2003.

Lister, Reginald Charles. *My Forty-Five Years on the Campus.* Edmonton: University of Alberta, 1958.

Lohnes, Donna, and Barbara J. Nicholson. *Alexander Calhoun.* Calgary: Calgary Public Library, 1987.

Macdonald, John. *The History of the University of Alberta, 1908–1958.* Toronto: W.J. Gage for the University of Alberta, 1958.

——. "In Memoriam: Donald Ewing Cameron." *The New Trail* 5, no. 1 (January 1947): 266–269.

Macleod, R.C. *All True Things: A History of the University of Alberta, 1908–2008.* Edmonton: University of Alberta Press, 2008.

Marble, Allan Everett. *The Archibald Family of Nova Scotia: No Reward without Effort.* Tantallon, NS: Glen Margaret Pub., 2008.

McCalla, Arthur G. *The Development of Graduate Studies at the University of Alberta, 1908–1983.* Edmonton: University of Alberta, 1983.

News from the Rare Book Room. Edmonton: University of Alberta Library, Special Collections Department, vol. 1, no. 1 (November 1964)–vol. 3, no. 2 (May 1970), no. 12 (October 1970)–no. 18 (December 1980).

Newton, Robert. "I Passed this Way, 1889 – 1964." UAA 71-87.

Peel, Bruce B. *History of the University of Alberta Library, 1909–1979.* [2nd ed.] Edmonton: University of Alberta Library, 1979.

——. *History of the Library, University of Alberta.* [1st ed.] Edmonton: University of Alberta, 1965.

——. "Miss Sherlock and her Times." *Library Editions* (Winter 1990): 5–8.

Riddell, John Henry. *Methodism in the Middle West.* Toronto: Ryerson, 1946.

Samuel, George. "An Early History of the U. of A." *The New Trail* 11, no. 4 (Winter 1953): 143–147, and 12, no. 1 (Spring 1954): 184–189.

Sanders, L.H.D. "Faculty Status for Academic Librarians." In *Encyclopedia of Library and Information Science* vol. 48, supplement 11 (1991): 130–150.

Schoeck, Ellen. *I Was There: A Century of Alumni Stories About the University of Alberta, 1906–2006.* Edmonton: University of Alberta Press, 2006.

Sherlock, Marjorie. "The Role of the University Library." *The New Trail* 11, no. 2 (Summer 1953): 61–64.

Thomas, Lewis G. *The University of Alberta in the War of 1939–45.* Edmonton: University of Alberta, 1948.

University of Alberta. *The University of Alberta, 1908–1933.* Edmonton: University of Alberta, 1933.

Name Index

Council of Prairie and Pacific University Libraries (COPPUL), 216

Coutts, Herbert T., see Education, Library

Cragg, Lawrence, 83, 86, 96

Craig, Carman, 27–29

Curwen Press, 126, 176

Cutter Expansive Classification System, 12, 13, 26, 50, 71, 73, 107

Cutter, Charles Ammi, n.15

Dairy Science Laboratories, 92

Dalhousie University, 12, 33

Data Library, 223

Data Research Associates (DRA), 199, 200, 206, 207, 216, 218

Davenport, Paul, 183, 186, 189, **203**, **204**, 205, 211

DeLong, Kathleen, 227

Delta Upsilon, 77

Dentistry, Faculty, 17, 27, 46

Dentistry, Library, n.96

Desmarais, Robert, 225

Development Office, 164

Distad, Merrill (author), 164, 175, 176, 202, 224, **226**

Dixon, Miss, 37

DOBIS, 145, 172–173, 184, 187, 199, 200

Dominion Art Gallery, Ottawa, 23

Doucette Library of Teaching Resources, 120

Dougherty, Richard, 192

Dovichi, Norm, 211–212

Duggan Street School, 6

East Asian Languages and Literature, 126, 177, 184

Eastpoint Project, 195, 196, 199, 200, 202

Ebdon, John, 143

Economics, Department, 59, 153

Edmonton Academy of Medicine, 30

Edmonton Journal, 73, 177

Edmonton Public Library (EPL), 33, 44, 222

Education Reading Room (Library), 56, 60, 67, 89, 134, 223

Education, Faculty, 30, 48, 117–118

Engineering, Faculty, 18, 117

Engineering, Library, 129, n.96

English, Department, 29

Ennis, Miss, 37

Evans, Brian, 177

Extension, Department, 9, 19, 31, 34, 50, n.13

Extension, Library, 9, **10**, 19, 44, 82, 89, 95, 135, 163–164, n.134

Facilities Development Committee, 149, 166

Faculté Saint-Jean, see Campus Saint-Jean

Faculty Association, 137, 193

Farnell, Peggy, 46, 50, n.67

Farquharson, Helen Elizabeth, 69, n.87

Film Studies, Library, 223

Fine Arts, Department, 34, 48, 58, 73

First Nations Information Connection (FNIC), 216

Fleming, Jamie, 199

Folio, 188

Folkways Records, 176–177

FolkwaysAlive!, 177

Forbes Library, Northampton MA, 12

Fraser, Doreen, 46, 50

Fraser, Roderick, 213

Freeman, Peter Leonard, 157–180, **158**, **160**, **170**, 183, 190, 216

Freifield, Norma Elizabeth, n.87, n.131

Gateway, The, 9, 25–26, 31, 33, 35, 36, 38, 39, 41, 51, 55, 62, 65, 67, 73, 77, 162, 163, 169, 171, 194, 197, 198, 200, 202, 207, 208, 211, 219

General Faculties Council (GFC), 97, 98, 99, 105–106, 111, 116, 132, 135, 141, 166, n.151

Genetics, Library, n.96

Geography, Department, 73, 77, 86

Geography, Library, 223

Geology, Library, 223, n.96

Georg Kaiser drama archive, 126

Gibb, Alexis, 218

Giffen, Blanche, 46, 48, n.87

Glyde, Henry George, 58, **66**, n.90

Gogo, John, 193, 207

Gordon, Robert K., 5, 11, 16, 17

Gould, Charles Henry, 8, 12, n.10

Gourlay, Hugh C., 40, n.58

Government Documents, 92

Govier, G.W., n.106

Graduate Student Association, 197

Graduate Studies, Faculty, 96

Grant, Mary Isobel, 118

Grayson-Smith, H., 78

Peel's Prairie Provinces, 225

Pembina Hall, 24, 30, 45

Peter, Richard, 212

Pharmacy, Department, 9, 17

Pharmacy, Library, n.96

Physical Education, Faculty, 73, 117

Physical Education, Library, 117, 129

Physical Sciences Reading Room (Library), 86,
99–100, 116, 129, 187, 210, 213, n.124

Physics, Department, 78, 86, 96, 213

Planning and Priorities Committee, 166, 167, 168

Plant Pathology, Library, n.96

Pocklington, Thomas C., 87

Poff, Douglas, 191, 218

Political Science, Library, 223

President's Advisory Committee on Campus
Reviews (PACCR), 188, 190–191, 194

Prins, Kees, 202

Printing Services, 185

Proposal for Cooperative Library Network
Development, 179

Public Archives of Nova Scotia, 12

Public Health Nursing, 23

Queen Alexandra School, 6

Queen's University, 15, 55, 65

Race, Cecil, **8**, 12, n.17

Race, Mrs, 37

Rankin, Allan Coates, 18

Rare Book Room, 42, 91, 125, 148, see also Bruce
Peel Special Collections Library

Rawlinson, H., n.105, n.106

Reed, Sarah Rebecca, 122

Rehabilitation Committee, 50

Reicher, Daniel, 125, n.174

Relais, 218

Remington-Rand Transcopy, 81

Research Council, Library, no.96

Revell, Daniel Graisberry, 18

Richard Abel Company, 111, n.153

Richards, Dorothy, 27

Riding the Wave, 191–193, 196

Riedel, Bernard Ewald, 89, 95, n.134

RLN, 146

Robert Woods Collection, 126, n.176

Rockefeller Foundation, 23, 34, 47

Romaniuk, Mary-Jo, 216, 220, 222

Rooney, Sieglinde E.H., 137, 160, 164, n.185, n.214

Ross, D.M., n.128

Rowan, William, 75, n.112

Royal Canadian Air Force, University Air Training
Corps, 45

Rutherford II, 134, 150

Rutherford II, Phase II, 164, 166, 167–168, 169

Rutherford North Library, **130**, **133**, 134–135, **136**,
145, 149–150, 164, 187, 220, 222

Rutherford South Library, 57–63, **64**, 65, 67, **68**, **69**,
70, **72**, 78, 82, 83, 85, 87, 89, 91, 95, 116, 118,
134–135, 159, 171, 183, 205, 207, 220, 222, **226**,
n.134

Rutherford West Library, 222

Rutherford, Alexander Cameron, 3, **3**, 5, 7, 9, 62, 76,
77, 135, 224

Rutherford, Cecil, 77, n.115

Rutkowski, Alan, n.244, n.250, n.252

Samarasekera, Indira, **226**

Save the Library Committee, 188–189, 192–195,
196, 197, 199, 204, 211, 212

Shastri Indo-Canadian Institute, 126

Sheldon, Ernest Wilson, 18

Sherban, Marlene, 173

Sherlock, Marjorie (Marjorie Grayson-Smith),
53–79, **54**, 83, 115, 119, n.78, n.86, n.87

Sifton, Arthur, 11

Sinclair, Robert David, 58

Skelhorne, G. Paul, 197–198

Small, Alastair, 196, 202

Smithsonian Folkways Recordings, 177

Social Sciences and Humanities Research Council
of Canada, 176

Soils Science, Library, n.96

South Labs, 92, 93

Southern Alberta Institute of Technology (SAIT),
118

Space Allocations Committee, 116

Spencer, Christopher, 204

St Andrews University, 19

Stanford, Lois, 193, 194, 208, 209, 210, 211, 212, 214

Steele Collection, 224

Stewart, Andrew, 60, 61–62, **65**, 70, 73, 82, 83

Strathcona Collegiate Institute, 6
Strathcona, 3, 6, n.8
Strathcona, Lord, 7
Student Union, 31, 38–39, 91, 149, 196, 198, 207
Student Union Council, 39, 163, 197
Supreme Court, 159
Systems Division, Library, 143

Talman, James, n.81
Tartar, John, 183, 185
TattleTape®, 148
Taylor, Karen, 201
Taylor, Malcolm G., 118
Technology Training Centre, 222
Teskey, John, 183–189, 201
The Alberta Library (TAL), 216, 217
Thornton, Harold Ray, 70
Timms Centre, 169, 183, n.223
Timms, Albert, 169
Toronto Public Library, 17
Tory, Henry Marshall, 3–8, **4**, **8**, 12, 16, 17, 18–19, 23, 29–30, 31, 48, 51, n.29, n.77
Transportation and Utilities, Library, 223
Turner, Geoffrey, 160, n.153, n.160

United Farmers of Alberta, 23
Universiade Pavilion, 152
University Act, 3, 48, 96, 114, 219
University Bookstores, 7, 30, n.7
University Microfilms International, 178
University Naval Training Division, 45
University of Alberta at Calgary, 118–120, 155
University of British Columbia, 35–36, 97, 118, 122, 189
University of Calgary, 97, 114, 178, 189, 190, 215, 216
University of California, 126
University of Chicago, Library School, 29
University of Edinburgh, 19
University of Manitoba, 31, 33, 157, 215
University of Michigan, 12
University of Regina, 178, 190, 216

University of Saskatchewan, 33, 55, 57, 59, 72, 81, 185
University of Toronto, 41, 43, 55, 97, 122, 163, 185, 225
University of Washington, 157
University of Wisconsin, 15, 16
University Planning Committee, 93
University Press, 219
University Senate, 5, 6, 8, 131
University Survey Committee, 48
UTLAS, 145–146, 199, 200, 201

Vaitkunas, Joe, **132**, 134, 135
Van de Pitte, Fred, 166, 185–186
Van Peteghem, Alfred, **226**
Van Vliet, Murray, 117
Vancouver Public Library, 12
Varley, Frederick, n.20
Viennese Theatre Playbills Collection, 126

Walker, Osman James, n.106
Walker, Thomas MacCallum, 120
Wallace, Robert Charles, 31–32, 33, 34, 38–39, 40, 65, **65**, 183, n.56, n.115
Walter C. Mackenzie Health Sciences Centre, **170**, 171
Western Economic Diversification Canada, 177
Wilson, Robert Starr Leigh, 18
Winspear Business Reading Room (Library), 171
Winspear, Francis, 171
Women's Common Room, 56
Wonders, William C., 77
Wood, W., 87
Woods, J.H., 42
Workflow and Reengineering International Association, 218
World University Games, 152
World War I, 17
World War II, 45–50

Zoology, Department, 75, 91